BE NOT DECEIVED

*A Berean Examination of the Rapture,
the Great Tribulation, and the Day of the Lord*

SUSAN E. JEANS

Master Design Publishing, a division of Master Design Marketing LLC
30 N Gould St, Ste R, Sheridan, WY 82801 | MasterDesign.org

Published 2026
Printed in the United States of America

ISBN: 978-1-941512-68-5 (paperback)
ISBN: 978-1-941512-69-2 (ebook)

For my husband, David, whose steadfast love has supported me for over fifty years of marriage and whose analytical and incisive mind has challenged and refined my thinking processes.

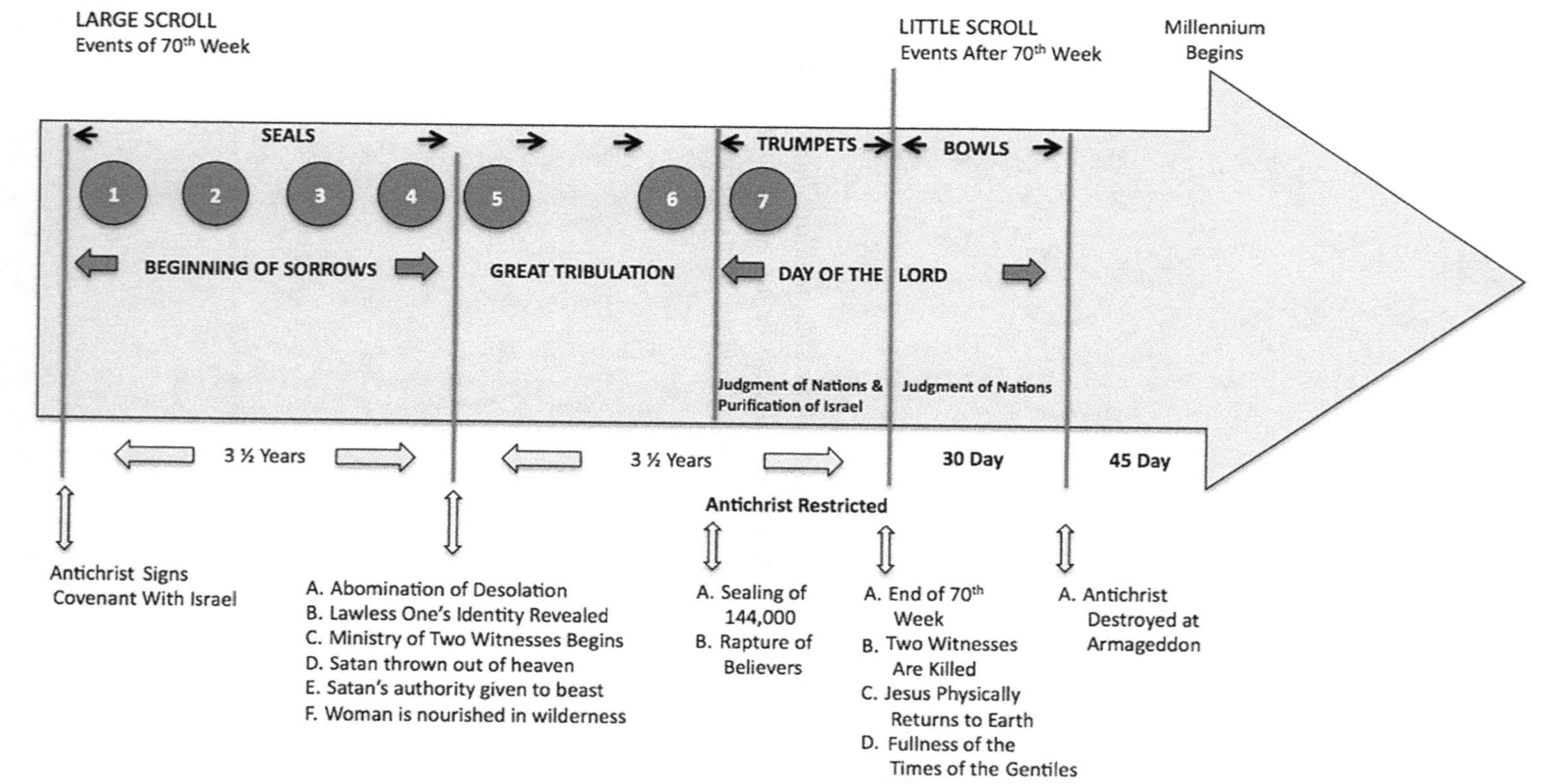

LARGE SCROLL
Events of 70th Week

LITTLE SCROLL
Events After 70th Week

Millennium Begins

SEALS
TRUMPETS
BOWLS

1 2 3 4 5 6 7

BEGINNING OF SORROWS
GREAT TRIBULATION
DAY OF THE LORD

Judgment of Nations & Purification of Israel
Judgment of Nations

3 ½ Years
3 ½ Years
30 Day
45 Day

Antichrist Restricted

Antichrist Signs Covenant With Israel

A. Abomination of Desolation
B. Lawless One's Identity Revealed
C. Ministry of Two Witnesses Begins
D. Satan thrown out of heaven
E. Satan's authority given to beast
F. Woman is nourished in wilderness

A. Sealing of 144,000
B. Rapture of Believers

A. End of 70th Week
B. Two Witnesses Are Killed
C. Jesus Physically Returns to Earth
D. Fullness of the Times of the Gentiles
E. "All Israel" Saved

A. Antichrist Destroyed at Armageddon

Contents

Foreword xvii

Preface xviv

Acknowledgments xxiii

Glossary xxvii

Section I: The Foundation

I. A foundation must be laid before a case can be built 1

  A. Misleading terminology clouds understanding. 1

  B. The predominant prophetic worldview today is shaped by modern dispensationalism 2

    1. What is dispensationalism?. 3

      (a) What are the dispensations?. 4

      (b) There are three indispensable elements of dispensationalism 6

    2. Pretribulationism derives from dispensationalism. 8

    3. How does dispensationalism relate to progressive revelation? 10

    (a) What is progressive revelation? 10

    (b) A biblical mystery explains progressive revelation . . .12

    (c) Are dispensationalism and progressive revelation different descriptions of the same thing?. 15

    (d) Is dispensationalism taught in the Bible?. 15

      (1) Luke 16:2, 3, 4 16

      (2) 1 Corinthians 9:17. 17

      (3) Ephesians 1:10 17

      (4) Ephesians 3:2 19

      (5) Ephesians 3:9 19

      (6) Colossians 1:25 20

      (7) 1 Timothy 1:4. 20

4. There are problems with dispensationalism. 21

    (a) God is not bound to act in accordance with a
man-made system 22

    (b) The inconsistencies controvert the dispensational
view that God will deal with the church and Israel
separately 24

    (1) Who decides when the church age began?. 26

    (2) Why does the church age have to end at the
beginning of the seventieth week?. 28

    (aa) Promises made in the Old Testament
regarding Israel's future have their fulfillment both in the church and in Israel. 28

    (bb) God the Holy Spirit does not have to leave
the earth, taking the church with Him,
before the seventieth week 32

    (cc) God the Holy Spirit is not the restrainer. 34

Section II: The Risk of Deception

II. Pretribulationism creates the risk of believers being deceived
and falling away from the faith 39

A. It is spiritually dangerous to fail to prepare for persecution . .39

B. It is important for all believers to be prepared to suffer
persecution and to be faithful unto death. 40

C. The prewrath rapture position is an alternative, though it,
too, has problems 42

Section III: The Pillars

III. The pillars of pretribulationism must be compared to the
biblical text. 43

A. Pillar 1. The seven years of the seventieth week of Daniel 9:24–27 are all a time of tribulation 44

B. Pillar 2: All seven years of that tribulation are God's
wrath in the day of the Lord 45

1. Tribulation versus the great tribulation 47

2. General wrath versus the wrath of the day of the Lord
versus the lake of fire/second death .59

C. Pillar 3. Believers are spared from God's wrath in the day
of the Lord 60

1. Romans 5. 62

2. 1 Thessalonians 1, 4, and 5 63

3. Revelation 3. 66

(a) What does "because you have kept the word of My
perseverance" refer to? 67

(b) What does "keep you from the hour of testing"
mean? 68

4. Other forms of calamity could be construed as tribulation or wrath but not as the wrath of the day of the Lord72

D. Pillar 4. The rapture is imminent 77

SECTION IV: THE DAY OF THE LORD

IV. The day of the Lord is a unique biblical period of time. 81

A. The day of the Lord has distinctive characteristics 81

1. The day of the Lord will be unique, unlike any other
time of judgment 81

2. The day of the Lord will demonstrate the side of God
that most Christians deny—His justice 82

3. The day of the Lord will be a time of reversal: It will
end humanity's wrath against God and initiate God's
wrath against those who are unrepentant 85

4. No human agency will be involved in the execution of
judgment in the day of the Lord .86

    5. The Lord alone will be exalted in the day of the Lord 88

B. Signs will herald the onset of the day of the Lord 90

    1. The first unmistakable sign will be cosmic-level up-heaval and disruption 90

    2. The second sign will be the silence that presages judgment..94

C. Is the day of the Lord the wrath from which believers are spared? 95

D. The day of the Lord does not fill the entire seventieth week but occurs only in the latter part of the second half of the seventieth week 96

    1. Pillars 2 and 3 of pretribulationism cannot both be true at the same time...................................96

        (a) Once the day of the Lord begins, there will be no further repentance and thus no new believers 96

        (b) God the Holy Spirit cannot be the restrainer of 2 Thessalonians 2:6–7 104

    2. Unbelievers will try to flee and hide when the day of the Lord begins.....................................108

    3. The day of the Lord cannot begin before the midpoint of the seventieth week of Daniel 109

    4. A different definition of the word *apostasy* found in 2 Thessalonians 2:3 does not resolve the fatal flaw of pretribulationism 112

    5. The seals of Revelation 6 cannot be the wrath of the day of the Lord 114

        (a) Jesus's warnings in Matthew 24 parallel the seals of Revelation 6, but He gave no warnings or information about the trumpets and bowls of Revelation.114

        (b) Jesus warned His followers to flee when the great tribulation begins 116

(c) The first seal cannot be a manifestation of the
wrath of the day of the Lord. 117

(d) The day of the Lord cannot begin until sometime
after the fifth seal of Revelation 119

(e) The text of the Bible itself tells us that the day of
the Lord begins at the seventh seal/first trumpet 121

6. There is no gap between the rapture and the outpour-
ing of God's wrath 122

(a) The two events are connected by Jesus. 122

(b) Prior historical events connected deliverance with
judgment. 123

(c) Paul connected the rapture and the day of the
Lord in both letters to the Thessalonians. 124

7. Jesus's description of the two halves of Daniel's seventieth week precludes the characterization of the
entirety of the week as the wrath of the day of the Lord .127

8. There will be no "peace and safety" in the day of the
Lord 128

9. There will be signs that precede the onset of the day of
the Lord 129

10. The rapture will not occur before the appearance of
the signs of the onset of the day of the Lord 131

11. The 144,000 Jews on earth are sealed for protection
from God's wrath just prior to its onset in the day of
the Lord 132

12. Elijah must appear before the commencement of the
day of the Lord 133

13. The future fulfillment of Jesus's prophecy of the end of
the age precludes a pretribulation rapture 134

Section V: Believers on Earth During Daniel's 70th Week

V. Other reasons believers will be on the earth for at least a portion, if not most, of the seventieth week of Daniel. 141

A. The Lord has always had witnesses on the earth 141

   1. The assumption that the 144,000 Jews will be witnesses to God during the great tribulation is unwarranted. . .141

     (a) There is not enough time between the breaking of the sixth and seventh seals to evangelize a host of people so great that it cannot be numbered 143

     (b) There is no text from which to draw an inference . . .144

     (c) Sealing denotes ownership and protection 145

     (d) The 144,000 are sealed as the time for evangelizing closes out. 146

     (e) Other biblical references, whether direct or indirect, do not imply that the 144,000 will evangelize the world. 147

     (f) The Bible tells us there will be witnesses to God during the great tribulation 149

   2. Israel and the church were meant to be the witnesses of God to the world 151

   3. God has always kept a remnant for Himself, both in Israel and in the church. 155

     (a) God preserved witnesses to Himself among the Jews155

       (1) 1 Kings 18–19 155

       (2) Genesis 45 156

       (3) Ezra 9 156

       (4) Isaiah 1 and 10. 157

       (5) Isaiah 11 158

       (6) Jeremiah 23, 31, and 50 158

       (7) Romans 9 and 11. 160

Contents

(b) God also preserves witnesses to Himself in the church 160

B. The church is not absent from Revelation after chapter 3 . . .162

  1. The words *church* and *saints* are synonyms 162

  2. The church is not among those who greet the multitude of Revelation 7 because the church *is* that innumerable throng 168

    (a) The passage in Revelation 4:1–2 does not describe a pretribulation rapture 170

    (b) There is no biblical support for the notion of two raptures 172

    (c) Three biblical texts discuss the timing of the rapture (singular) 173

    (d) Jesus Himself provided a clue to the timing of His return to gather His people to Himself 181

    (e) Because God is impartial, He would not arbitrarily treat one group of believers differently from another group of believers 185

  3. Gentiles were on earth for the first sixty-nine weeks of Daniel. 188

  4. Gentile believers, as sons of Abraham, will also be on the earth for the seventieth week. .189

C. The great tribulation will serve as God's cleansing, refining, and purifying of what is today's Laodicean/Thyatiran church, at least in America. 193

  1. New Testament believers need to learn about God's unchanging character from the Old Testament 193

  2. God's concern for the purity of His people has not changed 199

  3. The purpose of sanctification/purification is to make the believer more Christlike. 205

  4. The American church is not even close to being a pure

bride who has "no spot or wrinkle or any such thing" but is "holy and blameless" (Eph. 5:27) 209

    5. Judgment begins with the household of God 211

  D. The prewrath rapture position is based upon the belief that the rapture will occur just prior to the commencement of the day of the Lord. 214

    1. There are differences and similarities between pretribulationism and the prewrath position. 215

    2. There are problems even with the prewrath position. . . .216

      (a) If the rapture is modelled on Jewish betrothal and marriage, the pattern is not followed 216

      (b) Some Bible verses indicate that the church will be present even in the day of the Lord. 218

        (1) Isaiah 26:19–21 218

        (2) Psalm 30:4–5 219

        (3) Ezekiel 9:4–6 219

        (4) Zephaniah 2:3 220

        (5) 1 Thessalonians 5:1–4. .220

        (6) Other biblical examples 221

SECTION VI: "THE LAST DAY"

VI. Is "the last day" the millennium? 223

  A. The resurrection of the dead is associated with "the last day" 224

  B. There are differing opinions regarding the age of the creation 227

  C. What is the dispensationalist view of "the last day"? 231

    1. Some dispensationalists distinguish between different classes of saints, assigning them different resurrection dates 232

    2. There is yet another, very limited, dispensationalist

view of "the last day" 234

   3. Dispensationalists offer a solution to the contradictions.234

  D. There are other problems with limiting "the last day" to
the millennium 236

Section VII: Conclusion

VII. Believers cannot be complacent about deception. 241

  A. Each believer will be accountable to God. 242

  B. To avoid being deceived, each believer should study the
Bible thoroughly, as the end of days draws ever closer 244

   1. Spiritual deception occurs gradually. 246

   2. Spiritual deception makes one feel safe 250

Afterword 257
Appendix A: Biblical Texts Regarding Expected Tribulation in
This World 259
Appendix B: Biblical Texts Regarding God's Testing of His
People and in Afflicting Them as Punishment 265
Appendix C: Biblical Texts Regarding God's Corrective
Discipline and His Provision in Times of Testing 273
Appendix D: Biblical Texts Regarding the Identity of Daniel's
People, Israel 277
Appendix E: Biblical Texts Regarding the Day of the Lord 281

[3] As Jesus was sitting on the Mount of Olives, the disciples came to [H]im privately. "Tell us," they said, "when will this happen, and what will be the sign of [Y]our coming and of the end of the age?" [4] Jesus answered: "Watch out that no one *deceives* you."

Matthew 24:3–4 NIV (emphasis added)

[10] The brethren immediately sent Paul and Silas away by night to *Berea*; and when they arrived, they went into the synagogue of the Jews. [11] *Now these were more noble-minded* than those in Thessalonica, for they received the word with great eagerness, *examining the Scriptures daily, to see whether these things were so.*

Acts 17:10–11 (emphasis added)

FOREWORD

When my son introduced me to Susan Jeans's first book, *In the Strength of His Might*, I devoured it in a day! I was teaching an end-times Bible study and had been seeking a reference book our laity could understand. I gave each student a copy, spent a session on its overview, and asked them to read the book that week. They especially liked the time chart in the back.

Christ followers need to know *what* to expect in the end times, *when*, and *why*. Days before Jesus died on the cross for our sins, His disciples asked Him, "What will be the sign of [Y]our coming and of the end of the age?" (Matt. 24:3 ESV). Christ's answer included "great tribulation, such as has not been from the beginning of the world until now, no, and never will be. And if those days had not been cut short, no human being would be saved. But for the sake of the elect those days will be cut short" (Matt. 24:21–22 ESV). Open your Bible to Matthew 24:29–31. Read this paragraph aloud several times. Underline the phrases, "*after the tribulation of those days*" and "[H]e will send out [H]is angels with a loud *trumpet* call" (ESV; emphasis added).

This new book of Susan's will give you many pages and Bible verses to corroborate my paragraph above. Another key passage she exegetes and elaborates is 2 Thessalonians 2:1–12, that "the coming of our Lord Jesus Christ and our being gathered together to [H]im" (v. 1 ESV) will not occur until "the man of lawlessness [the Antichrist] is revealed" (v. 3 ESV) at the midpoint of *Daniel's seventieth week*—that is, earth's last seven years before Christ's return and reign.

I suggest you read this book with pencil in hand. Put a question mark by anything you are not sure about. Put an exclamation point by anything new to you but that you can now accept because of the author's explanation of it or her exegesis of pertinent passages. Put an *X* by anything you cannot accept now but are open to the Spirit giving you new information or understanding regarding it. Once you finally finish the book, I suggest you work back through your marks to see if you can then erase or change any of them.

If you bring strong convictions to this book that differ from the author's conclusions, you may want to reexamine what you believe and why you believe it. If you were taught dispensationalism, perhaps you should hold it with an open hand as to whether its perspective is relevant and helpful. I did not grow up in such a church and am a gentile Christian after the cross, so just being a New Testament believer simplifies things for me.

The Old Testament, especially the Prophets, *is* relevant for eschatology. Our author does an excellent job using Daniel's seventieth week as an exegetical framework to explain and mesh this earth's last seven years before Christ's return, noting numerous end-time prophecies from other Old Testament prophets.

Three types of people especially need to read this book. First are those with recent or revived interest in the end times who want a biblical framework for its specific components. Second are those who had long heard or assumed that Christians would be raptured out before the tribulation but are now having doubts or second thoughts about this. And third are people like me, who have long interpreted that the rapture will not precede the tribulation but are now realizing that we may have lived long enough to face even the great tribulation for ourselves.

Maranatha,

Dr. Jim Goodroe, ThM, DMin
(New Orleans Baptist Theological Seminary)

Author, *When the Bottom Falls Out:
Redemption's Greatest Story Never Told*

November 17, 2025

PREFACE

Like many believers, my first exposure to the concept of the pretribulation rapture came in the early 1970s, not from the Bible but from a book entitled *The Late Great Planet Earth*, by Hal Lindsey. Other Christians have a view of the pretribulation rapture that originates, again, not from the Bible but from the fictional *Left Behind* book series (and later movies) by Tim LaHaye and Jerry B. Jenkins. Still others have been taught pretribulationism by their respected and revered, seminary-trained church leaders. Indeed, the concept of a pretribulation rapture is extremely attractive because it means we Christians will not have to endure the torments of the great tribulation. I myself would love to agree with this position. However, many Christians do not realize that this is not a closed subject. The mere fact that there are at least four differing positions regarding the timing of the rapture demonstrates that the issue is far from clear in the Bible.

But God will hold each of us personally accountable for our failure to be like the "noble-minded" Bereans. They did not take as true even the teachings of the great apostle Paul—to whom the risen Jesus revealed Himself directly—but instead "examin[ed] the Scriptures daily, to see whether these things were so" (Acts 17:11). We cannot afford to blindly accept what anyone else tells us the Bible says when we have the ability to read the Bible and to reason and to seek the guidance of God the Holy Spirit ourselves.

Because Jesus warned us that deception in the end times will be so great, I have felt compelled to write this book to warn Christians to be prepared to enter into the great tribulation. If I am correct, many who put their trust in pretribulationism will become disillusioned and disheartened because *they were deceived*, and they may fall into unbelief.

All believers must be open to continued learning even if, or perhaps especially if, a position is counter to one's own, in order to defend one's biblical positions. For this reason, I challenge the reader to at least consider the possibility that pretribulationism may not be correct.

When believers in Jesus are discussing different interpretations of the Bible, there are several guiding principles that we must keep in the forefront of our minds:

1. When the Most High God provided mankind the Bible through the agency of selected men over the course of approximately fourteen hundred years, He did not provide the answers to every conceivable question people might have. What He did provide was precisely what *He* considered to be sufficient for salvation and for sanctified living.

2. The fundamental elements of the gospel of Jesus Christ are *not negotiable*, including the incarnation of God the Son; the perfect, sufficient, and complete payment for mankind's sins (atonement and propitiation) at the cross; His death and burial; the resurrection; the ascension; the coming of God the Holy Spirit; salvation by faith, not by works; the second coming of Jesus; and the millennium.

    If the subject of discussion involves one of the nonnegotiable elements of the gospel, *believers have an obligation* to "contend earnestly for the faith" (Jude 3), to "fight the good fight" (1 Tim. 1:18; 6:12; 2 Tim. 4:7), and to turn away from "those who cause dissensions and hindrances contrary to the teaching which you learned" (Rom. 16:17). We must all be equipped to be "ready to make a defense to everyone who asks you to give an account for the hope that is in you" (1 Peter 3:15).

3. There are, however, other elements of the Bible that are open to different interpretations. Believers should never quarrel over issues that are *not clear* in the Bible. If the issue is one for which different interpretations are biblically defensible (such as the timing of the rapture), there should be no disputing to the point of individual churches splitting or friendships ending (Titus 3:9).

4. Whether Christians are dealing with foundational truths or unclear issues, God demands that believers must stick to the text of the Bible, from beginning to end. Moses warned the younger generation that was about to enter the promised land:

Deuteronomy 4:1–2
¹ Now, O Israel, listen to the statutes and the judgments which I am teaching you to perform, in order that you may live and go in and take possession of the land which the LORD, the God of your fathers, is giving you. ² You shall not add to the word which I am commanding you, nor take away from it, that you may keep the commandments of the LORD your God which I command you.

Deuteronomy 12:32
Whatever I command you, you shall be careful to do; you shall not add to nor take away from it.

This warning was repeated to believers trying to understand the book of Revelation from the first century AD going forward. We are specifically warned at the end of the book not to add to nor to delete anything that has been written:

Revelation 22:18–19
¹⁸ I testify to everyone who hears the words of the prophecy of this book: if anyone adds to them, God shall add to him the plagues which are written in this book; ¹⁹ and if anyone takes away from the words of the book of this prophecy, God shall take away his part from the tree of life and from the holy city, which are written in this book.

When it comes to the subject of this book, most advocates of pretribulationism are interpreting Bible passages *without acknowledging* that their interpretation goes beyond the strict text or that they are ignoring other biblical passages that cannot fit into their position or both. (I will point out some of those in this book.) If any believer offers an interpretation on a biblical issue on which there are differing opinions, he or she is under obligation to clarify at the time that what is being written (or spoken) is their own thinking, subject to change as they continue to study, pray, and learn.

My request is that each reader be like the Bereans (Acts 17:11), give due consideration to the arguments presented in this book, and warn others of the dangers associated with pretribulationism, just in case Jesus does not come for us before the commencement of Daniel's seventieth week.

Susan E. Jeans

November 1, 2025

Acknowledgments

Alan Spencer

Approximately ten years ago, in 2015 or 2016, Alan Spencer, at that time the administrative pastor of Coronado Baptist Church in El Paso, Texas, called me to his office. He told me that in his quiet time that morning, he had received a word from the Lord for me. That word was Habakkuk 2:2: "Then the LORD answered me and said, 'Record the vision / And inscribe it on tablets, / That the one who reads it may run.'" Alan explained that this meant that I was being assigned to write another book. I asked what the subject was to be, as I myself had received no vision to do this. He responded that he didn't know—this was all he had received.

I did not forget this encounter, but every attempt to start another book ended in frustration and the certain knowledge that this was not *it*. Whatever the assigned subject was, "it" remained a mystery. In the summer of 2023, however, a series of conversations with other women at church not only confirmed what Alan had told me but at the same time made me wonder why almost everyone I knew believed in a pretribulation rapture, but I didn't (and still don't). In response to Peter's admonition in 1 Peter 3:15 to always be "ready to make a defense to everyone who asks you to give an account for the hope that is in you, yet with gentleness and reverence," I decided to organize my thoughts and write a defense of why I thought that believers (the church) would indeed go through the great tribulation. I know that Peter was talking about believers defending the gospel to unbelievers, but the principle could easily be applied to differences of interpretation among believers.

Although I thought I could summarize my defense in two to three pages, it resulted in eighteen. In addition, I began to collect and categorize Bible verses that provided the foundation for various biblical principles related to the subject.

Over the course of 2024, as I listened to various sermons (which were rarely on the subject of prophecy—I had to search for those) and read or reread many books, I would think of a response to what I had heard or read, and my paper began to grow organically, up to forty-nine pages, not including all the groupings of Bible verses by subject. At this point, I began to consider that the subject of the timing of the rapture might be "it," the divine assignment.

In January of 2025, my husband and I were watching some Hallmark® movie about an author with writer's block coming up on a deadline, and suddenly I was filled with the conviction and knowledge that what had been growing over the prior eighteen months was indeed the assignment and that I had better get to work!

This book, then, is the fulfillment of an assignment given approximately ten years ago. There were times when I worried that delayed obedience was disobedience, but I see now that it just took that much time for the seeds of ideas to germinate and sprout and grow into full expression.

This long history is given as a heartfelt thank-you to Alan. Although at the time of this writing he is in hospice care, I was able to convey to him that God's word through him to me did not return to Him void (Isa. 55:11).

Dr. Jim Goodroe

Although I have never met Jim personally, he initially contacted me as a result of having encountered my first book, *In the Strength of His Might*, on a bookshelf in his son's home. After he read the book, he contacted me to obtain additional copies. Then he sent me a copy of his own book, *When the Bottom Falls Out: Redemption's Greatest Story Never Told*, and from there we corresponded by email on occasion. He shared the outlines of Bible classes he was teaching, and we addressed other questions on prophetic material that, perhaps unbeknownst to him, contributed to my thinking as I wrote this book.

Jim is a retired pastor, with master of theology and doctor of ministry degrees from New Orleans Baptist Theological Seminary. Because of our shared interest in the Bible and our shared position on the timing of the rapture, he graciously agreed to read and proofread the manuscript and later to write the foreword.

I am indebted to you, Jim, for sharing your vast knowledge and your valuable time with me. If we never meet on this earth, I will seek you out in heaven to thank you in person!

David Jeans

My husband of over fifty years was a national champion of debate while an undergraduate and a moot court champion when we were in law school together. Since then, he labored forty-one years as a trial attorney. These activities have honed his thinking and reasoning skills to a sharp level, and I benefitted greatly from those skills in our frequent evening discussions about what I had read or written. Often he would make a remark or offer a suggestion about refining a point I was trying to make or about "connecting the dots" so that readers would better understand how one point related to another.

David was in full support of the long hours that I spent absorbed in a book, listening to a recorded sermon, or at the computer in my office, and he never objected to the amount of paper and ink our printer consumed. He was also my tech support when my computer acted as if it had been invaded by gremlins who had devoured the latest version of a new section I was working on. And he was my emotional support when my brain felt too fried to frame another argument.

Thank you, David, for your inestimable contribution to this labor of love.

God the Father, God the Son, and God the Holy Spirit

May the eternal, perfect, loving, just, merciful, omnipotent, omniscient, omnipresent triune Creator, Sustainer, Savior, Redeemer, Advocate, Protector, Ruler, the Word who is called Faithful and True, King of kings, Lord of lords, and ultimate Judge of all be exalted and glorified in the work of His servant, who offers back to Him her imperfect gift. May He use it to accomplish His purposes as He deems fit.

> All things come of [T]hee,
> and of [T]hine own have we given [T]hee.

1 Chronicles 29:14b KJV

Glossary

abomination of desolation: A sacrilegious act that defiles a holy place. Historically, it refers to the "desolation" (defilement) of the Second Temple in Jerusalem in approximately 168 BC by the Syrian ruler Antiochus IV Epiphanes, an event prophesied in Daniel 11:31 over four hundred years earlier. The "abomination" that "desolated" the temple was Antiochus's acts of entering the temple, erecting a statue of or an altar to Zeus, and sacrificing a pig, which is an unclean animal according to Jewish law.

Jesus referred to this historical act, which was well known to the Jews of His time, as an act that would be repeated by another person in the future. According to Matthew 24:15, He said, "Therefore when you see the abomination of desolation which was spoken of through Daniel the prophet, standing in the holy place (let the reader understand) ..." In other words, Jesus was warning His listeners (and future readers of the gospel) that an historical event which had happened a little over a century and a half earlier would be repeated in the future. And when it happened again, it would trigger "a great tribulation, such as has not occurred since the beginning of the world until now, nor ever will" (Matt. 24:21).

The future abomination of desolation is described in 2 Thessalonians 2:3–4, where Paul, speaking of the future antichrist, wrote, "The man of lawlessness is revealed, the son of destruction, who opposes and exalts himself above every so-called god or object of worship, so that he takes his seat in the temple of God, displaying himself as being God."

beginning of birth pangs: The phrase that Jesus used to describe the first three and a half years of the seven years of Daniel's seventieth week (see Matt. 24:4–8 [parallel passages Mark 13:5–8; Luke 21:8–11]), which corresponds to the first four seals of Revelation 6:1–8. It is important to note that Jesus never used the word *tribulation* in His description of this first half (three and a half years) of the seventieth week. Instead, He called this time period "the beginning of birth pangs."

church: The body of believers, who repented of their sins, turned to Jesus, and were saved "by grace … through faith, … not as a result of works" (Eph. 2:8–9), beginning with the time of Jesus's incarnation. The use of the word *church* in this book does not refer to any denomination or organization.

Daniel's seventieth week: A period of seven years. The Hebrew word for "weeks" is *shabuwa* (*Strong's* OT 7620[1]), which means "sevened, i.e., a week (specifically of years)." *Shabuwa* could mean seven days, seven weeks, or seven years. In hindsight, it is clear that God meant seventy sets of seven years—that is, 70x7 = 490 years. The seventieth week is the last of the seventy weeks decreed by God through His angel Gabriel in Daniel 9:24–27. The first sixty-nine weeks (483 years) were broken down into two periods of seven and sixty-two weeks, but together they add up to sixty-nine. The clock for those seventy weeks of years began in approximately 445 BC, and the sixty-ninth week included the last years of Jesus's life on earth.

Because the destruction of Jerusalem and the temple, which are described in Daniel 9:26, did not occur in the seven years after the end of the sixty-ninth week, we know that the seventieth week (a period of seven years) did not follow directly on the heels of the first sixty-nine weeks (483 years). There was a

---

1 Unless otherwise noted, all transliterations and definitions of Hebrew and Greek words are taken from James Strong, "Hebrew and Aramaic Dictionary" and "Greek Dictionary of the New Testament," in *The New Strong's Exhaustive Concordance of the Bible* (Nelson, 2010).

gap that began at the end of the sixty-ninth week; that gap has continued for approximately two millennia now, and the world watches for the sign that will herald the beginning of the seventieth week.

That sign is given in Daniel 9:27: "And he [the "prince who is to come" of v. 26, which points to the antichrist of the end times] will make a firm covenant with the many for one week [seven years]." Thus the sign that will trigger the seventieth week will be either the actual signing of a covenant/treaty or the confirmation/reaffirmation of an existing covenant between Israel and other countries. "The many" is the reference to Israel, indicating that there will be dissenters who are opposed to this treaty, since "many," but plainly not all, in Israel will agree.

Verse 27 goes on to say, in archaic language, that in the middle of the week (i.e., halfway through the seven years, meaning after three and a half years), he (the antichrist) will stop the sacrifices and grain offering (which means he will be standing in an, as of today, not-yet-rebuilt temple) and will commit what is commonly known as "the abomination of desolation."

day of the Lord: The period of time, more than a literal day, of God's devastating final judgment of apostate Israel and the nations. It is the time in which the Lord will punish, with no hope of restoration, all unrepentant unbelievers on the earth. It is a time of terror and darkness. There is no blessing associated with it. The day of the Lord is not synonymous with the *beginning of birth pangs*, which takes up the first half of the seventieth week; nor is it synonymous with the *great tribulation*, which begins at the midpoint of the seventieth week. The day of the Lord will begin when Jesus cuts short the days of the great tribulation. Since the great tribulation will take up most of the second half of the seven-year period, the day of the Lord will begin toward the end of that time. (See appendix E for biblical texts describing this awesome and terrible day.)

eisegesis: An approach to interpreting a biblical text by imposing onto it man-made ideas, beliefs, or biases. Bible verses are used selectively to support a preconceived conclusion, without considering the context in which the verses appear and while ignoring verses that contradict the conclusion.

eschatology: The study of the biblical presentation of the last things, the latter days, the last days, or the end times. Key themes include the apparent triumph of evil over the people of God, the rapture, the day of the Lord, God's wrath, the return of Jesus Himself to earth in great glory, the resurrection of the dead, the final judgment, and the establishment of God's kingdom in the millennium and in the eternal state.

exegesis: An approach to understanding and interpreting a biblical text by considering its historical, cultural, linguistic, and literary contexts and the content of the text itself.

hermeneutics: A method or principle of interpretation and explanation, especially of the text of the Bible.

millennium: The eschatological period of one thousand years in which Satan will be bound and Christ will reign on earth, together with those who had been martyred for refusing to worship the image of the beast (Rev. 20:1–6).

amillennialism: The belief that there is not literally one thousand years (Revelation 20) during which Jesus reigns and rules over the earth. Instead, this position holds that this millennial kingdom is neither future nor physical but is rather a present (i.e., currently existing) spiritual reality. One thousand is seen as a symbolic number.

premillennialism: The belief that Jesus will actually return to earth to reign over a physical kingdom for a period of one thousand years. His return will be at the beginning of that period. In contrast to postmillennialism, this position holds that before Jesus returns, the tribulations of the world will get worse—much worse—rather than better.

pretribulation dispensational premillennialism: A category of premillennialism and the prevalent end-times view in most evangelical churches today. For *pretribulationism*, which has to do with the timing of the rapture, see below under "tribulation." *Dispensationalism* is a man-made system that divides human history into distinct "dispensations" or time periods. According to this system, God deals differently with mankind in each dispensation. Dispensationalism is discussed further in section I.B below.

postmillennialism: Like amillennialism, this view also holds that Christ's reign is spiritual, not physical. He will return physically to earth after the passage of whatever indefinite number of years the number one thousand symbolizes. Postmillennialists believe that Jesus cannot return until the world has been improved by the spread of the gospel. Their view is that the tribulations of this world will become less as the "millennial" reign in people's hearts grows greater.

near/far or dual fulfillment: A unique characteristic of predictive prophecy in which the fulfillment occurs at two separate times and the first foreshadows the second, even though the second fulfillment may be hundreds or even thousands of years after the first.

rapture: The English translation of the Greek word *harpazo*, which means "to seize or snatch away." Like the word *Trinity*, the word *rapture* is not in the Bible, but the concept is. The rapture is an eschatological event in which believers, whether dead or alive, are gathered up, "caught up," to meet Jesus in the air, to be taken by Him into heaven. (See 1 Thess. 4:13–18; 1 Cor. 15:51–58.)

pretribulation rapture: The position that Jesus will rapture believers out of the world prior to the beginning of Daniel's seventieth week, all of which is incorrectly called "the tribulation period." (See the definition of *beginning of birth pangs* above.)

midtribulation rapture: The position that Jesus will rapture believers out of the world in the middle of Daniel's seventieth week—that is, after three and a half years. Thus, believers will not be on the earth to have to endure the great tribulation, which begins at that time.

posttribulation rapture: The position that the rapture will not occur until the very end of the seventieth week, after the great tribulation of the second half and even after the day of the Lord.

prewrath rapture: The position that places the rapture just prior to the onset of the day of the Lord. This position holds that this is the wrath from which Christians are promised deliverance and that the day of the Lord is a time period near the end of Daniel's seventieth week. It is believed to begin at the time that the Lord cuts short the days of the great tribulation, in accordance with Matthew 24:22.

tribulation: The English translation of the Greek word *thlipsis* (*Strong's* NT 2347), which means "pressure," literally or figuratively. It appears forty-five times in forty-three verses in the New Testament, where it is translated into English as "tribulation, trouble, affliction, anguish, persecution." As these words indicate, tribulation refers to a period of severe suffering, usually caused by external sources, such as persecution and hardship. In the Bible, Jesus warned that tribulation is the common experience for believers. They should expect it, not be surprised by it, and use it as an opportunity to grow spiritually by remaining steadfastly faithful to God as they endure it, knowing that ultimately God will deliver them safely to heaven. (See, e.g., Matt. 13:21; John 16:33; Rom. 5:3; 12:12; 2 Cor. 1:4; 4:17.)

References to tribulation in the New Testament in a nonprophetic context are different from the *great tribulation*, a term used by Jesus to describe *only* the relatively short (close to three and a half years) worldwide reign of the antichrist in the second half of the seventieth week (see below). Jesus described the first three and a half years as the beginning of birth pangs, followed by the great tribulation, which will last for most of the second half, until Jesus cuts the days of it short (Matt. 24:22).

great tribulation: Greek *thlipsis*, plus adjective *megas*, "great," referring to a period of time that begins at the midpoint of the seven years of Daniel's seventieth week. It will be triggered with the abomination of desolation by the antichrist—that is, the defiling of the (rebuilt) temple in Jerusalem by the antichrist proclaiming himself to be God and demanding that the world worship him.

This second half of the seventieth week, like the first half, will last three and a half years. While the great tribulation will begin at the midpoint of the seventieth week, it will not last to the end of the three and a half years because the days of the great tribulation will be cut short by the Lord. The days of the latter three and a half years will continue to the end of the seventieth week, but they will be filled with the day of the Lord.

The great tribulation will be a time of intense persecution by the antichrist and his forces against the Jews first and then Christians. (See Matt. 24:9–22; Mark 13:14–20; cf. Dan. 12:1–3.)

Section I

THE FOUNDATION

A FOUNDATION MUST BE LAID BEFORE A CASE CAN BE BUILT

At the outset, I want to acknowledge that the subject of this book is controversial. There are many who will stop reading at this point because they are already convinced that Jesus will rapture the church out of the world *before* the onset of Daniel's seventieth week.

Therefore, this book is expressly addressed

- to people who are adamantly pretribulationist and

- to advocates of other positions regarding the timing of the rapture, as well as

- to those who find all biblical terms of art (like *Daniel's seventieth week* and *rapture*) confusing or overwhelming.

There are two conceptual issues that must be dealt with before the substance of the book can be understood.

The first concerns the misleading use (which amounts to a misuse) of terminology. Many things in the Bible are hard enough to understand without humans further muddying the waters.

The second pertains to people's worldviews shaped by modern systems of theological interpretation, in particular modern dispensationalism.

A. MISLEADING TERMINOLOGY CLOUDS UNDERSTANDING

Most of the terms which are used to describe the timing of the rapture are based on an unfortunate misnomer—that is, a wrong or inappropriate name. Those terms are

- *pretribulation,*

- *midtribulation,*

- *posttribulation.*

> For definitions of these terms, see the glossary.

All three terms are based on the unbiblical notion that the whole of the seven years of Daniel's seventieth week are a time of tribulation. Indeed, most teachers and pastors call the entire seventieth week *the tribulation period.*

This is not, however, what Jesus taught. Jesus called the first half (the first three and a half years) "the beginning of birth pangs" (Matt. 24:8; Mark 13:8) and the second half (the last three and a half years) the "great tribulation" (Matt. 24:21). Even when He used the word "tribulation" in Matthew 24:9, He was referring to the great tribulation of the second half.

Thus, there is a "great tribulation" but *never* a "tribulation" in the context of the seventieth week. For this reason, it is incorrect to call the entire seven-year period of the seventieth week the tribulation period.

Unfortunately, all three terms (*pretribulation, midtribulation, post-tribulation*) are based on this incorrect naming of the entire seven-year period of the seventieth week the tribulation period.

Conclusion: It is a misnomer to call the entire seven years of Daniel's seventieth week the tribulation or the tribulation period because that is not what Jesus taught. Jesus referred to the first half of the seven years as "the beginning of birth pangs" and only the second half as the "great tribulation." There is no seven-year period of tribulation; there is only a *great* tribulation, and it begins at the midpoint of the seven years, not at the beginning.

B. The predominant prophetic worldview today is shaped by modern dispensationalism

It is important to recognize that people come to the Bible with differing mindsets or worldviews, and they read their Bibles through the lens of that mindset. If one has grown up in a church that teaches a particular interpretation of a biblical topic, then that might have become the lens through which that person reads his or her Bible.

Recognizing first the existence of the lens and then understanding its identity is critical regarding the interpretation of biblical prophecy.

For a little over a century, the predominant prophetic viewpoint in American evangelical churches on the timing of the rapture has been known as *dispensationalism* or *pretribulation dispensational premillennialism*. The latter is a long compound name that requires definition and just a bit of history.

Pretribulationism is the belief that believers will be raptured off the earth before the beginning of Daniel's seventieth week. That this view does not align with the Bible is the subject of this book.

Premillennialism is relatively straightforward; it holds that

- the millennium of Revelation 20 is a literal one thousand years,

- Jesus Christ will come again to earth at or just prior to the beginning of the one thousand years, and

- Jesus will rule and reign over the earth during that one thousand years.

There are many Old Testament passages that allude to this period of time—for example, Isaiah 2:2–4; 11:6–9; 51:4–5; 65:20–25; Daniel 2:44; Micah 4:1–3; Zechariah 14:9, 16–21. Because premillennialism does not affect the subject of this book, I will not go into any further detail, except to say that I agree with it as stated above.

1. WHAT IS DISPENSATIONALISM?

Dispensationalism is a theological framework of biblical interpretation that divides the Bible into set periods of time called *dispensations*, throughout which God has administered His divine will in history and on into the present time and even into the future, as it is revealed through biblical prophecy.

It is as if a grid of time periods were placed over the Bible, thus dividing it into different dispensations. In each of the different dispensations, God changes the ways He deals with mankind. This manner of interpreting the Bible assumes that God has adapted His means according to mankind's capacity to receive His revelation at different times in history.

The system was formulated by John Nelson Darby in the 1820s and 1830s, but its primary growth in the United States resulted from the publication of the *Scofield Reference Bible* in 1909 and from the founding of Dallas Theological Seminary in 1924 by Lewis Sperry Chafer.

(a) What are the dispensations?

Although Darby was a prolific writer, he was not always consistent. For example, his original dispensational scheme divided the Bible into nine dispensations, but he later decided that three of them were not really dispensations.

Some dispensationalists divide human history into three divisions:

- The patriarchal dispensation
- The Mosaic or Jewish dispensation
- The Christian dispensation

Other dispensationalists have concluded there are seven dispensations:

- Innocence (Genesis 1–3)
- Conscience (Genesis 4–8)
- Human government (Genesis 9–11)
- Promise (Genesis 12–Exodus 19)
- Law (Exodus 20–Acts 2)
- Grace (Acts 2–Revelation 19)
- Millennial kingdom (Revelation 20)

Unfortunately, over time, more and more divisions and varying permutations of dispensations were created, to the point that law and grace were deemed to be mutually exclusive dispensations, even though there have been elements of both throughout human history.

For example, in the dispensation of law, King David deserved the death penalty for adultery and for murder, but instead, God forgave him. It is true that God took the son of his adultery and that there were other lifelong consequences for David, but the Mosaic law, which required capital punishment, was not followed.

Conversely, even in the dispensation of grace, Christians are not free from the law of God. The Ten Commandments were not abrogated by the new covenant; indeed, Jesus taught that God looked not at outward behavior but at the heart. This means that God's standards of perfection ("you are to be perfect, as your heavenly Father is perfect," Matt. 5:48) had never been *only* about one's outward conduct, as the Jews had concluded.

Since the heart is the source of all that defiles a person, that was the starting point for all sinful behavior. And even if sinful thoughts never matured into sinful actions, the sinner was just as guilty as if they had.

Moreover, licentiousness and antinomianism were condemned in the strongest terms throughout the New Testament.

> See, e.g., Matt. 5:17–48; Rom. 6; and 1 Cor. 5–6.

Finally, the division of law and grace contradicted the biblical truth that there has never been a difference in the means by which any human of any time period has been saved.

Whether in the Old Testament (before the cross) or the New Testament (after the cross), the means of salvation has always been the same—by grace through faith (Eph. 2:8–9), not by the works of the law (Gal. 2:16). The content of one's faith before the cross was necessarily less full than the faith of those who looked back to the cross, but it was still faith that looked forward to something that they could not yet see.

> See Heb. 11:1–13.

A prime example is Abraham, who was saved by grace through faith over four hundred years before the giving of the law (Rom. 4:3, 16). Conversely, both before and after the giving of the Mosaic law, there were timeless moral laws of God. Cain's murder of his brother was a violation of God's law (Genesis 4). As well, New Testament saints, while not under the Mosaic law, had and have a law to fulfill (1 Cor. 7:19; 9:21; Gal. 6:2).

Despite the existence of both law and grace throughout God's dealings with His creation, the law vs. grace distinction led to another division of human history, which sandwiched the *church age* between two Jewish ages:

- law—the Mosaic/Jewish age

- grace—the church age

- law—the millennial kingdom

(b) THERE ARE THREE INDISPENSABLE ELEMENTS OF DISPENSATIONALISM

Despite the distorted and convoluted divisions and distinctions that compounded over time, there are three elements, developed by Dr. Charles Ryrie, that are accepted today as indispensably characterizing the system of dispensationalism:

1. The Bible should be interpreted consistently, literally, and at face value, unless it is clear that a metaphor or analogy is being used (e.g., the "Lamb of God" does not mean that Jesus was a sheep). In other words, the Bible must be interpreted by the consistent use of a plain, literal, grammatical, historical method of interpretation and with a futuristic, premillennial view of biblical prophecy.

2. (a) There is a distinction between the nation of Israel and the church. The nation of Israel will ultimately inherit all the blessings that were promised in the Old Testament. God has not finished with the nation of Israel, nor has Israel been assumed into and absorbed by the church.

   (b) Because God has different plans for the church and the nation of Israel, He will deal with them in different dispensations (time periods).

3. God's overall purpose is to bring glory to Himself.

I find it curious that only 2(b) actually addresses the heart of dispensationalism, which is that God gradually unfolds His plan of salvation through distinct dispensations—or time periods—of history. The others, 1, 2(a), and 3, are marvelous contributions to biblical hermeneutics, but really have nothing to do with the actual definition of dispensationalism.

What is the source of 2(b)? Why does the fact that God has different plans for the church and for the nation of Israel require that God deal with them in distinctly separate dispensations?

The answer goes back to John Nelson Darby, who established a new foundational method of all Bible interpretation. It is a major premise of dispensationalism, though many followers today have forgotten, or never knew of, this foundational principle of "rightly dividing." This method decides first whether a biblical passage concerns Israel or the church and then interprets the passage in light of this "division of the Word."

In other words, all Biblical interpretation depends upon an initial question that divides all Scripture into two divisions by asking, "In this passage of Scripture, is God dealing with Israel or with the church?" All interpretation flows from the answer to that question.

Application of this new hermeneutic principle to the book of Revelation results in the following:

- The seventy weeks are described in the book of Daniel. Since this book is in the Old Testament, God was dealing with Israel. After all, this was approximately six hundred years before Christ, so the concept of the church was utterly unknown.

- The first sixty-four-plus weeks occurred before Jesus was born. Jesus was crucified after the end of the sixty-ninth week. Despite the obvious fact that the gospels, which cover the life of Jesus, include some portion of the first sixty-nine weeks, dispensationalists conclude that God was dealing only with Israel during the first sixty-nine weeks; therefore, the seventieth week must also involve God's dealing solely with Israel.

- Thus, dispensationalists must insert a parenthesis, also known as an *intercalation* or a *redemptive parenthesis,* between God's dealings with Israel. This parenthetical dispensation is called the *church age,* in which God suspended His operations with

Israel. At the onset of the seventieth week, He must have concluded His dealings with the church because He must at that time resume His dealings with Israel.

SINCE the seventieth week deals only with Israel,

THEN

- the church must be out of the picture entirely by the beginning of the seventieth week; and

- Jesus' Olivet Discourse in Matthew 24 (with its parallels in Mark and Luke) and the book of Revelation, beginning either from chapter 4 or chapter 6 where the seals are broken, apply only to Israel.

Because of the disagreement over the names, dates, and durations of the varying dispensations, dispensational theology has evolved into three branches: classical, revised, and progressive. It is interesting to read about these branches, but that subject is not relevant for this book because all three branches still adhere to a pretribulational rapture of the church. Revised dispensationalism, for example, has softened the sharp, hard lines between dispensations but has not altered the conclusion that the rapture must occur prior to the seventieth week; this is because the church age is viewed as a parenthetical break between God's dealings with Israel as set out above.

2. PRETRIBULATIONISM DERIVES FROM DISPENSATIONALISM

Here is where dispensationalism intersects with pretribulationism, the subject of this book. **The eschatological doctrine of the pretribulation rapture of the church came out of dispensationalism.**

According to this doctrine, there are two peoples of God: ethnic Israel, consisting of the descendants of Abraham, Isaac, and Jacob; and the church, consisting of both gentiles and Jews who are saved during the dispensation called the church age. The church age will end when a seven-year period of "tribulation" (note the misnomer) begins. At that time, God will rapture the church up to heaven.

The purpose of the removal of the church from the earth is so that God can begin to deal with the nation of Israel. During the seven-year tribulation, God will execute His plan for the nation of Israel. At the end of the seven years, Jesus will return and inaugurate His millennial kingdom.

This sandwiching of the church age between the two Jewish ages is demonstrated in the chart below.

The Dispensations of Pretribulationism		
Dispensation of law; then	Dispensation of grace; then	Dispensation of law
Mosaic/Jewish age	Church age	Millennium/Jewish age
First sixty-nine weeks of Daniel	Gap	Seventieth week and thereafter
Daniel 9–Acts 2	Acts 2–Revelation 3	Revelation 4–20

Based on this chart, the church age ends after the events of Revelation 3 and just prior to the seventieth week of Daniel; thus the church has to be raptured out of the world at that point.

In other words, dispensationalism holds that because God still has a future for Israel and because that future is distinct from the church's future,

- God will rapture the church out of the world just before the seventieth week;
- the seventieth week will begin, including the great tribulation, in which He purges and then redeems Israel; and
- the millennial kingdom will come.

Many advocates of pretribulationism today may not understand that their position has its origin in and derives from dispensationalism. Nevertheless, the grid-like framework of dispensationalism laid over the Bible inexorably leads to these conclusions:

IF you believe that God deals with the church and with Israel in different dispensations (time periods),

THEN you also believe that the church's dispensation has to end so that God can deal with Israel in Israel's dispensation. And

IF you believe that the church's dispensation ends at the beginning of the seventieth week and that Israel's dispensation begins at that same time,

THEN you also believe that the church has to be raptured out of the world prior to the onset of the seventieth week.

3. HOW DOES DISPENSATIONALISM RELATE TO PROGRESSIVE REVELATION?

(a) WHAT IS PROGRESSIVE REVELATION?

Progressive revelation is the concept that God has revealed Himself and His plan for the redemption of mankind gradually over time, culminating in

- the revelation of Himself in the Person of Jesus Christ and
- the actual fulfillment of the eternal plan of redemption in the incarnation, life, ministry, death on the cross, burial, resurrection, and ascension of God the Son.

Passages from both the Old Testament and the New Testament describe this progression of revelation to mankind:

Isaiah 28:9–10 (KJV)

[9] Whom shall [H]e teach knowledge? and whom shall [H]e make to understand doctrine? them that are weaned from the milk, and drawn from the breasts. [10] For precept must be upon precept,

precept upon precept; line upon line, line upon line; here a little, and there a little.

Hebrews 1:1–2

[1] God, after He spoke long ago to the fathers in the prophets in many portions and in many ways, [2] in these last days has spoken to us in His Son, whom He appointed heir of all things, through whom also He made the world.

Each nugget of revealed truth builds upon prior revelations. Each new precept is a brick laid upon the growing structure of prior precepts, line upon line. Later precepts clarify and amplify earlier precepts.

The Most High God had a plan to redeem His fallen people, but this plan was only revealed to mankind in bits and pieces. Even His prophets struggled to understand what they were given, and not only they, who were human, but also the angels in the unseen realm longed to understand:

1 Peter 1:10–12

[10] As to this salvation, the prophets who prophesied of the grace that would come to you made careful search and inquiries, [11] seeking to know what person or time the Spirit of Christ within them was indicating as He predicted the sufferings of Christ and the glories to follow. [12] It was revealed to them that they were not serving themselves, but you, in these things which now have been announced to you through those who preached the gospel to you by the Holy Spirit sent from heaven—things into which angels long to look.

Jesus the Messiah, the Christ, the Anointed One, was the ultimate revelation of God:

John 1:1–2, 14 (emphasis added)

[1] In the beginning was the Word, and the Word was with God, and **the Word was God.** [2] **He was in the beginning with God.**

[14] And **the Word became flesh, and dwelt among us, and we saw His glory, glory as of the only begotten from the Father, full of grace and truth.**

John 14:9

[Jesus said to Philip] He who has seen Me has seen the Father.

Even after the ascension, God the Holy Spirit continued His work through the apostles, leading to further revelation, such as the inclusion of the gentiles in the plan of redemption.

In short, God's progressive revelation of Himself leads His people to a deeper understanding of His character and His means of redemption. The fulfillment of earlier prophecies, especially ones that seemed to be contradictory (e.g., that the Messiah would come from Bethlehem, that He would come out of Egypt, and that He would be a Nazarene) can give us confidence that the remaining prophecies will be fulfilled just as accurately.

An understanding of progressive revelation leads us to a discussion of biblical mysteries.

(b) A BIBLICAL MYSTERY EXPLAINS PROGRESSIVE REVELATION

In the Bible, a mystery is not a puzzle to be solved by sharp detectives sifting through clues. The Greek word is *musterion* (*Strong's* NT 3466), and it is defined within the very words of the Bible itself:

Romans 16:25–26 (emphasis added)

[25] Now to Him who is able to establish you according to my gospel and the preaching of Jesus Christ, according to the **revelation of the mystery which has been kept secret for long ages past,** [26] **but now is manifested, and by the Scriptures of the prophets, according to the commandment of the eternal God, has been made known to all the nations, leading to obedience of faith.**

A *musterion* is something (kept secret from mankind) that was always in the plans, purposes, and will of God but that God did not reveal to mankind (and which was undiscoverable by mankind) until He chose to do so. Here's another example of the biblical definition of *musterion* that focuses on God's timing of His revelation:

<u>Ephesians 1:9–10</u> (emphasis added, NIV)

[9] He made known to us **the mystery of [H]is will** according to [H]is good pleasure, which [H]e purposed in Christ, [10] **to be put into effect when the times will have reached their fulfillment—to bring unity to all things in heaven and on earth under Christ.**

In the context of Ephesians 3, the mystery was that gentiles would be included into the body of Christ. A similar passage from Colossians follows after it. Note how the definition of a mystery is included in both passages:

<u>Ephesians 3:1–11</u> (emphasis added)

[1] For this reason I, Paul, the prisoner of Christ Jesus for the sake of you Gentiles— [2] if indeed you have heard of the stewardship of God's grace which was given to me for you; [3] that **by revelation there was made known to me the mystery,** as I wrote before in brief. [4] By referring to this, when you read you can understand **my insight into the mystery of Christ,** [5] **which in other generations was not made known to the sons of men, as it has now been revealed to His holy apostles and prophets in the Spirit;** [6] **to be specific, that the Gentiles are fellow heirs and fellow members of the body, and fellow partakers of the promise in Christ Jesus through the gospel,** [7] of which I was made a minister, according to the gift of God's grace which was given to me according to the working of His power. [8] To me, the very least of all saints, this grace was given, to preach to the Gentiles the unfathomable riches of Christ, [9] **and to bring to light what is the administration of the mystery which for ages has been hidden in God who created all things;** [10] so that the manifold wisdom of God might now be made known through the church to the rulers and the authorities in the heavenly places. [11] **This was in accordance with the eternal purpose which He carried out in Christ Jesus our Lord.**

As a sidebar, note the *profound purpose* of God's revelation of His mysteries on His own timetable in verse 10, here quoting the Amplified Bible, Classic Edition:

Ephesians 3:10 (AMPC)

[The purpose is] that through the church the complicated, many-sided wisdom of God in all its infinite variety and innumerable aspects might now be made known to the angelic rulers and authorities (principalities and powers) in the heavenly sphere.

God is using the church (yes, us—pathetic, weak believers) to prove a point to the entire realm of heaven!

Colossians 1:25–27 (emphasis added)

25 Of this church I was made a minister according to the stewardship from God bestowed on me for your benefit, so that I might fully carry out the preaching of the word of God, 26 that is, **the mystery which has been hidden from the past ages and generations, but has now been manifested to His saints,** 27 **to whom God willed to make known what is the riches of the glory of this mystery among the Gentiles, which is Christ in you, the hope of glory.**

Another example of a biblical mystery appears in Romans 11. This relates to God's future plans for the salvation of Israel:

Romans 11:25–26 (emphasis added)

25 For I do not want you, brethren, to be uninformed of **this mystery**—so that you will not be wise in your own estimation—**that a partial hardening has happened to Israel until the fullness of the Gentiles has come in;** 26 **and thus all Israel will be saved.**

Even the concept of the rapture was a biblical mystery, not revealed to mankind until after Christ's ascension:

1 Corinthians 15:51–52 (emphasis added)

51 Behold, **I tell you a mystery**; we will not all sleep, but we will all be changed, 52 in a moment, in the twinkling of an eye, at the last

trumpet; for the trumpet will sound, and the dead will be raised imperishable, and we will be changed.

(c) ARE DISPENSATIONALISM AND PROGRESSIVE REVELATION DIFFERENT DESCRIPTIONS OF THE SAME THING?

On the one hand, both dispensationalism and progressive revelation emphasize that, while God had, from eternity past (an oxymoron, I know), ordained His plan of redemption for mankind, He chose to reveal His mysteries in stages, at different times in history. Whenever He deemed that "the times will have reached their fulfillment," (Eph. 1:10 NIV), He disclosed another element of His plan. Precept was laid upon precept, line upon line, until the proper moment:

<u>Galatians 4:4–5</u> (emphasis added)

[4] But **when the fullness of the time came**, God sent forth His Son, born of a woman, born under the Law, [5] so that He might redeem those who were under the Law, that we might receive the adoption as sons.

On the other hand, the difference between the two principles of interpretation lies in the specificity of the man-made grid of dispensationalism, with its sharp compartmentalization of dispensations (though there are many variations among the dispensationalists) and its complete separation between Israel and the church, requiring God to deal with them separately and having different plans for each. Progressive revelation approaches the Bible as a more unified whole, with God working on many different nations and individuals all at once, often accomplishing differing goals with the same actions on His part.

(d) IS DISPENSATIONALISM TAUGHT IN THE BIBLE?

Some modern theologians have advanced the argument that dispensationalism is explicitly taught in the Bible, citing the use of the English word *dispensation* four times in the King James Version of the New Testament:

- 1 Corinthians 9:17

- Ephesians 1:10; 3:2

- Colossians 1:25

In my research, I discovered that the corresponding Greek word appears three additional times in the New Testament in Luke 16:2, 3, 4.

The Greek word is *oikonomia* (*Strong's* NT 3622), defined as "administration (of a household or estate); specifically a (religious) 'economy.' "

The word *oikonomia* derives from *oikonomos* (*Strong's* NT 3623), a compound word made up of *oikos* (house) and *nomos* (distribute). Thus *oikonomos* means a "house-distributor (i.e., manager) or overseer," or figuratively, "a preacher."

The *Exegetical Dictionary of the New Testament* adds the following on *oikonomia* and its related words:

> The meaning … is characteristically nonspecific and diffuse and can be decided only case by case on the basis of context. The NT range of meanings, which extends from reference to the steward and his position or activity in the literal sense (Luke 12:42; 16:1–9) to metaphorical usage for ecclesiastical offices and functions (1 Cor. 4:1; 9:17; Col. 1:25, etc.) and to a circumlocution for God's plan of salvation (Ephesians), lacks the semantic structure that was already extant in secular Greek."[2]

Let's turn to all of the New Testament passages in which *oikonomia* is used and examine their respective contexts to determine whether they do teach dispensationalism.

(1) LUKE 16:2, 3, 4

In Luke, *oikonomia* occurs in the parable of the unfaithful manager, called to account for his "stewardship" or "management" of the owner's business; no English translation uses "dispensation." Obviously, these

---

2   Horst Kuhli, "οἰκονομία, οἰκονομέω, οἰκονόμος," in the *Exegetical Dictionary of the New Testament*, ed. Horst Balz and Gerhard Schneider, 3 vols. (Eerdmans, 1990–1993), 2:499.

verses do not have anything to do with the concept of dispensational-ism as a means of God's system of revealing His plan of redemption in different time periods or dispensations.

(2) 1 CORINTHIANS 9:17

In this passage, Paul is pointing out that, while those who proclaim the gospel have the right to make their living from that work, he himself did not claim this right because he did not want to cause any hindrance to the gospel of Christ. He went on to say that his preaching was under compulsion, and because it was against his will, he had a "stewardship entrusted" to him:

> For if I do this voluntarily, I have a reward; but if against my will, I have a **stewardship** entrusted to me. (emphasis added)

> "Stewardship" is the translation for *oikonomia* also found in the ESV, NKJV, and ASV. Other translations include "trust" (NIV), "dispensation" (KJV), "trusteeship" (AMPC), "administration" (DBT), and "commission" (RSV).

Note the synonyms:

- stewardship
- trusteeship
- administration
- commission

All of them fit the description better than *dispensation* unless dispensation is defined as the dispensing of the gospel rather than as a system or time period. Paul is describing the job given specifically to him by no other than God Himself, and he is answerable to God for his performance of the task assigned to him.

(3) EPHESIANS 1:10

Ephesians 1:9–10 (emphasis added)

[9] He made known to us the mystery of His will, according to His kind intention which He purposed in Him [10] with a view to an

administration suitable to the fullness of the times, that is, the summing up of all things in Christ, things in the heavens and things upon the earth.

Ephesians 1:9–10 (emphasis added, ESV)
[9] making known to us the mystery of [H]is will, according to his purpose, which he set forth in Christ [10] as a **plan** for the fullness of time, to unite all things in [H]im, things in heaven and things on earth.

> RSV also uses "plan."

Ephesians 1:9–10 (emphasis added, NIV)
[9] He made known to us the mystery of **[H]is will** according to [H]is good pleasure, which [H]e purposed in Christ, [10] **to be put into effect** when the times reach their fulfillment—to bring unity to all things in heaven and on earth together under Christ.

Ephesians 1:9–10 (emphasis added, KJV)
[9] Having made known unto us the mystery of [H]is will, according to his good pleasure which [H]e hath purposed in [H]imself: [10] That in the **dispensation** of the fulness of times [H]e might gather together in one all things in Christ, both which are in heaven, and which are on earth; even in [H]im.

> NKJV and ASV also use "dispensation."

This passage comes much closer than the prior ones to meeting one of the Merriam-Webster Dictionary definitions of *dispensation* in the religious sense—"a general state or ordering of things" or "a system of revealed commands or promises regulating human affairs."[3] It also fits definition 1.c of *dispensation* in the American Heritage Dictionary—"a specific arrangement or system by which something is dispensed."[4]

---

3   *Merriam-Webster's Collegiate Dictionary*, 11th ed. (2020), under "dispensation."
4   *The American Heritage Dictionary of the English Language*, 5th ed. (2022), under "dispensation."

In other words, the plan of salvation has been revealed in its fullness in Jesus Christ. This passage can also be used to explain progressive revelation and the biblical definition of a mystery, both of which are discussed in sections I.B.3.(a) and (b) above.

(4) EPHESIANS 3:2

<u>Ephesians 3:1-2</u> (emphasis added)

[1] For this reason I, Paul, the prisoner of Christ Jesus for the sake of you Gentiles— [2] if indeed you have heard of the **stewardship** of God's grace which was given to me for you.

> The ESV, AMPC, and RSV also use "stewardship"; the KJV, NKJV, and ASV use "dispensation"; and the NIV and DBT use "administration."

Like 1 Corinthians 9:17 above, the focus in verse 2 here is on the commission or assignment given to Paul rather than on the revelation of God's plan of salvation in the Person of Jesus Christ. A few verses later, however, Paul appears to be speaking of the master plan of God.

(5) EPHESIANS 3:9

<u>Ephesians 3:8-9</u> (emphasis added)

[8] To me, the very least of all saints, this grace was given, to preach to the Gentiles the unfathomable riches of Christ, [9] and to bring to light what is the **administration** of the mystery which for ages has been hidden in God who created all things.

> The NIV and DBT also use "administration"; the ESV, AMPC, and RSV have "plan"; and the KJV and NKJV use "fellowship." Only the ASV uses "dispensation."

In verse 8, Paul refers again (the first time was in 3:2) to the gift of the stewardship of God's grace that was given to him. But in verse 9 *oikonomia* appears again, and here the distinction between the various definitions becomes plain. Clearly, Paul has been assigned or commissioned with the stewardship (one meaning) of the gospel, but what he is stewarding or administering is the eternal plan of salvation (another meaning).

A cogent argument could be made, however, that even in Ephesians 3:9, it is the word *mystery* that really refers to the eternal plan of salvation, not the word *administration* or even the word *plan*. This argument is reinforced by the biblical definition of the English word *mystery*, discussed in section I.B.3.(b) above.

(6) Colossians 1:25

<u>Colossians 1:25</u> (emphasis added)

²⁵ Of this church I was made a minister according to the **stewardship** from God bestowed on me for your benefit, so that I might fully carry out the preaching of the word of God.

> The ESV, NKJV, and AMPC also use "stewardship"; the NIV uses "commission"; the KJV, DBT, and ASV use "dispensation"; and the RSV uses "divine office."

Once more, the reference here is to the commission, the stewardship bestowed on Paul; it does not refer to any system of revelation or governance.

(7) 1 Timothy 1:4

<u>1 Timothy 1:3–4</u> (emphasis added)

³ As I urged you upon my departure for Macedonia, remain on at Ephesus, so that you may instruct certain men not to teach strange doctrines, ⁴ nor to pay attention to myths and endless genealogies, which give rise to mere speculation rather than furthering the **administration** of God which is by faith. (emphasis added)

> The ESV uses "stewardship"; the NIV, "God's work"; the KJV, "godly edifying"; the NKJV, "godly edification"; the ASV and DBT, "dispensation"; the AMPC, "administration and the divine training"; and the RSV, "divine training."

All of these translations focus on the work of the steward entrusted with the gospel.

These seven Bible passages provide at best a very shaky foundation for constructing an entire system (dispensationalism) of God's dealing with mankind over the course of human history. At best, they—especially Ephesians 1:10 and maybe Ephesians 3:9—are a demonstration of God's progressive revelation of His eternal plan, but there are no pillars upon which to rest the varying and inconsistent (in terms of names and duration) bricks of dispensations.

Conclusion: Dispensationalism is a man-made addition to progressive revelation. As noted earlier, dispensationalism is a theological "grid" placed on the Bible that divides the progressive revelation of God's eternal plans into different dispensations, time periods, in history. As such, that is, as an addition to the Bible with many debates and disagreements regarding the naming, timing, and duration of each dispensation, it is not supported by the Bible itself. The next section deals with some of the problems with dispensationalism.

4. THERE ARE PROBLEMS WITH DISPENSATIONALISM

Because of the variety in the number, the naming, and the timing of the dispensations, dispensationalism has evolved into *classical, revised,* and *progressive dispensationalism.* As a result, many prominent dispensationalists have distilled the dispensations into the three shown in the chart above (section I.B.2) and paraphrased here:

- Israel's dispensation = the whole of the Old Testament, including the first sixty-nine weeks of Daniel; then

- the church's dispensation = the gap between the sixty-ninth and seventieth weeks of Daniel; then

- Israel's dispensation again = the entirety of the seventieth week and beyond.

They retain the three key elements of dispensationalism listed earlier and restated here for clarity:

1. The Bible should be consistently interpreted literally unless it is clear that a metaphor or analogy is being used.

2. (a) There is a distinction between Israel and the church. The nation of Israel will ultimately inherit all the blessings that were promised in the Old Testament. God has not finished with the nation of Israel, nor has Israel been assumed into and absorbed by the church.

    (b) Because God has different plans for the church and the nation of Israel, He will deal with them in different dispensations (time periods).

3. God's overall purpose is to bring glory to Himself.

I agree with 1, 2a, and 3 completely. It is only 2b that I disagree with, and that is the purpose of this book. In the following subsections, I will address some of the reasons I disagree with 2b—that is, that because God has different plans for the church and the nation of Israel, He will deal with them in different dispensations.

(a) GOD IS NOT BOUND TO ACT IN ACCORDANCE WITH A MAN-MADE SYSTEM

God is not bound by any man-made grid superimposed onto His Word. While God's unchanging character provides stability and consistency in our finite and limited understanding of Him and His ways, His patterns of behavior rarely change overnight so that He deals with people in one way today and in another way tomorrow. (Exceptions, of course, would be after the fall and after the flood.) The lines of demarcation are usually blurred over a time period—or in some cases, there was never a demarcating line at all, as, for example, in the division between law and grace.

In the case of Israel, Romans 11:25–26 teaches that God has allowed a partial hardening of Israel until the fullness of the gentiles has come in, at which time all Israel will be saved. Who are humans to say that those times (for Israel and for the gentiles) must not or cannot coincide? Who says that God is not already accomplishing both (the fullness of the gentiles and the partial hardening of the Jews) simultaneously?

God is not required to deal with Israel and the church separately, in different time periods, just because humans have assigned them separate dispensations. Indeed, God's partial hardening of the Jews during the time of the gentiles indicates the exact opposite. God is doing a work in the nation of Israel over the very same millennia that gentiles (and Jews too) are being brought to a saving faith.

And God continues to work with both Israel and the church, despite the fact that Daniel's seventieth week has not yet arrived. Who can deny that God Himself wrought the miracle of the rebirth of the nation of Israel in 1948—in a day (Isa. 66:8)? And what about His miracle of the Jews' retention of their culture and religion, despite approximately two millennia of exile from their land? No other nation in history that was conquered and dispossessed from its land retained its culture and religion; rather, they were assimilated into the conquering nation.

Clearly, God was at work in Israel throughout the millennia of the Diaspora. And He is still at work in Israel today, once again (the first time would be the return from the Babylonian exile) fulfilling His own prophetic word through His prophet Ezekiel—see Ezekiel 36:8–12 or the prophecy of the valley of dry bones in chapter 37:1–14. There are further prophecies yet to be fulfilled, but He is already in the process, and the seventieth week has not yet begun.

Not only can God work on two different entities, the church and Israel, at the same time but more importantly, God is perfectly capable of accomplishing multiple goals *through the same action* or sets of actions. For example, the passage in Romans 11:11–15 clearly demonstrates that God is using the Jews' rejection of Jesus to bring salvation to the gentiles—*and at the same time* using the salvation of the gentiles to make Israel jealous, which will ultimately lead to their salvation.

A future example of God's use of the same sets of actions to accomplish differing goals for the church and for Israel is this: He could accomplish (1) His goal of purifying His church (consisting of believing Jews and gentiles), while purging the tares, as well as (2) His goal of purging and redeeming whatever is left to constitute "all Israel" during the same time of the great tribulation.

> The subject of the presence of the church during the great tribulation is addressed in section V.B below.

Another inconsistency with splitting Jewish and Christian dispensations is that the first believers in Jesus were Jews. In fact, most of the early church was Jewish. As Paul explained in Romans 11, while God was partially hardening the nation of Israel for a time, He was also saving individual Jews. So where does one draw the line between God's dealings with Israel and the church when they are clearly occurring at the same time?

The point that I am making is that God can do anything He wants (except lie or be untrue to Himself) in whatever manner He deems best. While dispensationalism cannot limit God or constrain Him in accordance with human time schedules, the system presumes to understand His ways and then make predictions based on those presumptions. As I will demonstrate throughout the remainder of this book, this grid of dispensations, which divides and separates God's dealings with Israel from His dealings with the church, conflicts with the clear, literal language of other portions of the Bible.

(b) The inconsistencies controvert the dispensational view that God will deal with the church and Israel separately

Element 2(b) of dispensationalism states that God will deal with the church and with Israel separately in different dispensations. As I noted earlier, it is the only one of the three sine qua nons that actually deals with dispensationalism.

As mentioned earlier, charts often list seven dispensations:

- Innocence
- Conscience
- Human government
- Promise
- Law
- Grace
- Millennial kingdom

In many of these, the dispensation of grace (#6), also known as the church age, begins with Pentecost in Acts 2 and goes until Revelation 19. Others push the church age all the way to the beginning of the millennium. Since it is generally recognized that the seventieth week begins with the breaking of the seals in Revelation 6, some dispensationalist charts claim that the church age (and therefore the church) will go through the entirety of the seventieth week, including not only the great tribulation, which begins at the midpoint, but all the way to the end of the day of the Lord.

Other charts combine the ages of human government (#3) and promise (#4) into one renamed *authority*, so that a new dispensation called *tribulation* can be inserted between the dispensations of grace (#6) and the millennial kingdom (#7). Others keep the first five, but subdivide the dispensation of grace (#6) into the church and the tribulation, placing the rapture between the two. Curiously, there are even a few dispensationalist charts that place the end of the church age, and thus the rapture, between the books of Philemon and Hebrews.

Plainly, the parameters of the dispensations are completely subjective. What human being is the authority who gets to determine when God passes from one time zone to the next? Neither the Bible nor church history is nearly that clear-cut. The fact is, there is no clarity or even agreement among dispensationalists regarding

- the number of dispensations,
- their names,
- their duration, and
- their starting and ending points.

This highlights the weakness inherent in this man-made grid of interpretation. Any person who believes in pretribulationism should be very aware of the flawed system that gave rise to it.

(1) Who decides when the church age began?

An example of the problem of man-made assignments of dispensations within which God may deal only with a certain entity is the naming and the definition of the church age. Who are human beings to say that the church age began at Pentecost in Acts 2? Why is it called the church age and not the *age of believers* or the *age of the followers of the Way* or the *age of Christians*?

It should come as no surprise that there are actually two views about when the church was born. The dispensationalist view is that the coming of the Holy Spirit at Pentecost was the defining moment. But the other view is that the church (Greek *ekklesia* [*Strong's* NT 1577], meaning "a calling out") began when the *Head of that very ekklesia* began His ministry, calling out disciples and sending them out to proclaim the gospel. These men were the foundation of a new community centered around Him, the chief "corner stone" (Eph. 2:20).

It is obvious from even a cursory reading of the gospels that there were believers/saints before Pentecost, during the time when Jesus walked the earth—which, incidentally, was during the sixty-ninth week of Daniel. Jesus was laying the foundation of this new assembly of His followers when He told Peter that He would build *His church* upon the rock (Matt. 16:18).

Indeed, the fact that Jesus had already established His church is indicated by His own words in Matthew 18:

Matthew 18:15-17

[15] If your brother sins, go and show him his fault in private; if he listens to you, you have won your brother. [16] But if he does not listen to you, take one or two more with you, so that by the mouth of two or three witnesses every fact may be confirmed. [17] If he refuses to listen to them, tell it to **the church**; and if he refuses to listen even to **the church**, let him be to you as a Gentile and a tax collector. (emphasis added)

The fact that God the Holy Spirit had not yet come does not change the fact that believers in God the Son (also called saints) constituted the body of Christ just as surely as did post-Pentecost believers. They may not have had the indwelling of the third member of the Trinity, but they lived in *the physical presence* of the second member of the Trinity.

Nor does the descriptive noun utilized change the fact that the believing person was truly saved during Jesus's incarnation, even though God the Holy Spirit did not come until later. The thief on the cross is just one example. Indeed, throughout the New Testament, the words *church* and *saints* were employed interchangeably.

> See section V.B.1 below for further discussion on this point.

Regardless of the name (church, saints, believers, followers of the Way, Christians), a cogent argument can be made in defense of the view that is the alternative to the dispensationalist view: The body of Christ began to exist when the Head of the church—the Head of the body—walked the earth and called out men who followed Him and came to faith in Him during His lifetime.

Indeed, all of time is reckoned from the estimated time of the incarnation of God the Son (BC or AD), not from the time of the coming of God the Holy Spirit.

The problem for dispensationalists is that assigning the life or even just the ministry of Jesus Himself as the beginning of the church age dispensation would blur the hard lines of the dispensational chart in three ways:

- Jesus lived and ministered during the sixty-ninth week of Daniel and was not crucified until after the end of the sixty-ninth week. Thus, if the church age were to begin with Jesus's ministry, it would begin in the sixty-ninth week and not in the more convenient (from the dispensationalist view) gap between the sixty-ninth and seventieth weeks.

- There would be an overlap of the church age dispensation and the Israel dispensation (which was still ongoing in the sixty-ninth week).

- The absence of hard lines between the dispensations defeats the entire grid.

Again, the assignment of dispensations, being subjectively and variously determined by human beings, does not carry the weight of biblical authority.

> **(2) Why does the church age have to end at the beginning of the seventieth week?**

IF one removes

- the overlay of the man-made grid of dispensations—dispensations which are in turn based on

- the initial determination by humans regarding whether, in any given passage, God is dealing with Israel or with the church,

THEN a careful reader of the Bible in its entirety can see that there are no clean breaks between God's dealings with Israel and the church. Even though the nation of Israel has a future that is not subsumed under the church, there are threads throughout the Bible that connect both entities in the tapestry that is God's master plan for the whole of mankind.

> **(aa) Promises made in the Old Testament regarding Israel's future have their fulfillment both in the church and in Israel**

Most students of prophetic eschatology agree that the seventieth week begins with the breaking of the seals in Revelation 6.

Most pretribulationists today hold that the rapture of believers occurs at the beginning of John's vision in Revelation 4, and that the rest of the book of Revelation, including the millennium, relates only and entirely to God's dealings with Israel. This accords with the dispensational view that the church age is a parenthetical between God's dealings with Israel on either side of the parenthetical and that when the seventieth week begins, He will have completed His dealings with the church and will resume His dealings with Israel.

But what does the Bible, specifically Revelation, actually *say*? Where does it say that the seventieth week and, in particular, the great tribulation, are only for Jews or that God has finished with the church? It is apparent that this conclusion is merely an inference drawn from

- an initial determination, under the principle of *rightly dividing*, that the book of Daniel, being in the Old Testament, was part of the Jewish dispensation and had no relation to a church that would not come into existence for almost another six hundred years; and

- the grid of dispensationalism, which defines the seventy weeks of Daniel as a Jewish dispensation only, and the gap between the sixty-ninth and seventieth weeks as a parenthetical church age; and

- the resulting conclusion that, since the seventieth week begins with the breaking of the seals in Revelation 6, the Jewish age must resume at the latest at that point—if not before, at the beginning of Revelation 4—and therefore the church must be raptured out before that time.

Can such an inference be justified?

Consider other Old Testament prophetic promises made only to Jews, long before anyone had any inkling of a "church."

Search every word in the book of the prophet Joel, whose ministry was approximately eight hundred years before Christ, and you will find not one reference, direct or oblique, to the church. Yet, in the second chapter there are glorious promises of restoration of relationship that extend far beyond Israel. In the midst of these verses, this promise appears:

Joel 2:28–29 (emphasis added)

²⁸ I will pour out My Spirit **on all mankind;**

And your sons and daughters will prophesy,
Your old men will dream dreams,
Your young men will see visions.
²⁹ Even on the male and female servants
I will pour out My Spirit in those days.

This prophecy was made to Israel, to Jews. And yet dispensationalists have no problem understanding that this promise has a double fulfillment—to gentile and Jewish believers from the time of Christ and also to Israel when the prophecies of Romans 11:25–27 will be fulfilled. Of course, its New Testament application is hard to deny, because Peter quoted Joel 2 in his first public speech at Pentecost.

The same principle, that Old Testament prophecies have their fulfillment not just in Israel but also to the church, applies to Jeremiah 31, which was addressed explicitly to "the house of Israel and the house of Judah." Jeremiah prophesied approximately six hundred years before Christ. Again, there is not one word about the church.

Jeremiah 31:31–33 (emphasis added)

³¹ "Behold, days are coming," declares the Lord, "when I will make a new covenant **with the house of Israel and with the house of Judah,** ³² not like the covenant which I made with their fathers in the day I took them by the hand to bring them out of the land of Egypt, My covenant which they broke, although I was a husband to them," declares the Lord. ³³ "But this is the covenant which I will make **with the house of Israel** after those days," declares the Lord, "I will put My law within them and on their heart I will write it; and I will be their God, and they shall be My people."

Once again, dispensationalists have no difficulty applying to the church this prophecy, which was given exclusively to Israel. Like all Christians who have read Hebrews 8:6–13, dispensationalists understand that this promise is in effect with all believers in Christ, whether gentile or Jew, and when Romans 11:25–27 is fulfilled, "all Israel" as a people will also be saved and brought into this new covenant.

Despite this unity of God's purposes for both Israel and the church, seen first in the Old Testament and later in the New Testament, dispensationalists insist that, when it comes to Revelation, they must revert to their foundational principle of deciding first whether God is dealing with Israel or with the church. Once that decision is made, all interpretations must be made with that lens firmly in place.

SINCE the dispensationalist decision has already been made that

- the church age ends either at Revelation 4 or, at the latest, at Revelation 6, when the first seal is broken, signaling the beginning of the seventieth week, and

- the Jewish dispensation resumes at that point,

THEN it is only logical to conclude that the references in Revelation 13:7 and 17:6 to

- the saints,

- every tribe and people and tongue and nation, and

- the witnesses of Jesus

must refer only to Jews because the church age has ended and God can deal only with Jews from this point forward.

These conclusions are reinforced by Jeremiah 30:7, in which God, again speaking only to Israel, describes "the time of Jacob's distress." Having already concluded that the seventieth week applies only to Israel and forgetting their earlier application to the church of other Old Testament prophecies naming only Israel, dispensationalists are not even consistent in the use of their man-made hermeneutic that any Scripture deals only with either Israel or with the church.

SINCE dispensationalists have no problem applying Old Testament prophetic promises made to Israel to the church as well as to Israel (which breaks their cardinal rule about any given Scripture applying only either to the church or to Israel),

THEN why should the prophecies about the seventieth week, including the great tribulation, not apply to the church as well as to Israel? The assumption that suddenly God can deal only with Israel because any given Scripture applies only to either Israel or to the church is a man-made construct that is neither supported in the Bible nor even applied consistently by dispensationalists.

(bb) God the Holy Spirit does not have to leave the earth, taking the church with Him, before the seventieth week

Even if you choose the dispensational view that the church age began with the coming of God the Holy Spirit in Acts 2—that is, after the completion of the sixty-ninth week and during the gap between the sixty-ninth and seventieth weeks—there is no logical reason to conclude from this that God the Holy Spirit must leave the earth, taking the church with Him, before the seventieth week commences, for at least five reasons:

1. God the Holy Spirit did not just appear in the Bible in Acts 2 of the New Testament after the expiration of the sixty-ninth week so that He has to leave before the commencement of the seventieth week. He has been in the Bible from the beginning. Indeed, like God the Father and God the Son, He has existed before time was created and before the Bible was written. What is the logic in requiring Him to leave at *any* particular time?

2. The two witnesses of Revelation 11 will be on the earth during the seventieth week, and while their identity is not spelled out in the Bible, the very fact that they are God's witnesses is a strong indication that God the Holy Spirit will be present in them.

3. While God the Holy Spirit did not previously indwell believers as He did from the time of Pentecost going forward, the Bible explicitly teaches that He did indwell people in the Old Testament—in some cases for as long as it took to complete a God-given task but in other cases for the remainder of the person's life. Here is a sampling of examples:

    - Bezalel (Ex. 31:3; 35:31)

    - Moses and the 70 elders (Num. 11:17)

- Joshua (Num. 27:18)
- many of the judges of Israel in the book of Judges
- King Saul (1 Sam. 10:10, 11:6), with the Spirit later departing (1 Sam. 16:14)
- King David (1 Sam. 16:13)
- Azariah (2 Chron. 15:1).

4. According to the dispensationalist view, the church did not come into existence until the New Testament (i.e., it did not exist in the Old Testament), but that fact does not logically lead to the conclusion that it has to go out of existence (or at least out of this world) before the commencement of the seventieth week. Once in existence, why *can't* the church continue to exist into the seventieth week also (which is still in the New Testament)?

5. According to the alternate view of when the church came into existence (during Jesus's ministry), the church did not exist in the Old Testament, but it did exist before the expiration of the sixty-ninth week. Since Jesus's ministry—also in the New Testament—was in the sixty-ninth week, it means that both the sixty-ninth and seventieth weeks are in the New Testament. If the church existed in the sixty-ninth week, why should it have to cease to exist in the seventieth week?

Furthermore, since a "week" is seven years and since Jesus's life lasted approximately thirty-three years, that means the New Testament also includes about four and a half additional weeks (part of the sixty-fourth week and the whole of the sixty-fifth, sixty-sixth, sixty-seventh, and sixty-eighth weeks, as well as the sixty-ninth week). This would be a huge overlap of the dispensationalist's church age dispensation and Israel's dispensation! No wonder dispensationalists begin with Pentecost, after the sixty-ninth week is clearly over.

Later, I will make the argument that the church will indeed go into the seventieth week and into the great tribulation, which starts at the midpoint. I will address the dispensational argument that the absence of the word *church* after Revelation 3 requires the pretribulation rapture.

| See sections V.B and C below.

(cc) GOD THE HOLY SPIRIT IS NOT THE RESTRAINER

The assumption that God the Holy Spirit must remove the church before the commencement of the seventieth week is based on the further assumption that God the Holy Spirit is the restrainer of 2 Thessalonians 2:6–7. There are two problems with this assumption:

1. The view that God the Holy Spirit *alone* possesses the power to restrain Satan's evil intentions and assaults against His people is misguided. The Trinitarian God is omnipotent. He alone is God. Satan, though powerful beyond any human comprehension, is nevertheless a created being (whose ultimate destination is the lake of fire). His power is by no means equal to God's power.

   And God, the Commander of the host, has used those under His command to restrain evil in the world throughout history. One example of warfare in the unseen realm is given in Daniel 10:12–14, when in response to Daniel's prayers, an angel was dispatched from heaven. But the angel was waylaid by "the prince of the kingdom of Persia" and prevented from reaching Daniel for three weeks. But "Michael, one of the chief princes" came to help the ambushed angel, and he was able to get to Daniel.

   Consider another biblical example of angelic victory in the unseen realm, this time against Satan himself: Michael the archangel, when he disputed with the devil about the body of Moses, did not dare pronounce against him a railing judgment but said, "The Lord rebuke you!" (Jude 9).

   At first glance, this sounds as if Satan's power is at least equal to, if not greater than Michael's and, further, that Michael feared Satan because he "did not dare." But the Greek word for "railing" actually means blasphemy. The idea is that of language of reproach in terms that would be offensive to the Lord. Apparently,

Satan was insulting Moses, God's own servant, but Michael refrained from insulting Satan in turn for fear of offending God.

Instead, Michael, under God's authority, merely relayed the Lord's command to Satan to cease his activity and move away. The text is clear that the devil did not win the dispute over Moses's body; Michael won, in the power and authority of the Most High God, whom he served.

And finally, there is the example of Revelation 20:1–3, in which "an angel," (*one* angel) lays hold of the dragon (Satan), binds him with a great chain, and throws him into the abyss.

Thus, we can know that God is able to empower the celestial beings (singular or plural) under His command to restrain even all the world's evil against His people.

Even more important to the question as to whether God the Holy Spirit is the restrainer of 2 Thessalonians 2 is the following point.

2. The restrainer's removal (2 Thessalonians 2) is *not even related to the rapture*, because the removal of the restrainer is associated with the onset of the great tribulation *at the midpoint of the seventieth week, not at the beginning of the seventieth week* itself. The rapture will happen before the day of the Lord, *not* before the great tribulation and also *not* before the beginning of the seventieth week.

> Additional points about the restrainer will be developed in sections IV.D.1.(b) and 3 below.

Conclusion: Pretribulationism is based on the assumption that God can or must deal with Israel or with the church only individually—not both at the same time—simply because dispensationalism's man-made (and inconsistent) grid has placed God's dealings with Israel and with the church into separate dispensations. If one accepts this premise, it follows logically that God must remove the church from the world before He can deal with Israel again. The problem is that the premise, the assumption, the foundation upon which pretribulationism is based, is fatally flawed.

Elements 1, 2(a), and 3 of dispensationalism have made critical and necessary contributions to our understanding of God's Word. In contrast, element 2(b)—that God must deal with Israel and the church in different dispensations because any given Bible passage can address either only Israel or only the church—is an entirely human construct. It is unlike the others in two ways:

- It is the only element (or, more accurately, subelement of element 2) that actually deals with dispensationalism.

- It is not the result of exegesis, but is rather eisegesis, which means that a concept or doctrine is imposed upon the Bible rather than gleaned from it.

This is similar to what Calvin and Luther did as they attempted to correct a critical error of the Catholic Church by pointing out that the Bible explicitly teaches that salvation is by faith, not by the sacraments of the Church and by works. When the Catholic Church excommunicated these men, they began their own churches, which was led to the inception of Protestantism.

Among the Protestant Reformation's great gifts was its adherence to the Bible's clear teaching that salvation is by faith alone. However, Calvin and Luther did not address other biblical errors of the Catholic Church.

Errors retained by Calvin and Luther include the following:

- First are the unbiblical Catholic beliefs that the church has replaced Israel in God's economy, and that God had no further dealings with Israel after the advent of the Catholic Church. Such teachings resulted in rampant antisemitism both in the past and increasingly so in the present with the rise of neo-Calvinism in America today.

- In addition, *preterism*, the belief that all or most prophecy has been fulfilled in the past, led to the de-emphasis on all prophetic books—indeed, Luther believed that the book of Revelation should be removed from the Bible.

Just as Luther and Calvin corrected the Catholic doctrine of salvation through the sacraments and by works, dispensationalism

- corrected the Catholic/Calvinist replacement theology—but at the same time

- brought in a man-made grid of dispensations that separates God's dealings with the church from His dealings with Israel into different time zones.

Although the proliferation of dispensations resulted in a decline in the popularity of dispensationalism, the division of Israel and the church into different time zones remained because of the underlying principle of predetermining whether any particular biblical passage dealt with Israel or with the church. The natural consequence of that was and is the retention of the doctrine of a pretribulation rapture. Pretribulationism is the prominent product of dispensationalism.

Depending upon which chart one is using and whether one accepts the dispensationalist view that God can/must deal with Israel only after He has finished dealing with the church, I can see how someone might preemptively dismiss all the arguments I will present in this book.

My request, therefore, is that such people remember that

- I agree with elements 1, 2(a), and 3 of dispensationalism (and with premillennialism),

- I am addressing only element 2(b), and

- the *timing* of the rapture is not a foundational truth of the gospel (though the rapture itself is) and therefore should not ever be a cause of division among believers or among churches. There is absolutely no justification for churches excluding from their fellowship believers with differing views on this issue, as some pastors are doing today. Intolerance of differing views merely on the timing of the rapture should never be present in any believer.

I respectfully request that readers with views regarding element 2(b) that are different from mine set aside their grids, just for as long as it takes to read carefully and consider the arguments presented in this book.

Section II

THE RISK OF DECEPTION

PRETRIBULATIONISM CREATES THE RISK OF BELIEVERS BEING DECEIVED AND FALLING AWAY FROM THE FAITH

If pretribulationism is proved wrong in the passage of time, this may cause some who are unprepared to endure the great tribulation to fall away from their faith when it comes.

A. IT IS SPIRITUALLY DANGEROUS TO FAIL TO PREPARE FOR PERSECUTION

Many pastors/teachers/shepherds are teaching their flocks that they need not concern themselves with the coming life-or-death decision of whether to take the mark of the beast because Christians will be raptured out of the world before it all happens. For that reason, believers won't have to deal with cruel persecution or the vitriolic hatred of soon-to-be former friends and neighbors as Christians are blamed for all the economic and social and legal problems of the world.

But, what if? What if the shepherds are wrong and believers *do* have to suffer loss of jobs, income, health insurance, medical care, food, a roof over their heads, and even warm clothing? What if they have to go into hiding from the antichrist's massive police force, who will have all the sophisticated technological tools for tracking Christians down and incarcerating them, separating families, torturing them, and executing them?

In Ecclesiastes 1:9, Solomon wrote that "there is nothing new under the sun." But the great tribulation will be the first thing that is indeed new under the sun, because Jesus described it as tribulation "such as has not occurred since the beginning of the world until now, nor ever will" (Matt. 24:21).

How many people, utterly unprepared, will cave under that kind of unexpected and unprecedented tribulation? How many will turn on their pastors in anger because their teachings were wrong? Many will become bitter and decide that if the pretribulation teaching was wrong, all the rest of the church's teaching must also be wrong. Their "love will grow cold" (Matt. 24:12) as the society we all know crumbles into anarchy and then tyranny. People in desperation will do whatever they think they must do to keep their children from starving or being removed from them.

Americans in particular do not heed biblical warnings to expect tribulation in this world that is ruled by Satan, the prince of the power of the air (Eph. 2:2), simply because that has not been our experience, though it has been for Christians in other countries. But just as antisemitism is rearing its ugly head, it is only a matter of time before the world focuses its hatred on Christians. Yet there are few, if any, watchmen in the pulpits, warning Christians to strengthen their spiritual muscles while they can.

B. It is important for all believers to be prepared to suffer persecution and to be faithful unto death

All believers must be prepared to enter into the great tribulation, regardless of which rapture position they adopt. Since Jesus repeatedly warned about the eternal perils of the great deception that will be the hallmark of Daniel's seventieth week, there can be no substitute for each believer saturating himself or herself in the Word of God and hiding His Word in their heart, learning the signs of the seasons, and staying alert:

<u>**Psalm 19:7–13**</u>
[7] The law of the Lord is perfect, restoring the soul;
The testimony of the Lord is sure, making wise the simple.
[8] The precepts of the Lord are right, rejoicing the heart;
The commandment of the Lord is pure, enlightening the eyes.

9 The fear of the LORD is clean, enduring forever;
The judgments of the LORD are true; they are righteous altogether.
10 They are more desirable than gold, yes, than much fine gold;
Sweeter also than honey and the drippings of the honeycomb.
11 Moreover, by them Your servant is warned;
In keeping them there is great reward.
12 Who can discern [H]is errors? Acquit me of hidden faults.
13 Also keep back Your servant from presumptuous sins;
Let them not rule over me;
Then I will be blameless,
And I shall be acquitted of great transgression.

Psalm 119:9–11 (NIV)

9 How can a young person stay on the path of purity? By living according to [Y]our word. 10 I seek [Y]ou with all my heart; do not let me stray from [Y]our commands. 11 I have hidden [Y]our word in my heart that I might not sin against [Y]ou.

Mark 13:28–29, 33–37

28 Now learn the parable from the fig tree: when its branch has already become tender and puts forth its leaves, you know that summer is near. 29 Even so, you too, when you see these things happening, recognize that He is near, right at the door.

33 Take heed, keep on the alert; for you do not know when the appointed time will come. 34 It is like a man away on a journey, who upon leaving his house and putting his slaves in charge, assigning to each one his task, also commanded the doorkeeper to stay on the alert. 35 Therefore, be on the alert—for you do not know when the master of the house is coming, whether in the evening, at midnight, or when the rooster crows, or in the morning—36 lest he come suddenly and find you asleep. 37 What I say to you I say to all, "Be on the alert!"

Parallel passages in Matt. 24:32–33; Luke 21:28–36.

C. The prewrath rapture position is an alternative, though it, too, has problems

As an alternative to pretribulationism, I will take the prewrath rapture position in this book, though it, too, has problems. Those problems are addressed in section V.D.2 below. The point of this book, however, is not to advocate for the prewrath rapture position but rather to focus on the flaws of pretribulationism.

The prewrath rapture position is based on the premise that the day of the Lord is the wrath from which Christians are promised deliverance and that this day of the Lord is a time period near the end of Daniel's seventieth week. It is believed to begin at the time that the Lord cuts short the days of the great tribulation:

Matthew 24:22

Unless those days had been cut short, no life would have been saved; but for the sake of the elect those days will be cut short.

At Matthew 24:29 in the Olivet Discourse, Jesus describes cosmic disturbances that parallel Revelation 6:12–17, followed by His glorious appearance on the clouds of the sky (Matt. 24:30). He then describes (Matt. 24:31) what, on its face, appears to be the rapture of 1 Thessalonians 4 and 1 Corinthians 15:

Matthew 24:31

And He will send forth His angels with a great trumpet and they will gather together His elect from the four winds, from one end of the sky to the other.

There is less danger of apostasy and defection from the faith for those who are spiritually prepared (as much as it is possible) to appropriate the grace of God as and when needed to endure the horrors of the great tribulation, even knowing that most of them will not survive to the time when the Lord cuts those days short.

Section III

The Pillars

The pillars of pretribulationism
must be compared to the biblical text

Most Christians agree that Daniel's seventieth week, a period of seven years (Dan. 9:24–27), begins at Revelation 6 with the breaking of the first seal. From that point, the different rapture positions vary.

Remember that pretribulationism is a product of dispensationalism, which holds that God deals differently with different groups of people in distinct dispensations, though there is no consistency or objectivity in the number and names and lengths of each dispensation.

Nevertheless, dispensationalism requires that God will not or cannot or must not resume His dealings with Israel until after He has raptured the church out of the world. Because dispensationalists have concluded that the seventieth week is the beginning of another of God's dispensations dealing with Israel, the natural result is that the prior dispensation, the church age, must end at that same time. This grid is superimposed upon the text of the Bible, and the result is pretribulationism.

Pretribulationism rests upon the following foundational pillars:

- Pillar 1: The entire seventieth week (all seven years) is a time of tribulation.

- Pillar 2: All seven years of that tribulation are God's wrath in the day of the Lord.

- Pillar 3: Believers are spared from God's wrath in the day of the Lord.

Putting pillars 2 and 3 together leads to a corollary: The rapture must occur before the commencement of the seventieth week.

- Pillar 4: The rapture is imminent, likely to happen at any moment, because there is nothing more in biblical prophecy that needs to happen before the rapture.

A. PILLAR 1. THE SEVEN YEARS OF THE SEVENTIETH WEEK OF DANIEL 9:24–27 ARE ALL A TIME OF TRIBULATION

The events of Daniel's seventieth week are the skeletal framework for end-time prophecy. This skeleton was fleshed in by prophecies given

- by many other Old Testament prophets, such as Joel and Zechariah;

- by Jesus during His incarnation, as recorded in the three synoptic gospels (Matthew 24–25; Mark 13; and Luke 17 and 21);

- by Paul in his two letters to the Thessalonians and his first letter to the Corinthians; and later

- through John, who recorded his visions in the book of Revelation.

The seals of Revelation 6 are paralleled by Jesus's description in Matthew 24:4–31, Mark 13:4–27, and Luke 21:7–28. These parallels are set out in the chart in section III.B/pillar 2.1 below. For purposes of this discussion, I will focus on Matthew.

Referencing Daniel, which places an abomination of desolation at the midpoint of the week (i.e., at three and a half years into the seven years), Jesus calls the time period before that abomination "the beginning of sorrows" or "the beginning of birth pangs" (Matt. 24:8).

"*Then*," He says in verse 9, referring to the midpoint, "they will deliver you to tribulation." In verses 15 and 21, He clarifies that at the midpoint of the seven years, when the abomination of desolation occurs, there will be a "great tribulation, such as has not occurred since the beginning of the world until now, nor ever will."

Thus, Jesus referred to the first half of the seven years as "the beginning of birth pangs" and only the second half as the "great tribulation." There is no seven-year period of tribulation; there is only a *great* tribulation, and it begins at the midpoint of the seven years, not at the beginning. What begins at Revelation 6 with the breaking of the first seal is the beginning of birth pangs.

Conclusion: It is a misnomer to call the entire seven years of Daniel's seventieth week "the tribulation" or "the tribulation period" because that is not what Jesus taught. Unfortunately, it is this inaccurate designation that is the basis for the names of three of the four positions regarding the timing of the rapture: *pretribulation, midtribulation,* and *posttribulation.* All of these names are based upon the faulty assumption that the entire seven years is a tribulation period. Because of Jesus's designation of the first half of the seventieth week as "the beginning of birth pangs" and the second half as the "great tribulation," pillar 1—that all seven years of Daniel's seventieth week are a time of tribulation—is incorrect.

B. Pillar 2: All seven years of that tribulation are God's wrath in the day of the Lord

Dispensationalism is the reason why pillar 2 has to exist. And dispensationalism's structure, its division of time into dispensations, is also the source of the belief that the rapture must occur before the seventieth week.

IF one believes that God must get the church out of the way, in the form of the rapture, before He can deal with Israel, and

IF one also believes that the whole of the seventieth week is Israel's dispensation,

THEN it follows that one will believe that God must end the church age dispensation before the seventieth week, and rapture the church out of the world.

Furthermore,

IF the church's dispensation must end so that Israel's dispensation can begin and

SINCE the Bible promises that believers (the church) will be spared from God's wrath (which is pillar 3),

THEN not only must the rapture of the church occur at the beginning of the seventieth week but also

THEN the seventieth week must be, in its entirety, the wrath of the day of the Lord from which believers are spared.

The problem with this picture is that placing a man-made grid of dispensations onto the text of the Bible causes people to read and interpret the Bible in accordance with the grid that provides the mindset, the lens through which they see and think. The grid itself, rather than the text, leads to conclusions.

But when one removes the grid of dispensations and allows the Bible to speak for itself and to interpret itself, a different picture emerges.

In 1 Thessalonians 5:21, according to the NASB95, Paul admonished all believers to "examine everything carefully; hold fast to that which is good." The NIV and ESV have "test everything/all things" and the KJV has "prove all things." So let's carefully examine, test, and prove what Jesus actually said about tribulation and wrath.

Jesus expressly and explicitly warned people to count the cost (Luke 14:28–33) of following Him, because following Him involves hardship, sacrifice, suffering, persecution, and tribulation in this world.

| See appendix A for examples.

As God is sovereign, He has chosen to allow His people to suffer—for our good and for His glory. He either allows Satan to "sift" us (e.g., Luke 22:31; Rev. 12:12 and 17; and the book of Job), or He tests us directly to see whether we will remain faithful to Him. There are also times when God Himself punishes His people in His wrath for their obstinate refusal to turn away from their sin and return to Him.

| See appendix B for examples.

What, then, is the difference between, on the one hand, God's testing of His people in allowing or sending tribulation and, on the other hand, God's wrath? In other words, how is God's wrath different from the enormous range of suffering that God's people experience in this life? The answer is that it is not always possible to discern the difference. One reason this is so is that His wrath can be punitive or simply corrective discipline.

> Examples of the latter are listed in appendix C.

Nevertheless, apart from the obvious use of different words both in Greek (New Testament) and in English, the Bible does make a distinction not only between tribulation and wrath but also between

- tribulation and
- the great tribulation.

It also distinguishes among

- God's wrath,
- the wrath of the day of the Lord, and
- eternal wrath/hell/the second death/the lake of fire.

As noted earlier, it is important to use correct terminology to avoid being misled into incorrect conclusions.

1. Tribulation versus the great tribulation

When Jesus walked the earth, tribulation was a very real, ever-present, *and future* threat, and Jesus warned His followers, whether Jewish or gentile, about it. Trials in this life were and are common, and they can originate from the wrath of Satan or from the evil of fallen mankind or from the world system that has been in place since the fall of Adam. From the first century AD up to and including the present time, these warnings and encouragement of Jesus apply to every believer enduring various trials throughout their lifetimes:

John 15:18–19

[18] If the world hates you, you know that it has hated Me before it hated you. [19] If you were of the world, the world would love its own;

but because you are not of the world, but I chose you out of the world, because of this the world hates you.

John 16:33

In the world you have tribulation, but take courage; I have overcome the world.

Ephesians 6:11–12

[11] Put on the full armor of God, so that you will be able to stand firm against the schemes of the devil. [12] For our struggle is not against flesh and blood, but against the rulers, against the powers, against the world forces of this darkness, against the spiritual forces of wickedness in the heavenly places.

2 Timothy 3:12

Indeed, all who desire to live godly in Christ Jesus will be persecuted.

The Greek word that is translated into English as "tribulation" is *thlipsis* (*Strong's* NT 2347). It means "pressure," either literally or figuratively. It is translated into English as "tribulation, affliction, anguish, persecution, oppression, trouble."

This word, *thlipsis*, is used forty-five times in the New Testament but only six times in a clear prophetic context. Five of those are in Jesus's teachings in the gospels (Matt. 24:9, 21, 29; Mark 13:19, 24), and the sixth is in Revelation 7:14.

Jesus's warnings in the prophetic context are different from His general warnings about trials, tests, and tribulations common to all believers. In the context of His teaching about the abomination of desolation that will occur in the midpoint of the seventieth week, Jesus described the "great tribulation" that will follow on the heels of this dreadful event (the abomination of desolation).

The great tribulation will last up to three and a half years, until Jesus comes and cuts short the days of that great tribulation. While, in the course of His teaching, He occasionally used the word *tribulation* without the modifying adjective *great* (e.g., Matt. 24:9), it is clear that He is still referring to what He Himself called the great tribulation.

He *only* used the term *great tribulation* in the context of this particular period in the end times. Regarding this great tribulation, Jesus warned that His followers would suffer unprecedented persecution at the hands of the false christ (the antichrist) prior to His return, and He always peppered His teachings with particular warnings *not to be deceived*:

Matthew 24:4 (NKJV)

And Jesus answered and said to them, "Take heed that no one deceives you."

> Parallel passages in Mark 13:5; Luke 21:8.

Matthew 24:23–26 (NKJV)

23 Then if anyone says to you, "Look, here is the Christ!" or "There!" do not believe it. 24 For false christs and false prophets will rise and show great signs and wonders to deceive, if possible, even the elect. 25 See, I have told you beforehand. 26 Therefore if they say to you, "Look, He is in the desert!" do not go out; or "Look, He is in the inner rooms!" do not believe it.

> Parallel passages in Mark 13:21–23; Luke 17:22–23

Following all these warnings not to be deceived, Jesus provided a litany of both natural and man-made disasters that would precede His coming again. This list parallels the first six seals of Revelation 6. As Jesus continued His discourse, His words found their counterpart in the opening verse and verses 9–17 of Revelation 7. These parallels are set out in the chart below.

OLIVET DISCOURSE	REVELATION 6–7
"For many will come in My name, saying, 'I am the Christ,' and will mislead many." Matt 24:5	The first seal is the white horse and rider, and "he who sat on it had a bow; and a crown was given to him; and he went out conquering, and to conquer." Rev. 6:1-2 (He is understood to be the antichrist; note crown and bow but no arrow.)
"And you will be hearing of wars and rumors of wars; see that you are not frightened, for those things must take place, but that is not yet the end. For nation will rise against nation, and kingdom against kingdom." Matt 24:6-7a	The second seal is the red horse and "to him who sat on it, it was granted to take peace from the earth, and that men should slay one another; and a great sword was given to him." Rev. 6:3-4
". . . and in various places there will be famines. . . ." Matt 24:7b	The third seal is the black horse and rider. He is given a scale to measure the food supply. He will bring famine: "[H]e who sat on it had a pair of scales in his hand. And I heard as it were a voice in the center of the four living creatures saying, 'A quart of wheat for a denarius, and three quarts of barley for a denarius; and do not harm the oil and the wine.'" Rev 6:5-6

OLIVET DISCOURSE	REVELATION 6–7
"…and pestilences, and earthquakes. But all these things are merely the beginning of birth pangs." Matt 24:7c-8 NOTE: "Pestilences" is present only in variant mss, but it was not original. In English, it appears only in the KJV and NKJV.	The fourth seal is "an ashen horse; and he who sat on it had the name Death; and Hades was following with him. And authority was given to them over a fourth of the earth, to kill with sword and with famine and with pestilence [Greek thanatos: death] and by the wild beasts of the earth." Rev. 6:7-8

OLIVET DISCOURSE	REVELATION 6–7
"Then they will deliver you to tribulation, and will kill you, and you will be hated by all nations on account of My name. And at that time many will fall away and will deliver up one another and hate one another. And many false prophets will arise, and will mislead many. And because lawlessness is increased, most people's love will grow cold. Therefore when you see the abomination of desolation which was spoken of through Daniel the prophet, standing in the holy place (let the reader understand), then let those who are in Judea flee to the mountains . . . for then there will be a great tribulation, such as has not occurred since the beginning of the world until now, nor ever shall. And unless those days had been cut short, no life would have been saved; but for the sake of the elect those days shall be cut short. Then if anyone says to you, 'Behold, here is the Christ,' or 'There He is,' do not believe him. For false christs and false prophets will arise and will show great signs and wonders, so as to mislead, if possible, even the elect. Behold, I have told you in advance." Matt 24:9-25	"And when He broke the fifth seal, I saw underneath the altar the souls of those who had been slain because of the word of God, and because of the testimony which they had maintained; and they cried out with a loud voice, saying, 'How long, O Lord, holy and true, wilt Thou refrain from judging and avenging our blood on those who dwell on the earth?' And there was given to each of them a white robe; and they were told that they should rest for a little while longer, until the number of their fellow servants and their brethren who were to be killed even as they had been, should be completed also." Rev 6:9-11

OLIVET DISCOURSE	REVELATION 6–7
"But immediately after the tribulation of those days the sun will be darkened, and the moon will not give its light, and the stars will fall from the sky, and the powers of the heavens will be shaken." Matt 24:29 "But in those days, after that tribulation, the sun will be darkened, and the moon will not give its light, and the stars will be falling from heaven, and the powers that are in the heavens will be shaken." Mark 13:24-25 "And there will be signs in sun and moon and stars, and upon the earth dismay among nations, in perplexity at the roaring of the sea and the waves, men fainting from fear and the expectation of the things which are coming upon the world; for the powers of the heavens will be shaken." Luke 21:25-26	"[W]hen He broke the sixth seal, there was a great earthquake; and the sun became black as sackcloth made of hair, and the whole moon became like blood; and the stars of the sky fell to the earth, as a fig tree casts its unripe figs when shaken by a great wind. And the sky was split apart like a scroll when it is rolled up; and every mountain and island were moved out of their places. And the kings of the earth and the great men and the commanders and the rich and the strong and every slave and free man, hid themselves in the caves and among the rocks of the mountains; and they said to the mountains and to the rocks, 'Fall on us and hide us from the presence of Him who sits on the throne, and from the wrath of the Lamb; for the great day of their wrath has come; and who is able to stand?'" Rev 6:12-17

OLIVET DISCOURSE	REVELATION 6–7
"and then the sign of the Son of Man will appear in the sky, and then all the tribes of the earth will mourn, and they will see the Son of Man coming on the clouds of the sky with power and great glory. And He will send forth His angels with a great trumpet and they will gather together His elect from the four winds, from one end of the sky to the other." Matt 24:30-31 "And then they will see the Son of Man coming in clouds with great power and glory. And then He will send forth the angels, and will gather together His elect from the four winds, from the farthest end of the earth, to the farthest end of heaven." Mark 13:26-27 "And then they will see the Son of Man coming in a cloud with power and great glory. But when these things begin to take place, straighten up and lift up your heads, because your redemption is drawing near." Luke 21:27-28	After this I saw four angels standing at the four corners of the earth, holding back the four winds of the earth, so that no wind should blow on the earth or on the sea or on any tree. . . . [B]ehold, a great multitude, which no one could count, from every nation and all tribes and peoples and tongues, standing before the throne and before the Lamb, clothed in white robes, and palm branches were in their hands. . . . These are the ones who come out of the great tribulation, and they have washed their robes and made them white in the blood of the Lamb. Rev 7:1, 9, 14

The fact that Jesus provided this information in such great detail to His followers is a strong indication that *they would need this information.*

The reader should not be distracted by the fact that the apostles were all Jewish and think that therefore the information was provided only for Jews.

A similar misunderstanding exists regarding the Sermon on the Mount. Some dispensationalists believe that it, too, was addressed only to the Jewish audience. But did not the Sermon on the Mount set out God's *eternal* standard of perfection? Of course it did. And did that standard apply only to Jesus's immediate hearers and not to those who would read His words later? Of course not.

Remember that Jesus also provided the memorial of the Last Supper and the Great Commission to the same small group of Jewish followers, yet no one assumes that those were limited to Jewish followers. The words of Jesus were meant for all believers over the millennia.

For those readers who think that Jesus's warnings in His Olivet Discourse were meant only for the Jews or perhaps only for those people who would become believers during the great tribulation (meaning: after the rapture), I have addressed those beliefs in section IV.D below in most of the thirteen subsections.

It is important to note that these warnings regarding the great tribulation and the list of catastrophic events end with the triumphant return of Jesus coming on the clouds with power and great glory. The verses immediately following the cosmic disturbances in the gospels of Matthew and Mark describe what looks exactly like a description of the rapture in 1 Thessalonians 4—all three passages are quoted below:

<u>Matthew 24:29–31</u>

[29] But immediately after the tribulation of those days the sun will be darkened, and the moon will not give its light, and the stars will fall from the sky, and the powers of the heavens will be shaken, [30] and then the sign of the Son of Man will appear in the sky, and then all the tribes of the earth will mourn, and they will see the Son of Man coming on the clouds of the sky with power and great glory. [31] And He will send forth His angels with a great trumpet and they will gather together His elect from the four winds, from one end of the sky to the other.

<u>Mark 13:24–27</u>

²⁴ But in those days, after that tribulation, the sun will be darkened and the moon will not give its light, ²⁵ and the stars will be falling from heaven, and the powers that are in the heavens will be shaken. ²⁶ Then they will see the Son of Man coming in clouds with great power and glory. ²⁷ And then He will send forth the angels, and will gather together His elect from the four winds, from the farthest end of the earth to the farthest end of heaven."

<u>1 Thessalonians 4:16–17</u>

¹⁶ For the Lord Himself will descend from heaven with a shout, with the voice of the archangel and with the trumpet of God, and the dead in Christ will rise first. ¹⁷ Then we who are alive and remain will be caught up together with them in the clouds to meet the Lord in the air, and so we shall always be with the Lord.

Jesus provided *no further warnings after this*. Believers will not need them, because they will have been gathered together to be with the Lord prior to the onset of wrath on the day of the Lord.

In other words, Jesus's teaching regarding the great tribulation was replete with warnings about its terrors and the overpowering deception that will be its hallmark, but He said nothing after that about the day of the Lord.

The great tribulation, distinct from the wrath of the day of the Lord, will be the persecution of Jews and Christians at the hands of a world system in the control of the antichrist, who will be supernaturally empowered by Satan himself (Rev. 13:2).

Revelation 12 describes a war in heaven between Michael and his angels and Satan and his angels. Satan and his angels lose the war, and they are permanently evicted from the premises of heaven and thrown down to the earth. A loud voice in heaven announces,

"Woe to the earth and the sea, because the devil has come down to you, having great wrath, knowing that he has only a short time" (Rev. 12:12).

The text goes on to say that the devil persecutes the woman, who represents Israel/the Jews, but he is thwarted to some extent. Verse 17 says that "the dragon was enraged with the woman, and went off to make war with *the rest of her children, who keep the commandments of God and hold to the testimony of Jesus.*" We know this "dragon" from throughout the New Testament:

- the "great *dragon* ... the *serpent* of old who is called the *devil* and *Satan*, who deceives the whole world" (Rev. 12:9)

- the "prince of the power of the air" (Eph. 2:2)

- the "ruler of this earth" (John 12:31; 16:11)

- the "god of this world" (2 Cor. 4:4)

- the one who "had the power of death" (Heb. 2:14)

Revelation 12:17 explicitly states that this "dragon" will persecute, with a supernatural vengeance, *Christians,* who are described here as "the rest of her [Israel's] children, who keep the commandments of God and hold to the testimony of Jesus." A similar description of Christians appears in Revelation 14:12—"saints who keep the commandments of God and their faith in Jesus."

This great tribulation will be *the wrath of Satan* making war with and overcoming "the saints" (Rev. 13:7), which the Most High God will allow for a period of three and a half years (forty-two months = three and a half years, Rev. 13:5), though He Himself will cut the days of that time period short for the sake of the elect (Matt. 24:22). At that point, the day of the Lord will begin, and that is unquestionably the *time of God's wrath.*

Conclusion: Pillars 1 and 2 postulate that all seven years of Daniel's seventieth week are a time of tribulation and are also all the time of God's wrath. However, Jesus clearly described the two halves of the seventieth week of Daniel differently. For only the second half did He even use the word *tribulation,* and even then, the great tribulation is distinguished from the general tribulations of life that all Christians will experience as well as from God's wrath in the day of the Lord. Moreover, both the great tribulation and the day of the Lord take place in the second half of a definitive seven-year time frame in the end times. Therefore, pillar 1, that all seven years are a time of tribulation, clearly contradicts the plain teaching of Jesus and is incorrect.

Jesus called the first half of the seven-year period "the beginning of birth pangs." The second half is made up of, first, the great tribulation, and then later, the day of the Lord. Thus, the seventieth week is divided into three sections:

1. the beginning of birth pangs: the first three and a half years,

2. the great tribulation, beginning with the abomination of desolation at the midpoint of the seventieth week and lasting until Jesus cuts short the days of the great tribulation,

3. the day of the Lord, beginning at an unknown time in the later part of the second half of the seventieth week.

Jesus described the great tribulation with specificity in Matthew 24:21–22

> [21] Then there will be a great tribulation, such as has not occurred since the beginning of the world until now, nor ever will. [22] Unless those days had been cut short, no life would have been saved; but for the sake of the elect those days shall be cut short.

> See also Mark 13:19–20.

Thus it is probable that the great tribulation, *the wrath of Satan*, will be recognizable to believers when it comes. The great tribulation, however, is different from *the wrath of God in the day of the Lord*. For that reason, pillar 2, that all seven years of Daniel's seventieth week are God's wrath in the day of the Lord, is also incorrect.

In this lifetime, because we still see "through a glass, darkly" (1 Cor. 13:12 KJV) and because our thoughts and ways are not His thoughts and ways (Isa. 55:8–9), we cannot always know whether the hardships and tribulations we are suffering are caused by God's allowing Satan to sift us or whether He Himself is sending our suffering as a means of testing and refining us or even whether He is punishing us for recalcitrant refusal to respond appropriately to His correction. Whatever His motivation, what we *can* know is that these difficulties and trials are to be expected by believers. These are the normal tribulations that accompany every believer in this life.

| See relevant passages in appendix A.

During the specific time of the great tribulation (which will be limited to a three-and-a-half-year time period), because the persecution will be exponentially beyond anything that has occurred before in human history, believers can always trust that our Jehovah Jireh will provide the grace to endure the suffering.

| See relevant passages in appendixes B and C.

2. GENERAL WRATH VERSUS THE WRATH OF THE DAY OF THE LORD VERSUS THE LAKE OF FIRE/ SECOND DEATH

Just as we must distinguish between the general tribulation in every Christian's life and the specific period of three and a half years that Jesus called the great tribulation, we must also differentiate three distinct concepts of wrath:

- God's wrath in its various forms over the course of mankind's history—examples include the Assyrian and Babylonian captivities of the northern and southern kingdoms of Israel and Judah,

- the final wrath of the day of the Lord—as noted in the glossary, the day of the Lord refers to a specific period of time when God's wrath is poured out in final form against unrepentant believers in Israel and in the nations that have persecuted the Jews and the Christians,

- the judgment at the great white throne at the end of the millennium when those whose names are not written in the Lamb's book of life are thrown into the lake of fire prepared for the devil and his angels—this is the final destination of unbelievers and is also called the second death in Revelation 20:6, 14; 21:8 (the first death being, of course, physical death).

Since Jesus *did* warn His followers about tribulations in general and about the great tribulation in particular, it follows that He, in His incarnation, would *not* bother to warn His followers about something that would *not* affect them. But when specific Bible verses contain promises that believers will be spared from God's wrath, to which one of the three types above are those promises referring?

Pretribulationism takes the view that believers are spared from the wrath of God connected to the day of the Lord. This is pillar 3.

C. Pillar 3. Believers are spared from God's wrath in the day of the Lord

The verses most often cited to support the belief that believers are spared from God's wrath on the day of the Lord are the following:

Romans 5:9

Much more then, having now been justified by His blood, we shall be saved from the wrath of God through Him.

1 Thessalonians 1:10

… and to wait for His Son from heaven, whom He raised from the dead, that is Jesus, who rescues us from the wrath to come.

1 Thessalonians 5:9

For God has not destined us for wrath, but for obtaining salvation through our Lord Jesus Christ.

Revelation 3:10

Because you have kept the word of My perseverance, I also will keep you from the hour of testing, that hour which is about to come upon the whole world, to test those who dwell on the earth.

The operative question is: To which type of wrath do these verses refer? In attempting to answer this question, it is helpful to ask another: What was the purpose of the incarnation? Jesus's mission included, but was not limited to, the following:

- Doing the will of the Father (John 6:38, Heb. 10:7)
- Testifying to the truth (John 18:37)
- Fulfilling the Law and the Prophets (Matt. 5:17)
- Being the second and greater Adam (Rom. 5:14–15)
- Preaching the gospel (Luke 4:18–19, 43)
- Destroying the devil and his works (Heb. 2:14; 1 John 3:8)
- Calling sinners to repentance (Mark 2:17)
- Seeking and saving the lost (Luke 19:5, 9–10)
- Giving His life as a ransom for many (Mark 10:45; 1 Tim. 2:5–6; Titus 2:13–14)
- Giving eternal life to those who would believe in Him (John 3:16–18; 6:51; 17:3)
- Being the propitiation for our sins (1 John 2:2)
- Redeeming us from the curse of the law (Gal. 3:13; 4:5)
- Conforming believers to His image (Rom. 8:29)
- Rescuing believers from the domain of darkness (Col. 1:13–14)

For purposes of considering the rapture, let's focus on this one—saving sinners (1 Tim. 1:15; Heb. 9:26, 28; Rev. 1:5).

Saving sinners from what?—from hell, from eternal separation from the presence of God, from the second death, from the lake of fire:

Romans 6:23

For the wages of sin is death, but the free gift of God is eternal life in Christ Jesus our Lord.

Revelation 20:14–15

[14] This is the second death, the lake of fire. [15] And if anyone's name was not found written in the book of life, he was thrown into the lake of fire.

In addressing the question of from which wrath God is promising to spare believers, it is critical to look at each of the proof texts within their respective contexts to see whether they are referring only to one's eternal destiny, whether in heaven or in the lake of fire, or perhaps to the wrath of the day of the Lord as well. Since believers are clearly spared the eternal form of wrath in the lake of fire, the operative question is whether believers are also spared God's wrath in the day of the Lord.

1.　ROMANS 5

<u>Romans 5:1–11</u> (emphasis added)

[1]Therefore, **having been justified by faith, we have peace with God through our Lord Jesus Christ,** [2] through whom also we have obtained our introduction by faith into this grace in which we stand; and we exult in hope of the glory of God. [3] And not only this, but we also exult in our tribulations, knowing that tribulation brings about perseverance; [4] and perseverance, proven character; and proven character, hope; [5] and hope does not disappoint, because the love of God has been poured out within our hearts through the Holy Spirit who was given to us. [6] **For while we were still helpless, at the right time Christ died for the ungodly.** [7] For one will hardly die for a righteous man; though perhaps for the good man someone would dare even to die. [8] **But God demonstrates His own love toward us, in that while we were yet sinners, Christ died for us.** [9] **Much more then, having now been justified by His blood, we shall be saved from the wrath of God through Him.** [10] **For if while we were enemies we were reconciled to God through the death of His Son, much more, having been reconciled, we shall be saved by His life.** [11] **And not only this, but we also exult in God through our Lord Jesus Christ, through whom we have now received the reconciliation.**

Paul presents here the state of the unbeliever:

- helpless,

- ungodly,

- sinner,

- enemy of God.

And he contrasts that with the state of the believer who has been saved from eternal death to eternal life:

- justified by faith,

- at peace with God through Jesus,

- justified by His blood,

- saved from the wrath of God through Jesus,

- reconciled to God.

Clearly, then, the context of this passage is the eternal destination of those who remain enemies of God versus those who have been reconciled to God and therefore saved through Jesus Christ from the eternal wrath of God.

Although the additional argument that this passage also refers to God's wrath in the day of the Lord could still be made, it is not as strong a case as the next text.

2.   1 THESSALONIANS 1, 4, AND 5

The next set of passages listed above as proof texts for a rapture prior to the seven years of Daniel's seventieth week comes from 1 Thessalonians 1, 4, and 5.

<u>1 Thessalonians 1:9–10</u> (emphasis added)

For they themselves report about us what kind of a reception we had with you, and **how you turned to God from idols to serve a living and true God, [10] and to wait for His Son from heaven, whom He raised from the dead, that is Jesus, who rescues us from the wrath to come.**

Like the verses from Romans 5, this passage also contrasts the state of the unbeliever with that of the believer. The members of the Thessalonian church had once worshiped idols but had turned away (repented) from their idolatry to serve the true God (salvation) as they waited for the return of Jesus, who would deliver them from the wrath to come. Since the context of verse 9 is salvation, it follows that the "wrath to come" of verse 10 refers to one's eternal destiny.

A cogent argument could be made, however, that verse 10 is speaking of the day of the Lord because it mentions the believers waiting for Jesus's return from heaven. The wording of verse 10 might be a reference to Paul's description later in the same letter of the rapture in terms of Jesus's coming "from heaven":

<u>1 Thessalonians 4:13–17</u> (emphasis added)

13 But we do not want you to be uninformed, brethren, about those who are asleep, so that you will not grieve as do the rest who have no hope. 14 For if we believe that Jesus died and rose again, even so God will bring with Him those who have fallen asleep in Jesus. 15 For this we say to you by the word of the Lord, that **we who are alive, and remain until the coming of the Lord, shall not precede those who have fallen asleep.**

16 **For the Lord Himself will <u>descend from heaven</u> with a shout, with the voice of the archangel and with the trumpet of God; and the dead in Christ will rise first. 17 Then we who are alive and remain will be caught up together with them in the clouds to meet the Lord in the air, and so we shall always be with the Lord.**

Note, however, that Paul says nothing in this letter about the *timing* of the rapture relative to Daniel's seventieth week or to the onset of the day of the Lord before or within Daniel's seventieth week. Thus, even if Paul is teaching that the rapture of believers will occur just prior to the onset of the day of the Lord, there is nothing in his letter from which one might draw the conclusion that the whole of Daniel's seventieth week is the wrath of the day of the Lord from which believers will be spared. Indeed, Paul's second letter to the Thessalonians makes it plain that the day of the Lord cannot begin until, at the very earliest, the midpoint of the seventieth week.

> See section IV.D.3 below.

That believers will indeed still be on the earth (in other words, the rapture may not happen until, at a minimum, the onset of the day of the Lord or even possibly *after* the day of the Lord) is suggested by the next proof text, 1 Thessalonians 5:9. This verse appears in the context of the following passage:

<u>**1 Thessalonians 5:1–11**</u> (emphasis added)

[1] Now as to the times and the epochs, brethren, you have no need of anything to be written to you. [2] For you yourselves know full well that **the day of the Lord** will come just like a thief in the night. [3] While they are saying, "Peace and safety!" then destruction will come upon them suddenly like labor pains upon a woman with child, and they will not escape. [4] But you, brethren, are not in darkness, that the day would overtake you like a thief; [5] for you are all sons of light and sons of day. We are not of night nor of darkness; [6] so then let us not sleep as others do, but let us be alert and sober. [7] For those who sleep do their sleeping at night, and those who get drunk get drunk at night. [8] But since we are of the day, let us be sober, having put on the breastplate of faith and love, and as a helmet, the hope of salvation. [9] **For God has not destined us for wrath, but for obtaining salvation through our Lord Jesus Christ,** [10] who died for us, so that whether we are awake or asleep, we may live together with Him. [11] Therefore encourage one another and build up one another, just as you also are doing.

This passage explicitly discusses the onset of the day of the Lord. Paul describes unbelievers as

- they,
- them,
- others.

He says that for "them," that day will come like a thief in the night. In contrast, believers are described as

- you,
- we,
- us.

These will know in advance that the day of the Lord will come like a thief in the night and therefore, having been forewarned, will be alert and sober and watching for its arrival, so that "we" will not be overtaken by that day.

It is not clear, however, whether that means that believers will be raptured out of the world just prior to the onset of that day or that they will remain and have to endure it but will not be "overtaken" by it, even if they do not physically survive it. (Because believers will not be "overtaken," they will be "overcomers" in the context of Revelation 2 and 3.)

What *is* clear is the contrast between the unsaved and the saved. Verse 9 contrasts wrath with salvation, which once more places the emphasis on one's eternal destiny. Verse 10 follows this thought by pointing out that, whether believers are alive or dead, they will live together with Jesus.

3.   REVELATION 3

The final proof text above is Revelation 3:10, which appears in the context of the risen Jesus's letter to the church in Philadelphia:

<u>**Revelation 3:7–11**</u> (emphasis added)

[7] And to the angel of the church in Philadelphia write: He who is holy, who is true, who has the key of David, who opens and no one will shut, and who shuts and no one opens, says this: [8] "I know your deeds. Behold, I have put before you an open door which no one can shut, because you have a little power, and have kept My word, and have not denied My name. [9] Behold, I will cause those of the synagogue of Satan, who say that they are Jews and are not, but lie—I will make them come and bow down at your feet, and make them know that I have loved you. [10] **Because you have kept the word of My perseverance, I also will keep you from the hour of testing, that hour which is about to come upon the whole world, to test those who dwell on the earth.** [11] I am coming quickly; hold fast what you have, so that no one will take your crown."

Unlike the earlier passages, this letter to the church in Philadelphia is not contrasting salvation with wrath; in other words, it does not, on its face, appear to be about eternal destinies.

There are two key phrases in verse 10:

- The first is the dependent clause, "because you have kept the word of My perseverance," and the key word here is *perseverance*. (The word *kept* is the same as in the phrase below and is discussed there.)

- The second is the phrase, "keep you from the hour of testing," and the key words are *keep*, *from*, and *testing*.

(a) WHAT DOES "BECAUSE YOU HAVE KEPT THE WORD OF MY PERSEVERANCE" REFER TO?

In the dependent clause "because you have kept the word of My perseverance," the key word is *perseverance*, which is translated as "patience" in the KJV.

The Greek word is *hupomone* (*Strong's* NT 5281), which derives from *hupomeno* (*Strong's* NT 5278). *Hupomeno* is a compound word, made up of the prefix *hupo* (*Strong's* NT 5259), which means "under, beneath," or an "inferior position"; and the root *meno* (*Strong's* NT 3306), which means "to stay," and is translated as "abide, endure, remain." Put together, the related words *hupomeno* and *hupomone* mean "to bear trials, to have fortitude, persevere." They describe holding on and enduring hardship or misfortune and persevering in difficult circumstances.

Hupomeno is found in Matthew 24:13 and Mark 13:13, where Jesus warns believers in the context of the discussion of the great tribulation:

<u>Matthew 24:10–13</u> (emphasis added)

[10]At that time many will fall away and will betray one another and hate one another. [11] Many false prophets will arise, and will mislead many. [12] Because lawlessness is increased, most people's love will grow cold. [13] But the one who **endures** to the end, he will be saved.

<u>Matthew 10:22</u> (emphasis added)

You will be hated by all because of My name, but it is the one who **has endured** to the end who will be saved.

<u>Mark 13:13</u> (emphasis added)

You will be hated by all because of My name, but the one who **endures** to the end, he will be saved.

In the same context, Luke records the word *hupomone*, indicating the interchangeability of the two Greek words:

<u>Luke 21:16–19</u> (emphasis added)

[16] But you will be betrayed even by parents and brothers and relatives and friends, and they will put some of you to death, [17] and you will be hated by all on account of My name. [18] Yet not a hair of your head will perish. [19] By your **endurance** you will gain your lives.

Returning to Revelation 3:10, the point is that those who were faithful to Jesus in the church in Philadelphia had been suffering intense affliction at the hands of "those of the synagogue of Satan." In the midst of their adversity, they had endured and persevered in their fidelity to Jesus, and Jesus would reward their patience.

If this passage is to be claimed as a proof text of a rapture prior to the onset of the seventieth week, one must ask what terrible affliction or persecution or adversity will that future generation have suffered and faithfully endured that would qualify them to receive the benefits of this promise of Jesus? There is no currently known or even a prophesied calamity just *prior* to the onset of the seventieth week that they will have to have endured; if there were, imminence (pillar 4) would be nullified.

(b) What does "keep you from the hour of testing" mean?

At the outset, I must point out that there is no consensus among even conservative Greek scholars as to the meaning of the phrase "keep you from the hour of testing." Rather, interpretations seem to be based upon one's prior view of when the rapture will occur as well as upon one's interpretation of the Greek preposition *ek* (Eng. "from").

The Greek word that is translated into English as "keep" is *tereo* (*Strong's* NT 5083). The word means "to guard from loss or injury by keeping the eye upon." This same Greek word is used twice in verse 10, first of the Philadelphian faithful believers and second of the risen Christ Himself. Because the faithful believers had guarded His word, Jesus would also guard them, as discussed further.

The Greek word that is translated into English as "from" is *ek* or *ex* (*Strong's* NT 1537). The word is a preposition denoting origin, the place from which an action proceeds; it means "from, out (of place, time, or cause)."

The promise "to keep you **from** (*ek*) the hour of testing" neither implies nor requires physical bodily removal of the recipients of the promise. A comparison with other biblical texts in which *ek* is used in similar contexts proves that this is so:

John 17:15 (emphasis added)

I do not ask You to take them **out of** (*ek*) the world, but to keep them **from** (*ek*) the evil one.

Galatians 1:4 (emphasis added)

… who gave Himself for our sins, that He might rescue us **from** (*ek*) this present evil age.

In all these verses, there is no physical bodily removal involved, but rather deliverance from the power and control of evil. The same principle would apply to Revelation 3:10. Persecuted Christians who have been faithful to Christ are promised preservation and deliverance from the power of evil in the time ("the hour") of testing.

Unlike the other proof texts, Revelation 3:10 does not appear on its face to be about eternal destiny. Nevertheless, it is not clear what "the hour of testing" is. Does the phrase refer to the day of the Lord or to the great tribulation (two different events within the second half of the seventieth week)?

The Greek word that is translated into English as "testing," is *peirasmos* (*Strong's* NT 3986). It is defined as "a putting to proof … adversity."

Vine's explains that the word "is used of trials with a beneficial purpose and effect ... divinely permitted or sent."[5]

Further, "This testing is accompanied by burdening, risk, uncertainty, and even danger and mistrust. Depending on the intention at hand, the test can be, positively, a test in which one proves oneself or, negatively, an enticement to failure."[6]

This definition rules out the day of the Lord as the hour of testing. The day of the Lord has no test or putting to proof associated with it. It is a time of undiluted wrath, with no blessing or hope of lessons learned or of any form of redemption whatsoever. It is a time of divine judgment, not of testing.

In contrast, the great tribulation *is* a time of testing. The fact that the Greek word for testing refers more to trials or temptations meant for our benefit or purification or sanctification is a clear indication that this hour of testing refers to the great tribulation. Once the antichrist demands the world's worship at the midpoint of the seventieth week, all people will be required to choose whom they will serve: Will they give allegiance to the antichrist and take his mark on their foreheads or hands, or will they maintain their believing loyalty to Jesus Christ and suffer intense persecution and mass execution as a result?

A careful reading of the text demonstrates that the promise to be kept from the hour of testing is limited to those who "have kept the word of My perseverance." Again, the Greek word for "perseverance" is *hupomone*, discussed above.

If the "hour of testing" refers to the great tribulation, then it is clear to whom the promise of Jesus applies. While the first three and a half years are described by Jesus as "the beginning of birth pangs," that means only that, while they will be very trying and difficult, they will not be nearly as severe as the unprecedented terror of the great tribulation which begins at the midpoint.

---

5   W. E. Vine, Merrill F. Unger, and William White Jr., *Vine's Complete Expository Dictionary of Old and New Testament Words*, (Nelson, 1985), under "temptation."

6   Wiard Popkes, "πειράζω," in the *Exegetical Dictionary of the New Testament*, ed. Horst Balz and Gerhard Schneider, 3 vols. (Eerdmans, 1990–1993), 3:65.

But in those first years of the seventieth week, the antichrist will have made his entrance onto the world stage (even if his true identity is not revealed until the midpoint), and there will be wars, shortages, rationing and famine, disease, and high rates of death from all of the above. There will be rampant chaos, lawlessness, and violence. False christs and false prophets will arise and begin their satanic work of deceiving people everywhere. Families will disintegrate as members betray one another, and believers in Jesus will be hated and blamed above all.

It will be extraordinarily difficult for any Christian to maintain their believing loyalty to Jesus Christ and to live out their faith even in those first three and a half years. But some will have "kept His word," and they are the ones whom Jesus will "keep from the hour of testing"—that is, the great tribulation. He will do it in one of two ways:

- Those in and around Jerusalem will get out before the midpoint, just as a believing remnant fled Jerusalem before the Romans destroyed it in AD 70.

- For those in other locations, He will provide direct divine protection. The specific means and provisions would be as varied as He wishes; there are no limitations on His power.

Thus, faithful believers who kept the word of His perseverance during the first three and a half years of the seventieth week will be either divinely protected in the midst of the great tribulation or divinely strengthened for endurance through it. During the great tribulation, all believers can call upon the Lord for His grace, strength, and perseverance so that they may glorify Him in their faithful endurance, even if they do not physically survive.

Conclusion regarding proof texts: The contrast of unbelievers with believers in the passage from Romans 5 indicates that the context is one of eternal destination. An argument that it might also apply to God's wrath in the day of the Lord could be advanced.

Such an argument has stronger support in 1 Thessalonians 1:9–10 because of its possible tie to 1 Thessalonians 4 and Paul's explicit description of the rapture.

While the passage in 1 Thessalonians 5 addresses the day of the Lord expressly, it does not address whether believers will be raptured out prior to the onset of that day or will remain on earth but endure and not be "overtaken" by it.

The passage in Revelation 3 is the weakest in its support for the argument that believers will be raptured out of the world before the day of the Lord because the word *testing* in that context does not refer to God's wrath. The great tribulation is most likely the hour of testing in Revelation 3:10. The days of this terrible trial, unparalleled in its ferocity against Christians and Jews, will be cut short by the Lord when He comes to rescue His own and to inaugurate His own great and terrible day of the Lord.

- Despite pillar 1's misnomer of the whole seventieth week as "the tribulation" and

- despite pillar 2's claim that the entire seven years of Daniel's seventieth week are the wrath of the day of the Lord,

- there is a clear distinction between the *great* tribulation and the day of the Lord.

Furthermore, it is clear that both of these events happen in the second half of the seventieth week.

4. OTHER FORMS OF CALAMITY COULD BE CONSTRUED AS TRIBULATION OR WRATH BUT NOT AS THE WRATH OF THE DAY OF THE LORD

The Bible repeatedly records that Jesus does not save believers from catastrophic weather events, from disease, from emotional or physical pain, or from the tyranny and cruelty of human beings, up to and including even the antichrist. While He may use any of those things or people as agents of His judgment (e.g., the Assyrians' and the Babylonians' conquests of Israel and Judah), He does not promise His people that they will be spared in the midst of it. Indeed, since Jesus "humbled Himself by becoming obedient to the point of death, even death on a cross" (Phil. 2:8), should His disciples expect any less? Here is Jesus's answer:

<u>Matthew 10:21–25</u> (emphasis added)

[21] Brother will betray brother to death, and a father his child; and children will rise up against parents and cause them to be put to death. [22] **You will be hated by all because of My name, but it is the one who has endured to the end who will be saved.** [23] But whenever they **persecute you** in one city, flee to the next; for truly I say to you, you shall not finish going through the cities of Israel until the Son of Man comes. [24] **A disciple is not above his teacher, nor a slave above his master.** [25] It is enough for the disciple that he become like his teacher, and the slave like his master. If they have called the head of the house Beelzebul, **how much more will they malign the members of his household!**

Moreover, consider that God's wrath in judgment can be, has been, is, and will be visited upon both individuals and nations. Individual persons will experience various forms of His wrath both in this life and when this life is over, but nations, which will not exist in the eternal state, can experience His wrath only in time, that is, in this age and in the millennial kingdom.

Because nations are made up of people, when God punishes a nation, it is the people who make up that nation who suffer. When God judged the northern and southern kingdoms of Israel via Assyria and Babylon, it wasn't only the wicked and idolatrous who suffered. The righteous were not spared. Not even God's prophets were spared.

- Daniel was taken into captivity as a teenager. He was ripped from his family, most likely castrated, and marched eight hundred miles with other captives to Babylon, where he spent the rest of his life.

- Ezekiel, at the age of 25, and his wife were taken in the second wave of captivity into the Babylonian exile. Her death in exile is recorded in Ezekiel 24. Like Daniel, he never returned to his homeland.

- Jeremiah was left behind with the poorest of the poor in the land and was forced to go with them to Egypt, against the explicit directions given by the Lord through Jeremiah. A rabbinic note claims that when Babylon invaded Egypt in 568/567 BC, Jeremiah was taken captive to Babylon.

- We don't know what happened to Habakkuk and Zephaniah, who prophesied shortly before the first wave of the Babylonian invasion. They may have been among the untold numbers of Jews who either died of starvation during the siege of the Babylonians or were slaughtered by them.

Going back even further, when God punished the whole world for its evil, even righteous Noah was not spared the trauma of His judgment. While he and his family did not drown, it was no small task to spend 120 years building a boat while his friends and neighbors mocked him. And who can even imagine the terror of seeing "all the fountains of the great deep burst open" along with "the floodgates of the sky" (Gen. 7:11), even from the relative safety of the ark? Anyone who has survived a hurricane, tsunami, rogue wave, tornado, or other catastrophic weather event still has only an inkling of the divine power that was unleashed at that time.

Moreover, in addition to their own apprehension (and perhaps seasickness), Noah and his family may have had to address the alarm of the animals as the ark pitched about on the turbulent waters flooding the earth. And then, when the waters eventually subsided and Noah and his family emerged from the ark, they faced a world entirely unlike the world they had known before, with a different environment, ecology, and weather system. What a shock they must have endured as they labored to build new lives for themselves in utterly unfamiliar surroundings.

While these catastrophic judgments (Babylonian captivity and the flood) were unquestionably forms of God's wrath, no one was spared the experience. Even though Noah and his family survived, they still lived on the earth—and on the waters—throughout the time of the flood. In contrast to all tribulations, judgments, and various forms of human wrath, Satan's wrath, and God's wrath, however, the day of the Lord will be a one-of-a-kind time period that has not happened yet and that will be different from all the horrors that preceded it.

It is the subject of the next major division of this book, section IV.

Conclusion: The question for us has been whether the day of the Lord is part of the wrath of God from which believers will be spared (which is the claim of pillar 3) or if it is only to the believer's eternal destiny that the promise applies.

A search through God's Word does not enable us to pinpoint the moment that the wrath from which believers are promised to be spared begins. For the length of each believer's life, he or she will experience the joys and pains that come with living as a follower of Jesus in a fallen world ruled by Satan. We live in enemy territory, and we should not be surprised that the citizens of this world hate us and persecute us.

Believers have been promised that they will be delivered from the wrath of God, but it is not clear whether the wrath of God upon the nations that comes with the day of the Lord is included in that promise. Since hell/gehenna/the lake of fire/the second death is the only wrath that has, *without a doubt*, been paid for by Jesus with His own sinless blood, all we can *know with certainty* is that the moment of each believer's death is the moment that the wrath from which he or she is most assuredly spared begins.

Nevertheless, both pretribulationism and prewrath rapturism take the position that believers are *also* spared from God's wrath in the day of the Lord and will be raptured out of the world before its onset. The two positions disagree about when the day of the Lord begins.

> For purposes of full disclosure, I have taken in this book the prewrath rapture position, in which the rapture occurs immediately prior to the onset of the day of the Lord. Unlike pretribulationism, however, the prewrath position deduces that the day of the Lord not only does *not* take up the entirety of the seventieth week but actually occurs near the end of the great tribulation (which begins at the midpoint).
>
> The prewrath position is that the day of the Lord, which will begin when the Lord cuts short the days of the great tribulation, will be a once-for-all-time period with unique characteristics that will distinguish it from all prior forms of tribulation or judgment or wrath. The day of the Lord will be the subject of the entire next division of the book. I frankly acknowledge, however, that, like all the other positions regarding the timing of the rapture, there are

> problems with the prewrath position. See section V.D below for further discussion.

Returning to pretribulationism, pillar 3 postulates that believers are spared from God's wrath on the day of the Lord. Standing alone, apart from the other pillars of pretribulationism, this pillar is the same as in the prewrath rapture position. Both presume that the day of the Lord is the wrath from which believers are spared (in addition to being spared from the eternal wrath of final separation from God in hell).

If, however, pillar 3 (that believers are spared from God's wrath in the day of the Lord) is taken in conjunction with pillar 2 (that all seven years are God's wrath in the day of the Lord), the result is a corollary pillar—namely, that the rapture must occur before the commencement of the seventieth week. As shown in the preceding section, pillar 2 is incorrect because there is a clear distinction between the great tribulation and the day of the Lord and because the great tribulation also occurs within the seventieth week of Daniel.

Since pillar 2 is incorrect, the corollary pillar that is drawn from pillars 2 and 3 fails as well.

As I pointed out in the prior subsection on pillar 2,

- dispensationalism is the reason why pillar 2 (that all seven years of the seventieth week are God's wrath in the day of the Lord) has to exist, and

- dispensationalism is also the reason why the corollary of pillars 2 and 3 (that the rapture must occur before the seventieth week) has to exist.

Pillars 1 and 2 and the corollary of pillars 2 and 3 simply contradict what Jesus plainly taught. Jesus taught that there will be a great tribulation that will begin at the midpoint of the seventieth week and that when He cuts the days of that great tribulation short, *then* the day of the Lord will commence.

Like pretribulationism, the prewrath position holds that the rapture will occur before the day of the Lord, but because it is not bound by dispensations, it relies only on the biblical text for the conclusion that the day of the Lord happens when Jesus cuts short the days of the great tribulation and *not* at the beginning of the seventieth week.

D. PILLAR 4. THE RAPTURE IS IMMINENT

Imminence means that the rapture is likely to happen at any moment because there is nothing more in biblical prophecy that needs to occur *before the beginning of the seventieth week*. Imminence is integrally connected to the other pillars of pretribulationism. This means that imminence also postulates that there is nothing more in biblical prophecy that needs to happen *before the onset of the day of the Lord*, because other pillars claim that the entirety of the seventieth week is the wrath of the day of the Lord from which believers will be spared by being raptured prior to the beginning of the seventieth week.

A secondary argument offered by dispensationalists in favor of imminence is the command, both in the gospels and in the epistles of the New Testament, to "watch" or "be ready." But the context of this command, whenever it appears, is the uncertainty of the time of the Lord's return, not its imminence. Jesus and the writers of the epistles emphasized the possibility of delay.

For example, the servants in Luke 12:36–40 were told to be on the alert for their master's return, whether that time should be in "the second watch, or even in the third." In the following verses, Jesus contrasted a "faithful and sensible" slave who continued to work at his master's business, regardless of the length of the master's absence, with a lazy slave who, because of his master's delay, began to beat other slaves and to get drunk.

Delays of the return of the master or bridegroom were also an integral part of the parables of Matthew 25—that is, the parable of the ten virgins and the parable of the master who entrusted his servants with talents to invest in his absence. See Matthew 25:5 ("the bridegroom was delaying") and 25:19 ("after a long time the master of the slaves came").

Peter noted, in 2 Peter 3, that even then, approximately two thousand years ago, people were complaining about the delay in Jesus's return, concluding that it was never going to happen. But Peter reminded his readers that the Lord has purpose in His delay, and until He does come, they (and we) need to be diligent to be found faithful when He does finally come.

Thus, being ready and watchful is not so much looking for an event that could happen at any time (imminence) as it is a state of faithful service and spiritual alertness, no matter how long the delay should last.

In 1 Thessalonians 5, Paul used the metaphor of being asleep and awake to contrast those who were consumed with worldliness with those who were spiritually alert and sober, and therefore consumed with their Lord's business while they awaited His return, no matter how late that should be.

The point to be made here is that the Lord's delay brings out the true character of His servants as they wait. They either continue to work faithfully at the Master's business, or being spiritually lazy, they pursue their own desires, and His return comes upon them like a thief in the night.

Conclusion: Because there *are* some prophesied events that are as yet unfulfilled, which may occur either before or within the seven years of the seventieth week, imminence as an integral part of pretribulationism is not coherent.

> See sections IV.B and D.

Imminence is predicated on the prior pillars, and since pillar 1 (that the entire seven years are a time of tribulation) and pillar 2 (that the same, entire seven years of tribulation are God's wrath at the day of the Lord) are incorrect, then imminence falls as well. The day of the Lord is an event that will occur within the seventieth week but will not consume the entirety of it. There are other prophesied events that must occur before the onset of the day of the Lord. They may occur before the seventieth week begins, or they may occur within the seventieth week but still before the day of the Lord. Thus, the rapture is not imminent and pillar 4 is incorrect.

Secondarily, the command to watch or to be ready relates to the attitude of the heart and the conduct of those who profess to be followers of Jesus. Will we be faithful in service to Him, even if He should not return before our lives on this earth are over?

This concludes a summary response to the pillars of pretribulationism. The remainder of the book will address them more fully.

Section IV

The Day of the Lord

The day of the Lord is a unique biblical period of time

A. The day of the Lord has distinctive characteristics

1. The day of the Lord will be unique, unlike any other time of judgment

The judgment of the day of the Lord will be different from everything that precedes it. The purpose of the day of the Lord will not be disciplinary, corrective, or restorative. In all prior judgments, God disciplined His people to correct them because of His great love for them; His chastening rod was intended to build, shape, mold, purify, and sanctify their character, and in that sense, it was forward-looking. In contrast, the day of the Lord will be wholly punitive. It will be final, and it will be focused backward. It will be the time when a holy God pours out His wrath in its full, undiluted strength on people and nations for their unrepentant rebellion against Him.

Describing the wrath of the day of the Lord, Zephaniah 1:17–18 states,

[17] I will bring distress on men
So that they will walk like the blind,
Because they have sinned against the Lord;
And their blood will be poured out like dust
And their flesh like dung.
Neither their silver nor their gold
Will be able to deliver them

On the day of the LORD's wrath;
And all the earth will be devoured
In the fire of His jealousy,
For He will make a complete end,
Indeed a terrifying one,
Of all the inhabitants of the earth.

> See appendix E for over fifty references in both the Old and New Testaments regarding the day of the Lord.

2.   THE DAY OF THE LORD WILL DEMONSTRATE THE SIDE OF GOD THAT MOST CHRISTIANS DENY—HIS JUSTICE

Most Christians readily embrace the abundant love of God. Even though the depth of that love, as it is demonstrated in the cross, is infinitely outside and beyond the minds of mere mortals to fully comprehend, we who believe in Jesus can at least try to appreciate the cost of our salvation.

Unfortunately, most Christians take this love for granted and view it very lightly. Romans 6:1 asks, "Are we to continue in sin that grace might increase?" Paul's answer in verse 2 is emphatic: "May it never be! How shall we who died to sin still live in it?"

People underestimate the wickedness of their sin because they use other, relatively more sinful people as their frame of reference; by comparison, *they* have not behaved so badly. What they fail to understand is what God's holiness demands. His standard is absolute perfection:

<u>Leviticus 11:44–45</u> (emphasis added)

⁴⁴ For I am the LORD your God. Consecrate yourselves therefore, and **be holy, for I am holy**. And you shall not make yourselves unclean with any of the swarming things that swarm on the earth. ⁴⁵ For I am the LORD, who brought you up from the land of Egypt to be your God; thus **you shall be holy, for I am holy**."

Leviticus 19:2 (emphasis added)

Speak to all the congregation of the sons of Israel and say to them, **"You shall be holy, for I the Lord your God am holy."**

Habakkuk 1:13 (NIV)

Your eyes are too pure to look on evil; [Y]ou cannot tolerate wrongdoing.

Matthew 5:48

Therefore you are to be perfect, as your heavenly Father is perfect.

Ephesians 1:4 (emphasis added)

… just as He chose us in Him before the foundation of the world, that **we would be holy and blameless before Him**.

1 Peter 1:14–16 (emphasis added)

[14] As obedient children, do not be conformed to the former lusts which were yours in your ignorance, [15] but **like the Holy One who called you, be holy yourselves** also in all your behavior; [16] because it is written, **"You shall be holy, for I am holy."**

It is only when a person understands the depth of his offenses against a holy and perfect Creator that he can understand the need for the cross. Consider these levels of offense:

- If one man punches another man, he may be charged with criminal assault and battery; depending on many factors, the price he will pay will vary, but it is unlikely he would spend much, if any, time in jail.

- If this same man punches a police officer, however, the consequences will be worse.

- If he punches the president of the United States, his crime will be elevated from a state crime to a federal crime, and from a misdemeanor to a felony. His sentence will involve the loss of assets and a lengthy prison term.

- But what if his offense is against his own Creator, the Creator of the universe, Who is infinite, holy, perfect, and just? What penalty would be sufficient to cover the cost of that crime? How many lifetimes of life sentences could ever pay off an infinite debt?

If a person thinks that telling little white lies or gossip or petty theft of office supplies or the grudge he or she holds against their own siblings doesn't matter to God, they haven't begun to comprehend God's standard. The penalty for the least sin against a perfect and perfectly holy and perfectly just God is eternal separation from Him and all that He is—all light and good and love and met needs and joy and fellowship with Him and with other believers, and on and on the list goes.

Only a perfect and sinless human being could pay the price of mankind's sins, and that is the plan of salvation that God the Father implemented through God the Son. The Son's death was sufficient to pay the price for the sins of the world.

> See, e.g., John 1:29; 3:16–17; 4:42; 12:47; 2 Cor. 5:19; Eph. 2:11–16; Heb. 9:26; 1 John 4:9–10, 14.

But if any person refuses to admit his need of a Savior and to repent, he has rejected the only pardon made possible—the payment for his sins by the substituting Savior. As a human judge would not be just if he overlooked and refused to exact punishment for a heinous crime committed by one human being against another, so the perfect Judge will not overlook and refuse to punish all the injustices done by human beings against each other and against Himself.

Some argue that it is not fair for God to judge, asking "What about all those people who had no exposure to the gospel?" But here are some things to consider:

- A perfect God knows exactly how much light each person has been exposed to.

- Romans 1:20 says that the created order is sufficient to show His existence: "For since the creation of the world His invisible attributes, His eternal power and divine nature, have been clearly seen, being understood through what has been made, so that **they are without excuse**" (emphasis added).

- If you really want God to be "fair," you will get the exact level of justice that you deserve. What we need is His mercy, because "there is none righteous, not even one" (Rom. 3:10, quoting Pss. 14:1–3; 53:1–3).

- God's standard for entrance into heaven is perfection. James 2:10 warns, "For whoever keeps the whole law and yet stumbles in one point, he has become guilty of all."

- Humanity's inability to be perfect, regardless of the number of chances given, points to the need for a Savior. Without the cross and Jesus's perfect and complete payment for the sins of mankind, no pardon for us sinners would be possible.

In the day of the Lord, God will judge and punish—with perfect justice, taking every ameliorating factor into account—those who have refused the proffered grace and pardon obtained at infinite cost to Himself. There will be no turning back at that point.

God's justice will be meted out to those who have refused His mercy. That side of our Creator will be apparent to all in the day of the Lord.

3. **THE DAY OF THE LORD WILL BE A TIME OF REVERSAL: IT WILL END HUMANITY'S WRATH AGAINST GOD AND INITIATE GOD'S WRATH AGAINST THOSE WHO ARE UNREPENTANT**

> The argument that the entire seventieth week of Daniel does not consist of the wrath of the day of the Lord is developed in greater detail in section IV.D below.

For purposes of the discussion of the day of the Lord, it is necessary to address the contrast between the offensive and defensive lines that are developed in the battle between the creatures and their Creator in the seventieth week, before and after the onset of the day of the Lord.

The first five seals of Revelation 6:1–11 depict, under God's sovereign permissive supervision, the entrance of the ultimate antichrist onto the world stage and the havoc and chaos that he will unleash among the nations and peoples of the world. This will be orchestrated by Satan, the ruler of this world (John 12:31; 16:11). Having been evicted from the premises of heaven (Rev. 12:7–9), he will empower, perhaps even possess, the antichrist to persecute Jews and Christians. His campaign will be vicious and merciless, an unprecedented great tribulation so terrible that, "unless those days had been cut short, no life would have been saved" (Matt. 24:22).

Thus, this seventieth week will be an explosive era of furious rebellion by people against God.

But God will, at His appointed time, turn the tables. At the breaking of the sixth seal (Rev. 6:12–17), the long-suffering patience of God will at last come to an end, as He initiates the day of the Lord. The offensive that people were relentlessly pursuing against God and His people will suddenly be flipped by God Himself, and they will find themselves on the defensive side. At that point, it will be God's wrath directed at unrepentant humanity.

And it will be a rout. The blood of the martyrs of the fifth seal will be avenged by Him Who said, "Vengeance is Mine. I will repay" (Rom. 12:19 quoting Deut. 32:35).

4. No human agency will be involved in the execution of judgment in the day of the Lord

While the events of at least some of the seals of Revelation 6 (war, famine, death) have been used by God over the course of biblical history to judge either His own people or another group, in every case, the judgment was delivered by *human agency*. For example, when the Israelites were about to enter the promised land, God instructed them to absolutely annihilate the people who were in the land. The reason was that the "cup of iniquity" of those people was full, and the time of God's judgment of them had arrived. God used, or intended to use, His own people to deliver His judgment upon these people.

Another example involves God's judgment of His own people. He raised up the cruel and barbaric Babylonians and brought them in judgment upon the people of Judah. Untold numbers of Judeans were slaughtered outright, and most of the rest were taken into captivity for a period of seventy years; only the poorest of the poor were left on the land in Judah.

Like the two examples above, the first five seals of Revelation 6 are authorized, within circumscribed parameters, by God, acting through His four living creatures, but they are carried out on earth by people:

- The first seal represents the emergence onto the world stage of the antichrist; his going out "conquering and to conquer" (Rev. 6:2) is not the work of God's angels.

- The second seal represents war; again, this has been a common activity of people and nations against other people and nations since Cain murdered his brother. No angels are involved.

- The third seal represents famine; this is a natural result of the shortages and the disruption of commerce caused by war. No angels' activity is noted.

- The fourth seal and the fifth seal represent death caused by war, famine, pestilence, and the activity of the "beasts of the earth."

> Some English translations say, "wild beasts of the earth," but the Greek says only "beasts of the earth." The adjective, "wild," is not in the Greek.

While the phrase "death by the beasts of the earth" could refer to a population explosion in wild animals like bears and lions, in this context, it could also be a reference to the first beast (the antichrist) and the second beast (his false prophet) of Revelation, because the same Greek word (*therion*, *Strong's* NT 2342, defined as "a dangerous animal") is used in both passages. Indeed, in all thirty-nine times that *therion* appears in Revelation, it refers to the antichrist or his false prophet.

Whether "death by the beasts" refers to dangerous animals or is a metaphor for the antichrist and his false prophet, the point here is that the widespread death represented by the fourth and fifth seals is the result of human activity, not of angels.

In contrast, when God pours out His unmitigated and full wrath in the time period known as the day of the Lord, *no human agency* will be involved. With the breaking of the seventh seal, the seven trumpets of judgments begin in Revelation 8. From that point forward, the Lord will act either through angels or directly.

> See Rev. 8:2, 7, 8, 10, 12; 9:1–2, 13–15 for the trumpet judgments; see Rev. 15:1, 6–7; 16:1–4, 8, 10, 12, 17 for the bowl judgments.

Even *unbelievers* will recognize the difference between all the events that have transpired before and after the coming of the day of the Lord. They will not be able to say that the cataclysmic upheavals in the heavens and on earth, which herald the onset of the day of the Lord, are so-called natural phenomena. When God unleashes His wrath, He will be intervening in human history, and all unbelievers will recognize what is happening.

Revelation 6:15–17 (emphasis added)

[15] Then the kings of the earth and the great men and the commanders and the rich and the strong and every slave and free man hid themselves in the caves and among the rocks of the mountains; [16] and they said to the mountains and to the rocks, "Fall on us and **hide us from the presence of Him who sits on the throne, and from the wrath of the Lamb;** [17] **for the great day of their wrath has come, and who is able to stand?"**

The Lord may *use* the material of the universe, such as meteors, but they will not be "natural" disasters. The insurance industry has a term that would actually be accurate in this case; what will happen next will truly be "acts of God."

5. THE LORD ALONE WILL BE EXALTED IN THE DAY OF THE LORD

In *that* time, God alone will be exalted, and all proud men will be abased. Indeed, no one will be *able* to stand against Him:

Isaiah 2:11–12, 17

[11] The proud look of man will be abased

And the loftiness of man will be humbled,
And the Lord alone will be exalted in that day.
¹² For the Lord of hosts will have a day of reckoning
Against everyone who is proud and lofty
And against everyone who is lifted up,
That he may be abased.
¹⁷ The pride of man will be humbled
And the loftiness of men will be abased;
And the Lord alone will be exalted in that day

Isaiah 13:9, 11

⁹ Behold, the day of the Lord is coming,
Cruel, with fury and burning anger,
To make the land a desolation;
And He will exterminate its sinners from it.
¹¹ Thus I will punish the world for its evil
And the wicked for their iniquity;
I will also put an end to the arrogance of the proud
And abase the haughtiness of the ruthless.

Jeremiah 10:10

But the Lord is the true God;
He is the living God and the everlasting King.
At His wrath the earth quakes,
And the nations cannot endure His indignation.

Joel 2:11

The Lord utters His voice before His army;
Surely His camp is very great,
For strong is he who carries out His word.
The day of the Lord is indeed great and very awesome,
And who can endure it?

Revelation 6:16–17

¹⁶ And they said to the mountains and to the rocks, "Fall on us
and hide us from the presence of Him who sits on the throne, and

from the wrath of the Lamb; [17] for the great day of their wrath has come, and who is able to stand?"

B. Signs will herald the onset of the day of the Lord

1. The first unmistakable sign will be cosmic-level upheaval and disruption

Throughout the Bible, the day of the Lord is heralded by cosmic disturbances involving the sun and the moon as well as tectonic upheavals on the earth that affect both land and sea. Note that in the New Testament, the timing is also provided—it is *after* the great tribulation. In other words, this is the time that the Lord cuts short the days of the great tribulation (Matt. 24:21–22).

Revelation graphically describes the onset of the day of the Lord:

Revelation 6:12–17

[12] I looked when He broke the sixth seal, and there was a great earthquake; and the sun became black as sackcloth made of hair, and the whole moon became like blood; [13] and the stars of the sky fell to the earth, as a fig tree casts its unripe figs when shaken by a great wind. [14] The sky was split apart like a scroll when it is rolled up, and every mountain and island were moved out of their places. [15] Then the kings of the earth and the great men and the commanders and the rich and the strong and every slave and free man hid themselves in the caves and among the rocks of the mountains; [16] and they said to the mountains and to the rocks, "Fall on us and hide us from the presence of Him who sits on the throne, and from the wrath of the Lamb; [17] for the great day of their wrath has come, and who is able to stand?"

This description of disruption in the heavens and earth aligns with Jesus's words in the synoptic gospels. Note that what follows in these passages appears to be a description of the rapture, just prior to the onset of the day of the Lord:

Matthew 24:29–31

29 But immediately after the tribulation of those days the sun will be darkened, and the moon will not give its light, and the stars will fall from the sky, and the powers of the heavens will be shaken. 30 And then the sign of the Son of Man will appear in the sky, and then all the tribes of the earth will mourn, and they will see the Son of Man coming on the clouds of the sky with power and great glory. 31 And He will send forth His angels with a great trumpet and they will gather together His elect from the four winds, from one end of the sky to the other.

Mark 13:24–27

24 But in those days, after that tribulation, the sun will be darkened and the moon will not give its light, 25 and the stars will be falling from heaven, and the powers that are in the heavens will be shaken. 26 Then they will see the Son of Man coming in clouds with great power and glory. 27 And then He will send forth the angels, and will gather together His elect from the four winds, from the farthest end of the earth to the farthest end of heaven.

While the arrival of the day of the Lord will be like a thief in the night for unbelievers (see 1 Thess. 5:2, 4; 2 Peter 3:10; Rev. 3:3; 16:15), believers will know to look for the signs and will not be caught unprepared. Instead, they will straighten up and lift up their heads as their redemption draws near:

Luke 21:25–28

25 There will be signs in sun and moon and stars, and on the earth dismay among nations, in perplexity at the roaring of the sea and the waves, 26 men fainting from fear and the expectation of the things which are coming upon the world; for the powers of the heavens will be shaken. 27 Then they will see the Son of Man coming in a cloud with power and great glory. 28 But when these things begin to take place, straighten up and lift up your heads, because your redemption is drawing near.

As one would expect, Jesus's descriptions of these heavenly upheavals align with those of the prophets. Here is a sampling:

Isaiah 13:9–10

⁹Behold, the day of the LORD is coming,
Cruel, with fury and burning anger,
To make the land a desolation;
And He will exterminate its sinners from it.
¹⁰ For the stars of heaven and their constellation
Will not flash forth their light;
The sun will be dark when it rises
And the moon will not shed its light.

Ezekiel 32:7–8

⁷ And when I extinguish you,
I will cover the heavens and darken their stars;
I will cover the sun with a cloud
And the moon shall not give its light.
⁸ "All the shining lights in the heavens
I will darken over you
And will set darkness on your land,"
Declares the Lord GOD.

Joel 2:1–2, 10–11, 30–31

¹ Blow a trumpet in Zion,
And sound an alarm on My holy mountain!
Let all the inhabitants of the land tremble,
For the day of the LORD is coming;
Surely it is near,
² A day of darkness and gloom,
A day of clouds and thick darkness.
¹⁰ Before them the earth quakes,
The heavens tremble,
The sun and the moon grow dark
And the stars lose their brightness.
¹¹ And the LORD utters His voice before His army;

Surely His camp is very great,
For strong is he who carries out His word.
The day of the Lord is indeed great and very awesome,
And who can endure it?
30 I will display wonders in the sky and on the earth,
Blood, fire and columns of smoke.
31 The sun will be turned into darkness
And the moon into blood
Before the great and awesome day of the Lord comes.

Joel 3:14–16

14Multitudes, multitudes in the valley of decision!
For the day of the Lord is near in the valley of decision.
15 The sun and moon grow dark
And the stars lose their brightness.
16 The Lord roars from Zion
And utters His voice from Jerusalem,
And the heavens and the earth tremble.

Habakkuk 3:10–12

10 The mountains saw You and quaked;
The downpour of waters swept by.
The deep uttered forth its voice,
It lifted high its hands.
11 Sun and moon stood in their places;
They went away at the light of Your arrows,
At the radiance of Your gleaming spear.
12 In indignation You marched through the earth;
In anger You trampled the nations.

Zephaniah 1:15

A day of wrath is that day,
A day of trouble and distress,
A day of destruction and desolation,
A day of darkness and gloom,
A day of clouds and thick darkness.

> See also Isa. 24:21–23; 34:4; Jer. 4:23–24, 27–28; Amos 5:18–20; 8:9;
> Hag. 2:6–7, 21–22; Zech. 14:6–7.

2. THE SECOND SIGN WILL BE THE SILENCE THAT PRESAGES JUDGMENT

There is one other sign that follows the terrifying chaos in the heavens and on the earth and signifies/signals (that's what signs do, after all!) that the day of the Lord is commencing. This sign appears both in the Old and New Testaments:

<u>Habakkuk 2:20</u> (emphasis added)
But the LORD is in His holy temple.
Let all the earth be silent before Him.

<u>Zephaniah 1:7</u> (emphasis added)
Be silent before the Lord GOD!
For the day of the LORD is near,
For the LORD has prepared a sacrifice,
He has consecrated His guests.

<u>Zechariah 2:13</u> (emphasis added)
Be silent, all flesh, before the LORD; for He is aroused from His holy habitation.

Even Hannah's prayer acknowledged the eschatological truth that the Lord will one day deal out final judgment against the wicked and that all will be silent before Him:

<u>1 Samuel 2:9–10</u> (emphasis added)
[9] But **the wicked ones are silenced in darkness;**
For not by might shall a man prevail.
[10] Those who contend with the LORD will be shattered;
Against them He will thunder in the heavens,
The Lord will judge the ends of the earth.

<u>Revelation 7:1</u> (emphasis added)

After this I saw four angels standing at the four corners of the earth, **holding back the four winds of the earth, so that no wind should blow on the earth or on the sea or on any tree.**

<u>Revelation 8:1–2</u> (emphasis added)

¹ When the Lamb broke the seventh seal, **there was silence in heaven** for about half an hour. ² And I saw the seven angels who stand before God, and seven trumpets were given to them.

> Silence on the earth corresponds to the silence in heaven in Revelation 8:1.

Conclusion: Throughout the Bible, the consistent signs that the day of the Lord is commencing are disruptions in the heavens and on the earth. As well, absolute silence on earth and in heaven immediately precedes and presages the impending judgment.

C. Is the day of the Lord the wrath from which believers are spared?

The prewrath rapture position is based upon the Bible verses in the preceding section and answers the question in the affirmative: Yes, the wrath of the day of the Lord is the wrath from which believers are spared, *as well as* being spared from an eternity apart from God in hell. Jesus sets out the chronology in the synoptic gospels. The church goes into the great tribulation, which is so severe, according to Matthew 24:22, that "unless those days had been cut short, no life would have been saved; but for the sake of the elect those days shall be cut short." At that time, the cosmic disturbances signal the afflicted believers still alive on the earth to straighten up and lift up their heads because the time of their redemption is drawing near. The Lord comes on the clouds and sends forth the angels with a great trumpet, and they gather together His elect from the four winds, from the farthest end of the earth, to the farthest end of heaven. This is the rapture described in 1 Thessalonians 4:

1 Thessalonians 4:16–17

¹⁶ For the Lord Himself will descend from heaven with a shout, with the voice of the archangel and with the trumpet of God; and the dead in Christ shall rise first. ¹⁷ Then we who are alive and remain will be caught up together with them in the clouds to meet the Lord in the air, and so we shall always be with the Lord.

Revelation confirms this chronology. The great tribulation, represented by the fifth seal, is followed by cosmic disturbances, represented by the sixth seal. Those on earth recognize that the great day of the wrath of "Him who sits on the throne" and "of the Lamb" has come, and ask, "Who is able to stand?" (Rev. 6:16–17). There is a pause, or interlude, that follows in Revelation 7, in which the 144,000 Jews are sealed to protect them from the wrath of God that is about to fall upon the earth. Then the great, innumerable throng appears in heaven, having come out of the great tribulation. Finally, Revelation 8 opens with the breaking of the seventh seal, and the trumpets begin the great and terrible day of the Lord.

D. THE DAY OF THE LORD DOES NOT FILL THE ENTIRE SEVENTIETH WEEK BUT OCCURS ONLY IN THE LATTER PART OF THE SECOND HALF OF THE SEVENTIETH WEEK

1. PILLARS 2 AND 3 OF PRETRIBULATIONISM CANNOT BOTH BE TRUE AT THE SAME TIME

(a) ONCE THE DAY OF THE LORD BEGINS, THERE WILL BE NO FURTHER REPENTANCE AND THUS NO NEW BELIEVERS

Pillars 2 and 3 of pretribulationism posit that the entire seven years of Daniel's seventieth week, including whatever portion of that week is the great tribulation, constitute the wrath of the day of the Lord (pillar 2) and that therefore the church—that is, all true believers—will be raptured off the earth before the beginning of the seventieth week (pillar 3). At first glance, these two statements do not appear to be inconsistent with one another, but that is only until they are considered in the context of other biblical passages.

Whenever the day of the Lord does actually begin, the Bible makes it plain that there will be no more opportunities for people to repent from their hostility to God and turn to Him for forgiveness and salvation. That this is so (that is, that no one still on the earth will come to faith during the day of the Lord) is confirmed by several passages in Revelation in which the inhabitants of the earth curse and blaspheme God as they are suffering from the outpouring of His wrath. From the end of Revelation 6, they recognize that God's wrath is about to begin:

<u>Revelation 6:12–17</u> (emphasis added)

[12] I looked when He broke the sixth seal, and there was a great earthquake; and the sun became black as sackcloth made of hair, and the whole moon became like blood; [13] and the stars of the sky fell to the earth, as a fig tree casts its unripe figs when shaken by a great wind. [14] And the sky was split apart like a scroll when it is rolled up, and every mountain and island were moved out of their places. [15] Then the kings of the earth and the great men and the commanders and the rich and the strong and every slave and free man hid themselves in the caves and among the rocks of the mountains; [16] and they said to the mountains and to the rocks, "Fall on us and **hide us from the presence of Him who sits on the throne, and from the wrath of the Lamb;** [17] **for the great day of their wrath has come, and who is able to stand?"**

But they never respond with repentance and prayers for forgiveness:

<u>Revelation 9:20–21</u> (emphasis added)

[20] The **<u>rest of mankind</u>, who were not killed by these plagues, did not repent of the works of their hands, so as not to worship demons, and the idols** of gold and of silver and of brass and of stone and of wood, which can neither see nor hear nor walk; [21] and **they did not repent of their murders nor of their sorceries nor of their immorality nor of their thefts.**

Revelation 16:9 (emphasis added)

Men were scorched with fierce heat; and **they blasphemed the name of God** who has the power over these plagues, and **they did not repent** so as to give Him glory.

Revelation 16:11 (emphasis added)

And **they blasphemed the God of heaven** because of their pains and their sores; and **they did not repent** of their deeds.

Revelation 16:21

And huge hailstones, about one hundred pounds each, came down from heaven upon men; and **men blasphemed God** because of the plague of the hail, because its plague was extremely severe.

There is one other reaction to the judgment of God's trumpets and bowls in Revelation; just before the seventh trumpet sounds, we are told the following:

Revelation 11:13 (emphasis added)

And in that hour there was a great earthquake, and a tenth of the city fell; and seven thousand people were killed in the earthquake, and **the rest were terrified and gave glory to the God of heaven.**

At first glance, it may appear that there is actually some sign of repentance here. But giving glory to God is not the equivalent of conviction of sin and repentance and submission to Him as Savior. All that is meant here is merely that the people were stunned and terrified because they recognized and acknowledged that there is indeed a God and that it was He Who was causing this upheaval.

Despite the fact that some commentators think these people were actually saved, there are two factors that militate against that conclusion:

1. The first is that no interpretation of a biblical passage can be valid if it contradicts another biblical passage whose meaning is clear. The interpretation of Revelation 11:13 as people being saved during the day of the Lord contradicts a passage in 2 Thessalonians 2. Verses 3–10 describe the revelation of the

identity of the antichrist at the midpoint of the seventieth week, at which time the great tribulation will also begin. In verse 10, this description includes the antichrist's "deception of wickedness for those who perish, because they did not receive the love of the truth so as to be saved." The next two verses are critical:

<u>**2 Thessalonians 2:11–12**</u> (emphasis added)

[11] For this reason **God will send upon them a deluding influence so that they might believe what is false**, [12] in order that they all may be judged who did not believe the truth, but took pleasure in wickedness.

The "deluding influence" is part of God's judgment for their rejection of the truth. This cross reference thus reinforces the conclusion that the people in Revelation 11:13 did not repent of their sins and were not saved. It also is consistent with all the other verses in Revelation cited above, which state plainly that the people on the receiving end of God's judgment in the day of the Lord did not repent.

2. The second factor is the context in which Revelation 11:13 appears. Consider that, since these people are still alive on the earth as the day of the Lord begins, they will have taken the mark of the beast during the preceding time of the great tribulation. If they had not taken the mark, they would either be dead (see Rev. 13:15–17; 14:12–13) or raptured out before the day of the Lord began. And there is no turning back once the mark of the beast is taken (see Rev. 14:9–11), because to take the mark of the beast and to worship him is to unequivocally and irrevocably renounce Jesus Christ and believing loyalty to Him.

The Bible makes it abundantly and painfully clear that taking the mark of the beast is a sin that will not be repented of, nor will it be forgiven.

- Revelation 13:14 states that they are **deceived** by the signs that the false prophet performs; **because they are deceived**, they obey the command to make an image of the beast and to worship him. Revelation 19:20 reiterates that the false prophet **deceived** those who had received the mark of the beast and those who worshiped his image.

- The third angel in Revelation 14 warns the people on earth not to take the mark, because of the terrifying eternal consequences:

  > **<u>Revelation 14:9–11</u>**
  >
  > If anyone worships the beast and his image, and receives a mark on his forehead or on his hand, [10] he also will drink of the wine of the wrath of God, which is mixed in full strength in the cup of His anger; and he will be tormented with fire and brimstone in the presence of the holy angels and in the presence of the Lamb. [11] And the smoke of their torment goes up forever and ever; they have no rest day and night, those who worship the beast and his image, and whoever receives the mark of his name.

- Revelation 16:2 reveals that the contents of the first bowl judgment will affect those who took the mark:

  > So the first angel went and poured out his bowl on the earth; and it became a loathsome and malignant sore upon the men who had the mark of the beast and who worshiped his image.

Another reason we know that the door for salvation has closed when the day of the Lord opens is that, if people were saved during the day of the Lord, they would be treated differently from those who had already been raptured and had attended the marriage feast. This would be contrary to the character of God, Who deals with human beings impartially.

See section V.B.2.(e) for further development of this argument.

Returning to the comparison of two of the pillars of pretribulationism, we can see that the context of the above passages highlights the pillars' inconsistency, demonstrating that both cannot be true at the same time.

To reiterate, the two pillars are as follows:

- Pillar 2. The entire seven years of the seventieth week of Daniel constitute God's wrath in the day of the Lord;

- Pillar 3. Because all true believers are promised to be spared from God's wrath, all true believers will be raptured out of the world before the beginning of the seven-year period of the seventieth week.

Here is the inconsistency:

IF the whole seven years, including the great tribulation, is characterized as God's wrath, and

IF all believers have been raptured out of the world before that seven years begins, and

SINCE no one will repent once the actual wrath of God on the day of the Lord begins to be poured out on the world,

THEN how can the great throng of Revelation 7 consist of new believers who came to faith during the great tribulation (which takes up most of the second half of the seven years)?

Indeed,

IF/SINCE people *are* still coming to Jesus in repentance during the great tribulation (Revelation 7 states that the throng of people come out of the great tribulation),

THEN how can the great tribulation even be characterized as part of God's wrath since the Bible shows no repentance but only further hostility and hardening of hearts during the day of the Lord?

Conclusion: The great tribulation, during which there will unquestionably be believers on the earth, cannot be characterized as God's wrath because no one will come to a saving faith once His wrath begins.

In other words, whatever portion of that seven years (something less than the full second half, which is three and a half years) that makes up what Jesus called the great tribulation *cannot be God's wrath.*

Stated another way, the great tribulation cannot be God's wrath if new believers are still coming to faith.

It follows, then, that the entire seven years of Daniel's seventieth week cannot be God's wrath.

It also follows that both the pillars listed above cannot be true at the same time.

This also means that the church will go into the great tribulation.

Further, it means that the great throng of Revelation 7—which most likely *is* a description of the rapture, since the wrath of the day of the Lord begins with the breaking of the seventh seal and the appearance of the seven trumpets—will include all the saints, both those already in the church and those who will come to faith as a result of the church's evangelistic outreach during the great tribulation.

Here is a restatement of the problem using the dispensational approach.

A purely dispensational point of view of pretribulationism sets out the scenario in this way:

- The church age ends as the seventieth week begins.

- All believers are raptured at that time.

- The seventieth week, which is now *Israel's dispensation*, begins.

Within the new dispensation of Israel—the seventieth week—the following actions occur:

1. The 144,000 Jews of Revelation 7:4–8 are sealed and become mighty evangelists.

2. As a result of their evangelistic endeavors, there is an unprecedented, massive, worldwide revival, and these new believers are seen in heaven in Revelation 7:9–17.

3. The two witnesses on earth also testify about God, and their testimony is corroborated by signs and wonders, according to Revelation 11:3–12.

4. The angel of Revelation 14:6–7 preaches the eternal gospel to the world from mid-heaven.

The problem with this dispensational picture is that pillar 2 of pretribulationism declares that the entire seventieth week is God's wrath on the day of the Lord. And the ramifications of that declaration include the following:

SINCE at the commencement of the day of the Lord,

- the time of Romans 2:4, in which the riches of God's kindness, forbearance, and patience ought to have led all to repentance, will have passed,

- the time of 1 Timothy 2:4, in which God has desired all people to be saved and to come to the knowledge of the truth, will have passed, and

- the time of 2 Peter 3:9, in which the Lord has waited patiently, not wishing for any to perish but for all to come to repentance, will have passed; as a result of which

- no new believers can come to faith,

THEN God's gracious offer of salvation will have been irrevocably withdrawn, and the door of repentance, redemption, and restoration will close forever. Like the five foolish virgins of Matthew 25, all people to whom the door is permanently closed will no longer have the opportunity to repent.

The consequences of these facts are as follows:

- NO evangelistic activity on the part of the 144,000 sealed Jews will be possible, because no one can be saved during the day of the Lord.

- NO revival of any size will be possible, for the same reason. Therefore, in contravention of the express language in

Revelation 7:9–17, there can be NO great multitude that no one can count appearing in heaven at this time.

- God's two witnesses are wasting their breath, because no one can be saved.

- The gospel angel is also wasting his breath, for the same reason.

BUT SINCE the Bible explicitly places the two witnesses and the gospel angel inside the context of the seventieth week,

THEN those two facts alone suffice to nullify the declaration of pillar 2 of pretribulationism, and the entire seventieth week simply cannot be the wrath of the day of the Lord. The day of the Lord must begin at some time well into the seven years of the seventieth week.

> The issue of the activity of the 144,000 sealed Jews is discussed further in section V.A.1 below.

Furthermore,

BECAUSE the day of the Lord cannot begin at the beginning of the seventieth week, and

IF the wrath of the day of the Lord is the wrath from which believers are promised to be spared,

THEN this means that the rapture of believers must also be postponed until just prior to the actual onset of the day of the Lord at some point in the second half of the seventieth week.

(b) God the Holy Spirit cannot be the restrainer of 2 Thessalonians 2:6–7

> Although earlier verses of this passage in 2 Thessalonians are discussed in section IV.D.3 below, I am placing this section here because it relates directly to the argument just made in the previous subsection (IV.D.1.(a)), where I pointed out the inconsistency between two of the pillars of pretribulationism.

There is another inconsistency between these two pillars that becomes apparent in verses 6 and 7 of 2 Thessalonians 2:

<u>2 Thessalonians 2:3–7</u> (emphasis added)

³ Let no one in any way deceive you, for it will not come unless the apostasy comes first, and **the man of lawlessness is revealed**, the son of destruction, ⁴ who opposes and exalts himself above every so-called god or object of worship, so that he takes his seat in the temple of God, displaying himself as being God. ⁵ Do you not remember that while I was still with you, I was telling you these things? ⁶ And you know **what restrains him now, so that in his time he will be revealed**. ⁷ For the mystery of lawlessness is already at work; only **he who now restrains will do so until he is taken out of the way.**

While it is not a pillar of pretribulationism, most adherents of this position also believe that the restrainer is God the Holy Spirit. The problem with this belief is it highlights yet another inconsistency between these two pillars, which I will restate for clarity now:

- Pillar 2: The entire seven years of the seventieth week of Daniel constitute God's wrath at the day of the Lord.

- Pillar 3: Because believers are promised to be spared from God's wrath, the church will be raptured out of the world before the beginning of the seven-year period of the seventieth week.

Here is the inconsistency:

IF the Holy Spirit leaves the earth along with all believers at the rapture, thus allowing the antichrist unfettered and unrestrained rule over the earth for the time that God has allotted to him, which, you will remember, is only three and a half years, not seven (Rev. 13:5),

THEN no one *can* be saved after that, because God the Holy Spirit will no longer be on the earth to regenerate unbelievers into believers.

Stated differently,

SINCE God the Holy Spirit will have departed from this earth with the believers prior to the entire seven-year period, and

SINCE pillar 2 states that the whole seven years, including the time of the great tribulation, constitute the outpouring of the wrath of the day of the Lord, and

SINCE pillar 3 states that believers are spared from God's wrath, and

SINCE God's wrath is directed at unbelievers,

THEN there can be no new believers on the earth during the entire seven-year period, which includes the great tribulation in the second half.

So, either God the Holy Spirit *is or is not* the restrainer of 2 Thessalonians 2.

EITHER God the Holy Spirit is the restrainer, in which case

- He is absent from the earth during the entire seven years, which means

- there can be no believers coming to faith during that seven years, and

- there is no explanation for the presence and ministry of God's two witnesses on earth during the latter half of the seventieth week, and

- there is no explanation for the proclamation of the gospel by the evangelistic angel in Revelation 14:6–7, also during the seventieth week, and

- there is no explanation for the throng of believers coming out of the great tribulation in Revelation 7, also during the seventieth week, and

- there is the same inconsistency as in section IV.D.1.(a) above—namely, that pillars 2 and 3 of pretribulationism cannot both be true at the same time.

OR God the Holy Spirit is not the restrainer, in which case

- He remains on the earth through "the beginning of birth pangs" (the first three and a half years) and also through the great tribulation (which begins at the midpoint), which means that

- the great tribulation is not the wrath of the day of the Lord from which believers are spared, which means that

- new believers can come to faith during the great tribulation through hearing the Word

  1. from other human believers (who have not yet been raptured off the earth, because the day of the Lord has not yet begun) or

  2. from God's two witnesses or

  3. from the evangelist angel of Revelation 14:6, and in all cases,

  4. by being regenerated by God the Holy Spirit.

Conclusion: All of the reasons listed in this latter option lead inexorably to the following conclusion:

- God the Holy Spirit cannot be the restrainer of 2 Thessalonians.

- This reinforces the earlier conclusion in section IV.D.1.(a) above that both pillars 2 and 3 cannot be true at the same time.

One final point can be made regarding the restrainer, which ties in with section IV.D.3 below. According to 2 Thessalonians 2, the restrainer is not taken out of the way until the identity of the antichrist is revealed, which will be at the midpoint. If God the Holy Spirit were the restrainer, the associated rapture of the church could not happen until the beginning of the great tribulation, which starts not at the onset of the seventieth week but *halfway through it.*

This removal of the restrainer at the halfway point also means that his removal is associated with the onset of the great tribulation and *not* with the day of the Lord. Believers are not promised any exemption from the great tribulation. Thus any connection between the restrainer of 2 Thessalonians 2 and God the Holy Spirit is precluded.

2. Unbelievers will try to flee and hide when the day of the Lord begins

For *unbelievers*, the natural response to God's wrath when He cuts short the days of the great tribulation will be to flee. Two parallel passages, one from the Old Testament and the other from the New Testament, confirm that this is exactly what unbelievers will do, and the reason is also spelled out—they will recognize that the great and terrible day of the Lord is beginning:

Isaiah 2:19–21

[19] Men will go into caves of the rocks
And into holes of the ground
Before the terror of the LORD
And the splendor of His majesty,
When He arises to make the earth tremble.
[20] In that day men will cast away to the moles and the bats
Their idols of silver and their idols of gold,
Which they made for themselves to worship,
[21] In order to go into the caverns of the rocks and the clefts of the cliffs
Before the terror of the LORD and the splendor of His majesty,
When He arises to make the earth tremble.

Revelation 6:15–17

[15] Then the kings of the earth and the great men and the commanders and the rich and the strong and every slave and free man hid themselves in the caves and among the rocks of the mountains; [16] and they said to the mountains and to the rocks, "Fall on us and hide us from the presence of Him who sits on the throne, and from the wrath of the Lamb; [17] for the great day of their wrath has come, and who is able to stand?"

Conclusion: If God's wrath on the day of the Lord were to begin with the first seal, as pretribulationism claims, then why do men not flee and try to hide from God's wrath until the sixth seal? The Bible is clear that when the wrath of the day of the Lord is unleashed, the world will know it.

3. THE DAY OF THE LORD CANNOT BEGIN BEFORE THE MIDPOINT OF THE SEVENTIETH WEEK OF DANIEL

The midpoint of the seventieth week is the absolute earliest time that the day of the Lord can begin, and the prewrath and posttribulation positions posit that it begins later than that. Paul's second letter to the Thessalonians explains why the day of the Lord cannot begin until, at the earliest, the midpoint:

<u>2 Thessalonians 2:1–4</u> (emphasis added)

[1] Now we request you, brethren, with regard to the coming of our Lord Jesus Christ and our gathering together to Him, [2] that you not be quickly shaken from your composure or be disturbed either by a spirit or a message or a letter as if from us, to the effect that the day of the Lord has come. [3] Let no one in any way deceive you, for **it will not come unless the apostasy comes first, and the man of lawlessness is revealed, the son of destruction,** [4] who opposes and exalts himself above every so-called god or object of worship, so that he takes his seat in the temple of God, displaying himself as being God.

This text plainly states that two things have to occur before the onset of the day of the Lord:

- the apostasy
- the revelation of the identity of the "man of lawlessness" or "son of destruction," both of which refer to the end-times antichrist.

That there is widespread and ever-growing apostasy in America and in Western countries today is undeniable. But throughout church history, there have been periods of both apostasy and revival. What makes Paul's reference to apostasy different in this case is the use of the definite article (the) in the Greek. This indicates that this apostasy is a definable event in the end times and refers to a mass defection of so-called believers from the true faith. It could refer as well to the apostasy of the Jews in Israel, as they willingly follow and give their allegiance to the antichrist. This mass apostasy is associated in verse 3 with the revelation of the identity of the antichrist. Does the Bible tell us when the antichrist's identity will be revealed? It does.

Daniel 9:27 states:

> And he ["the prince who is to come" of v. 26—a reference to the antichrist] will make a firm covenant with the many for one week [a period of seven years], but in the middle of the week [i.e., at the three-and-a-half-year mark] he will put a stop to sacrifice and grain offering; and on the wing of abominations will come one who makes desolate, even until a complete destruction, one that is decreed, is poured out on the one who makes desolate.

Most scholars believe that the abomination of desolation of this verse will be a violation of a rebuilt temple in Jerusalem, similar to the desecration of the Second Temple by Antiochus IV Epiphanes in 168 BC (see Dan. 11:31). What will the antichrist's abominable desecration be? We are told the answer in 2 Thessalonians 2:4: He will oppose and exalt "himself above every so-called god or object of worship, so that he takes his seat in the temple of God, displaying himself as being God." The same answer appears in Daniel 11:36 and in Revelation 13:5–8:

Daniel 11:36 (regarding the events of the end times [see v. 35])
Then the king [the antichrist] will do as he pleases, and he will exalt and magnify himself above every god and will speak monstrous things against the God of gods; and he will prosper until the indignation is finished, for that which is decreed will be done.

Revelation 13:5–8
5 There was given to him [the "beast," i.e., the antichrist] a mouth speaking arrogant words and blasphemies; and authority to act for forty-two months was given to him. 6 And he opened his mouth in blasphemies against God, to blaspheme His name and His tabernacle, that is, those who dwell in heaven. 7 It was given to him to make war with the saints and to overcome them, and

authority over every tribe and people and tongue and nation was given to him. 8 All who dwell on the earth will worship him, everyone whose name has not been written from the foundation of the world in the book of life of the Lamb who has been slain.

These verses establish that the antichrist will demand the worship of *the world*, not just the Jews, whose temple he has just defiled with his abomination of desolation. Later, in Revelation 13:11–14, John reiterates that the antichrist's false prophet (the second beast) deceives "those who dwell on the earth" and demands that they worship him. In addition, he requires everyone to take the mark of the beast in order to buy and sell. When people are faced with the starvation of their families, they will do whatever they feel is expedient to survive. Many, many so-called believers will make the fatal assumption that taking the mark is not a sin, or if it is, God will forgive it. This will be "the" apostasy that is associated with the revelation of the identity of the antichrist.

When will these two related events— the apostasy and the revelation of the identity of the antichrist (2 Thess. 2:3)— occur? It will be at the midpoint of Daniel's seventieth week. (See Dan. 9:27, quoted above.) That this is so is confirmed by Revelation 13:5 (forty-two months = three and a half years; also quoted above) and by Jesus Himself:

Matthew 24:15, 21

15 Therefore when you see the abomination of desolation which was spoken of through Daniel the prophet, standing in the holy place (let the reader understand), ...
21 For then there will be a great tribulation, such as has not occurred since the beginning of the world until now, nor ever will.

The onset of the great tribulation will occur at the midpoint of the seventieth week, when the antichrist will

- reveal his identity,

- commit the abomination of desolation by somehow desecrating the rebuilt temple,

- declare himself to be God,

- demand the worship of all the people of the world, on pain of death, and

- require all people to take his mark in order to survive.

These requirements will shock many people, including so-called believers, into compliance, though in saving their lives, they will be losing their souls. (See Matt. 16:25; Mark 8:35; Luke 9:24.)

Conclusion: For these reasons, Paul's reassurance to the believers in the Thessalonian church that the day of the Lord had not come yet spells out for believers of all times that the day of the Lord *cannot* come until, at the very earliest, the midpoint of the seventieth week.

Since, however, we know that the great tribulation begins at the midpoint (See Matt. 24:15, 21), the day of the Lord must begin even later.

In his explanation and reassurance to the believers, Paul ruled out the possibility of a pretribulation rapture (i.e., before the beginning of the seventieth week) because pillar 2, that all seven years are the wrath of the day of the Lord, cannot be true.

4. **A DIFFERENT DEFINITION OF THE WORD** *APOSTASY* **FOUND IN 2 THESSALONIANS 2:3 DOES NOT RESOLVE THE FATAL FLAW OF PRETRIBULATIONISM**

As in the prior subsection, this subsection addresses the following passage from 2 Thessalonians:

<u>2 Thessalonians 2:1–4</u> (emphasis added)

[1] Now we request you, brethren, with regard to the coming of our Lord Jesus Christ, and our gathering together to Him, [2] that you not be quickly shaken from your composure or be disturbed either by a spirit or a message or a letter as if from us, to the effect that the day of the Lord has come. [3] Let no one in any way deceive you, for **it will not come unless the apostasy comes first, and the man of lawlessness is revealed, the son of destruction,** [4] who opposes and exalts himself above every so-called god or object of worship,

so that he takes his seat in the temple of God, displaying himself as being God.

As noted in the prior subsection, this text plainly states that two things have to occur before the onset of the day of the Lord:

- the apostasy and
- the revelation of the identity of the "man of lawlessness" or "son of destruction," both of which refer to the end-times antichrist.

There is a minority view among pretribulationists today that translates the Greek word *apostasia* in 2 Thessalonians 2:3 into English as "departure" instead of "apostasy."

Translated as "departure,"

- the word could either have a spiritual meaning, in which case it would refer to a spiritual departure, ostensibly from orthodoxy (the usual meaning of apostasy); or
- it could refer to a physical departure, meaning the rapture of believers out of this world.

The minority view holds the latter view—that is, that "the apostasy" refers to the rapture. Bypassing an argument on the merits of this alternate definition, I see a problem of consistency again. The problem is that both of the events Paul listed in 2 Thessalonians—the apostasy and the revelation of the identity of the antichrist—are related events, one leading to the other.

SINCE both events, the departure/apostasy/rapture and the revelation of the identity of the antichrist, will happen at the midpoint of the seventieth week,

THEN the rapture cannot occur before the midpoint, much less before the commencement of the seventieth week.

A counterargument to solve this problem may be anticipated: If the Greek word *apostasia* refers to the rapture, perhaps the two events in 2 Thessalonians 2:3 are not related. The first, the rapture, will happen before the commencement of the seventieth week; and the second, the revelation of the identity of the antichrist and his abomination of desolation, will happen three and a half years later, at the midpoint of the seventieth week. The wrath of the day of the Lord will begin sometime in the second half, after the second event has occurred at the midpoint.

The problem with this "solution" is that the Bible clearly teaches that deliverance of the just immediately precedes the delivery of judgment. Jesus Himself gave the examples of Noah's entry into the ark and Lot's hasty exit from Sodom.

> See section IV.D.6 below for further development of this point.

Conclusion: Changing the usual definition of the Greek word *apostasia* from "apostasy" to "departure" nullifies pillar 2 of pretribulationism (i.e., that all seven years of the seventieth week are the wrath of the day of the Lord) because the different definition acknowledges that the day of the Lord will not start until after the "departure" *and* after the revelation of the antichrist, both of which do not occur until the midpoint of the seventieth week.

Alternatively, changing the time of the rapture to at least three and a half years before the onset of the wrath of the day of the Lord nullifies pillar 3 (believers are spared from the wrath of the day of the Lord) because it removes believers from the world at least three and a half years before the time from which they are to be spared arrives. Further, putting a three-and-a-half-year gap between the time of the rapture and the time of the onset of the day of the Lord contradicts Jesus's teaching, set out in section IV.D.6 below.

5. THE SEALS OF REVELATION 6 CANNOT BE THE WRATH OF THE DAY OF THE LORD

(a) JESUS'S WARNINGS IN MATTHEW 24 PARALLEL THE SEALS OF REVELATION 6, BUT HE GAVE NO WARNINGS OR INFORMATION ABOUT THE TRUMPETS AND BOWLS OF REVELATION

The parallels between Matthew 24 and Revelation 6 are set out in the discussion and the charts in section III.B/pillar 2.1 above. Jesus gave

His followers the warnings they would need to heed in the last days. Nowhere in the teaching of Matthew 24 did Jesus say that these events are His wrath. The purpose of the warnings was that believers, having been forewarned, would not be caught off guard and thereby be deceived by these events as they begin to transpire.

Warnings such as the list below would be unnecessary if all believers in Jesus would be raptured off the earth before the events of Matthew 24 and the parallel passages in Mark and Luke:

- See that no one misleads you. Matthew 24:4

- See that you are not frightened, for those things must take place. Matthew 24:6

- The one who endures to the end, he will be saved. Matthew 24:13

- If anyone says …, do not believe him. Matthew 24:23, 26

- I have told you in advance. Matthew 24:25

- Therefore, be on the alert. Matthew 24:42

- You also must be ready, too. Matthew 24:44

- Be on the alert. Matthew 25:13

In addition, Jesus called believers to

- be faithful (Matt. 24:45–47),

- be prepared (Matt. 25:1–13),

- be fruitful (Matt. 25:14–30).

Moreover, while Jesus taught His followers about events that paralleled the seals of Revelation 6, conspicuous by its absence in Matthew 24 is any mention by Jesus of events that would have paralleled the trumpets and the bowls of Revelation. The most obvious reason for the omission is that his followers would not need any warnings to watch for those events because they would no longer be on the earth to experience them.

Conclusion: The events of the seals are the activities of human beings (and of Satan, acting through the agency of humans, though circumscribed by God), and therefore Jesus warned His followers regarding those events so that they would not be deceived, unprepared, unfruitful, frightened, and unable to endure.

In contrast to the seals, the trumpets and bowls are *God's* wrath, and therefore believers will have been raptured off the earth just prior to that time. For that reason, Jesus gave no warnings or information to His followers about those.

(b) Jesus warned His followers to flee when the great tribulation begins

In Matthew 24, Jesus advised His followers that the great tribulation would be triggered by the abomination of desolation spoken of by Daniel the prophet. Daniel 9:27 tells us that the abomination of desolation will occur at the midpoint of the seventieth week.

<u>Matthew 24:15–21</u> (emphasis added)

[15] Therefore **when you see the abomination of desolation which was spoken of through Daniel the prophet, standing in the holy place (let the reader understand),** [16] **then those who are in Judea must flee to the mountains.** [17] Whoever is on the housetop must not go down to get the things out that are in his house. [18] Whoever is in the field must not turn back to get his cloak. [19] But woe to those who are pregnant and to those who are nursing babies in those days! [20] But pray that your flight will not be in the winter, or on a Sabbath; [21] **For then there will be a great tribulation, such as has not occurred since the beginning of the world until now, nor ever will.**

At that point, the midpoint of the seventieth week, Jesus warned His people *to flee*. If the great tribulation were the wrath of the day of the Lord, the only appropriate response for followers of Jesus would be to fall on their faces in repentance, not to flee.

Conclusion: Thus, another reason why the seals cannot be part of God's wrath in the day of the Lord judgment is that Jesus would not tell His followers to flee from the great tribulation (the fifth seal) if it were part of His wrath.

(c) The first seal cannot be a manifestation of the wrath of the day of the Lord

The first seal, the emergence of the antichrist, by its very nature cannot be a manifestation of God's wrath. It is true that one form of God's judgment is that He "gives mankind over"—to use the expression of Romans 1:24, 26, 28—to their own evil desires and allows them to suffer the consequences of their own evil. It is also true that God has in the past used evil people to discipline His own. A prime example is that, in response to the ongoing idolatry of the southern kingdom of Judah, God sent the barbaric and completely idolatrous Babylonians to destroy His own temple in Jerusalem and to carry off His people into captivity for seventy years—after which, it should be remembered, He then judged the Babylonians by allowing the Persians to conquer them. His sovereignty over all things, including those who are evil, is never diminished.

The Lord will allow the rise of the antichrist; remember that Revelation 6:2 says that "a crown was given to him"—that is, in the passive voice. The antichrist may think that he has gained his own crown for himself, but the reality is that it will be only because it has been given him by the Lord's permission. And the Lord knows *exactly* how long the antichrist will be allowed to wreak havoc in the world.

For example, Daniel 7:21 says that the little horn, which is the antichrist, will wage war with the saints and will overpower them. Verse 25 of the same chapter of Daniel says that "he [the antichrist] will speak out against the Most High and wear down the saints of the Highest One, and he will intend to make alterations in times and in law; and they [the saints of the Highest One] **will be given into his hand for a time, times, and half a time.**"

That means that the sovereign Lord will allow the saints to be given into the hand of the antichrist for a specified period of time. The expression, "a time, times, and half a time," is a term of art that means three and a half years; in Revelation 11:2 and 13:5, the same period of time is referred to as forty-two months, and in Revelation 12:6, it is referred to as 1,260 days.

How can we know that the first seal, the emergence of the antichrist, is not a part of God's wrath in the day of the Lord? While this seal and the next few seals are very similar to forms of God's judgment that He has used in the past, they are not the *wrath of the Lord* which is described throughout the Bible as the day of the Lord because in *that* time, the day of the Lord, God alone will be exalted, and all proud men will be abased.

It is true that, from the midpoint of the seventieth week, the antichrist will be exalting himself, but when the Lord cuts short the days of the great tribulation and the day of the Lord begins, the antichrist will no longer be able to exalt himself. He will not lose his position immediately, but he will be rendered impotent to do anything beyond calling the nations to Armageddon (Rev. 16:13–16). Indeed, when the day of the Lord begins, no one will be *able* to stand against Him.

> See section IV.A.5 above.

For this reason, it is completely contradictory that during this time of the day of the Lord, God would allow the ultimate Satan-inspired and possibly Satan-possessed blasphemer to, according to 2 Thessalonians 2:4, oppose and exalt "*himself* above every so-called god or object of worship, so that he takes his seat in the temple of God, displaying *himself* as being God" (emphasis added). Daniel 11:36 says something very similar: "He will exalt and magnify himself above every god and will speak monstrous things against the God of gods."

During the time period known as the day of the Lord, the antichrist simply could not

- rise to power,
- consolidate the entire world into his *own* kingdom under his *own* authority,
- commit the abomination of desolation in the rebuilt temple in Jerusalem,
- declare himself to be God,
- demand that the world worship him as God, and

- immediately thereafter begin slaughtering Jews and Christians wholesale.

This is because *the Lord alone* will be exalted in that day. The only logical conclusion is that those events, those actions by the antichrist (i.e., the great tribulation), will precede the day of the Lord.

Conclusion: The first seal represents the emergence of a final world ruler, and his rule during the day of the Lord would be inconsistent with the exaltation of the Lord *alone* in that day. For that reason, the first seal cannot be part of the day of the Lord.

(d) The day of the Lord cannot begin until sometime after the fifth seal of Revelation

<u>Revelation 6:9–11</u> (emphasis added)

[9] When the Lamb broke the fifth seal, I saw underneath the altar the souls of those who had been slain because of the word of God, and because of the testimony which they had maintained; [10] and they cried out with a loud voice, saying, **"How long, O Lord, holy and true, will You refrain from judging and avenging our blood on those who dwell on the earth?"** [11] And there was given to each of them a white robe; and they were told that they should rest for a little while longer, until the number of their fellow servants and their brethren who were to be killed even as they had been, would be completed also.

The plaintive cry of the martyrs under the altar clearly demonstrates that the day of the Lord has not begun. Because they are asking Him how long He will *refrain from judging and avenging* their blood, it clearly means that He has not yet begun the judgment of the day of the Lord, in which He *will* judge and avenge their blood. These martyrs long to see evil expunged from the earth, but it has not yet happened. In fact, the response to their question is that the killing of saints will continue until the number of them should be completed.

That the outpouring of God's wrath in the judgment of the day of the Lord has not yet begun by the time the fifth seal is broken is confirmed by the following verses of Revelation 6. These verses indicate that those who dwell on the earth suddenly recognize that *that* "great day of their wrath has come" and is about to begin:

<u>**Revelation 6:12–17**</u> (emphasis added)

¹² I looked when He broke the sixth seal, and there was a great earthquake; and the sun became black as sackcloth made of hair, and the whole moon became like blood; ¹³ and the stars of the sky fell to the earth, as a fig tree casts its unripe figs when shaken by a great wind. ¹⁴ The sky was split apart like a scroll when it is rolled up, and every mountain and island were moved out of their places. ¹⁵ Then the kings of the earth and the great men and the commanders and the rich and the strong and every slave and free man hid themselves in the caves and among the rocks of the mountains; ¹⁶ and they said to the mountains and to the rocks, "Fall on us and hide us from the presence of Him who sits on the throne, and **from the wrath of the Lamb;** ¹⁷ **for the great day of their wrath has come, and who is able to stand?"**

Since it is probable that the persecution and executions associated with the fifth seal begin with the abomination of desolation at the midpoint of the seventieth week—at which time the antichrist will demand the worship of all the people of the world and after which time Jews and Christians who refuse to worship him will be killed—it means that the day of the Lord cannot begin prior to the middle of Daniel's seventieth week.

Indeed, since the mass executions will continue throughout the great tribulation, until Jesus cuts short those days, the day of the Lord cannot begin until, according to Revelation 6:10–11, all "who were to be killed" are killed. Only then will the Lord no longer "refrain from judging and avenging [their] blood." The fact is that, at the time of this fifth seal, He has not yet done it. Therefore, the day of the Lord cannot have yet begun.

In addition, if this fifth seal were the time of God's final wrath, then God would be killing off His own children through the agency of the antichrist. But we know that this cannot be the case because the martyrs are asking God to *avenge their deaths*, which were caused by the persecution of the antichrist and his followers. Because the judgment of the Lord is always just and true, they could hardly be asking Him to avenge their deaths if He were responsible for their deaths.

Conclusion: During the wrath of the day of the Lord, the Lord will avenge the blood of every martyr. Since, as of the time of the fifth seal, He will not yet have done so, the day of the Lord cannot have begun before the fifth seal.

Incidentally, the same principle regarding the first seal applies to the fifth: Because the antichrist will be executing Christians and Jews on an unprecedented scale, it is clear that he will be exalting himself. Once the day of the Lord begins, however, even the antichrist will be abased and rendered powerless, as the Lord alone will be exalted in that time period.

(e) THE TEXT OF THE BIBLE ITSELF TELLS US THAT THE DAY OF THE LORD BEGINS AT THE SEVENTH SEAL/FIRST TRUMPET

The text of the Bible itself states that the day of the Lord begins *after* the sixth seal. In Revelation 6:12, when the Lamb breaks the sixth seal, there are huge cosmic disturbances. The sun becomes black as sackcloth, and the moon becomes like blood; the stars of the sky fall to the earth, and the sky is split apart like a scroll when it is rolled up. Back on the earth, there is a tremendous earthquake, so intense that all mountains and islands are moved out of their places.

At this point, people try to hide in the caves and among the rocks of the mountains, because they recognize what is about to happen and, in their terror, they want to escape from "Him who sits on the throne, and from the wrath of the Lamb; for **the great day of their wrath has come, and who is able to stand?**" (Rev. 6:15–17).

This is the first time in Revelation that the wrath of God is mentioned. It is never used in the descriptions of the first six seals. The word *wrath* appears an additional seven times in the book of Revelation but never before this point. There is no reason to make it retroactive to cover the prior seals.

Conclusion: The fact that the great tribulation begins with the fifth seal at the midpoint of the seventieth week and that the saints are given into the hand of the antichrist, as he rules through the great tribulation for forty-two months (Rev. 13:5–7), clearly demonstrates that the day of the Lord will not occur until well into the second half of the seventieth week, when the Lord cuts short the days of the great tribulation. Thus, this passage from Revelation is yet another reason why the seals cannot be the wrath of God during the day of the Lord.

6. THERE IS NO GAP BETWEEN THE RAPTURE AND THE OUTPOURING OF GOD'S WRATH

Recently added to the concept of imminence (that the rapture could happen at any time) is the idea that the rapture could happen not only just before the beginning of the seventieth week but also *at any time prior* to the beginning of the seventieth week. Popular pretribulation authors opine that the rapture could happen at any moment, and once it does, it will cause absolute chaos on the earth. Consider the *Left Behind* books and movies.[7] Into that chaos will step a charismatic leader (the antichrist), who will bring stability and peace to the world. His success will be spectacular, but not instant. For that reason, such authors conclude that a period of perhaps even years may elapse between the rapture of the saints and the beginning of the seventieth week.

The problem with this gap theory is that it is not biblically supported. In the Bible, deliverance of the just is always tied directly to the delivery of judgment. *Every description of the rapture takes place in the context of the onset of the day of the Lord.*

(a) THE TWO EVENTS ARE CONNECTED BY JESUS

Jesus Himself tied the rapture and the onset of the day of the Lord together:

---

7   *Left Behind* is a fiction series dealing with the events of the end times as portrayed in the Book of Revelation. The books were written by Tim LaHaye and Jerry B. Jenkins and published from 1995–2007 by Tyndale House. Some of the books were later turned into movies.

<u>Matthew 24:29–31</u>

[29] But immediately after the tribulation of those days the sun will be darkened, and the moon will not give its light, and the stars will fall from the sky, and the powers of the heavens will be shaken. [This is the sixth seal, *the sign of the onset of the day of the Lord.*] [30] And then the sign of the Son of Man will appear in the sky, and then all the tribes of the earth will mourn, and they will see the Son of Man coming on the clouds of the sky with power and great glory. [31] And He will send forth His angels with a great trumpet and they will gather together His elect from the four winds, from one end of the sky to the other.

> Parallel passages in Mark 13:24–27 and Luke 21:25–28.

This is the rapture.

This is consistent with the warnings of the Old Testament prophets that cosmic disturbances would signal the onset of the day of the Lord.

> See section IV.B above.

(b) PRIOR HISTORICAL EVENTS CONNECTED DELIVERANCE WITH JUDGMENT

In addition, Jesus also compared the rapture and the onset of the day of the Lord to prior historical events recorded in the Bible, events in which deliverance of the righteous immediately preceded the delivery of judgment:

<u>Matthew 24:37–41</u> (emphasis added)

[37] For the coming of the Son of Man will be just like the days of Noah. [38] For as in those days before the flood they were eating and drinking, marrying and giving in marriage, **until the day that Noah entered the ark,** [39] and they did not understand until the flood came and took them all away; so will the coming of the Son of Man be. [40] Then there will be two men in the field; one will be taken and one will be left. [41] Two women will be grinding at the mill; one will be taken and one will be left.

> Parallel passage in Luke 17:26–31.

Luke makes the same point, and adds the example of Sodom and Gomorrah.

<u>Luke 17:27, 29</u> (emphasis added)

[27] They were eating, they were drinking, they were marrying, they were being given in marriage, until **the day** that Noah entered the ark, and the flood came and destroyed them all.

[29] But on **the day** that Lot went out from Sodom it rained fire and brimstone from heaven and destroyed them all.

Deliverance of the just immediately preceded the delivery of judgment.

(c) PAUL CONNECTED THE RAPTURE AND THE DAY OF THE LORD IN BOTH LETTERS TO THE THESSALONIANS

The same connection between the rapture and the day of the Lord is repeated in 1 Thessalonians. Chapter 4 closes with a graphic description of the rapture, and chapter 5 opens with a discussion of the day of the Lord.

Paul's second letter to the Thessalonians reiterates this connection. This second letter was in response to some confusion that had arisen. The Thessalonian church had received another letter, ostensibly from Paul, but which, in fact, had not been written by him, and this fake letter contained false teachings about the day of the Lord. Specifically, it said that the day of the Lord had arrived already and that, therefore, since these Thessalonian believers had not been participants in the preceding rapture, they had been, in the ultimate sense of the phrase, truly left behind. Since the Thessalonian believers were suffering intense persecution, this news was extremely distressing to them. Word of this fake letter had reached Paul, and he wrote this second letter to the Thessalonians to correct this false teaching, directly addressing their concern:

<u>2 Thessalonians 2:1–5</u> (emphasis added)

[1] Now we request you, brethren, with regard to the **coming of our Lord Jesus Christ and our gathering together to Him,** [2] that you

not be quickly shaken from your composure or be disturbed either by a spirit or a message or a letter as if from us, to the effect that the day of the Lord has come. ³ Let no one in any way deceive you, for it will not come unless the apostasy comes first, and the man of lawlessness is revealed, the son of destruction, ⁴ who opposes and exalts himself above every so-called god or object of worship, so that he takes his seat in the temple of God, displaying himself as being God. ⁵ Do you not remember that while I was still with you, I was telling you these things?

> Verses 3 and 4 are discussed in sections I.B.4.(b)2(bb) and IV.D.1.(b) above.

The point to be made here is that, consistent with Jesus's teachings in Matthew, Mark, and Luke, Paul connects the two events. Verse 1 speaks of the coming of our Lord Jesus Christ and our gathering together to Him in one breath, so to speak. They appear to be two descriptions of the same event. This verse describes it first from the heavenly point of view and secondly from the earthly point of view. That is, from the heavenly point of view, the Lord Jesus Christ comes out of heaven, and from the earthly point of view, believers are gathered together up into the skies to meet Him. This is the rapture. The following verses, beginning with verse 2, speak of the day of the Lord.

This would accomplish the same dual purpose that Paul sets out in verses 7 and 8 of chapter 1 in the same letter.

2 Thessalonians 1:6–8 (emphasis added)

⁶ For after all it is only just for God to repay with affliction those who afflict you, ⁷ and **to give relief to you who are afflicted** and to us as well **when the Lord Jesus will be revealed from heaven** with His mighty angels in flaming fire, ⁸ **dealing out retribution to those who do not know God and to those who do not obey the gospel of our Lord Jesus.**

The first purpose of Jesus's coming will be to give relief to those who are afflicted when He is revealed from heaven. This is a reference to the rapture. Then, with believers safely out of the way, He will begin to fulfill the second purpose of His coming—that is, to deal out "retribution to those who do not know God and to those who do not obey the gospel." This is a description of the day of the Lord. Once more, the rapture and the day of the Lord are tied together, with no intervening gap of time.

Finally, I will include two Old Testament passages which also confirm the deliverance of the righteous just prior to the day of the Lord:

Joel 2:31–32

[31] The sun will be turned into darkness
And the moon into blood
Before the great and awesome day of the Lord comes.
[32] And it will come about that whoever calls on the name of the Lord
Will be delivered.

This passage could not be more clear. As the sun and the moon signal the arrival of the day of the Lord, those who belong to the Lord will be delivered (raptured) from His wrath.

Daniel 11:45; 12:1–2

[45] He [the antichrist] will pitch the tents of his royal pavilion between the seas and the beautiful Holy Mountain.
[12:1] And there will be a time of distress such as never occurred since there was a nation until that time; and at that time your people, everyone who is found written in the book, will be rescued. [2] Many of those who sleep in the dust of the ground will awake, these to everlasting life, but the others to disgrace and everlasting contempt.

These verses in Daniel describe the antichrist's rise to power; then the great tribulation, following which will be the rapture of believers in the first resurrection; and later, the second resurrection for unbelievers. While this passage does not go on to address the day of the Lord, it is consistent with other biblical passages that indicate both that Old Testament saints will be included in the rapture and that this first resurrection will follow the great tribulation.

Conclusion: The Bible makes it clear that there is no gap of time between the rapture and the onset of the day of the Lord. Deliverance of the just immediately precedes the delivery of judgment.

7.   JESUS'S DESCRIPTION OF THE TWO HALVES OF DANIEL'S SEVENTIETH WEEK PRECLUDES THE CHARACTERIZATION OF THE ENTIRETY OF THE WEEK AS THE WRATH OF THE DAY OF THE LORD

Pillar 1 of pretribulationism asserts that the entire seven-year period of Daniel's seventieth week is a time of tribulation that, according to pillar 2, is also the wrath of the day of the Lord. These two pillars conflict with Jesus's characterization of the same seven-year time period.

According to Matthew 24:8, Jesus described the first half of the seventieth week, prior to the abomination of desolation at the midpoint, as "merely the beginning of birth pangs." Even people who have not endured the process of labor and delivery know that the pains of labor begin relatively slowly, with intervening spaces of time between the contractions. As labor progresses, however, the contractions increase in frequency and in intensity. This means that Jesus was teaching that the first three and a half years will be bad, but not nearly as severe as the second three and a half years. He did not even characterize the first half as tribulation *at all* but as "merely the beginning of birth pangs."

The *great* tribulation will begin with the abomination of desolation at the midpoint of the seven years, when the antichrist declares himself to be God and demands that the world worship him as God (Matt. 24:9, 15–22; 2 Thess. 2:3–4). This second half of the seventieth week is similar to the hard labor that precedes the delivery of a child.

Finally, the onset of the day of the Lord is the worst. It is described by Paul as destruction that comes suddenly—"like labor pains upon a woman with child, and they will not escape" (1 Thess. 5:3). Isaiah described it in a similar fashion:

<u>Isaiah 13:6–8</u>
⁶ Wail, for the day of the LORD is near!
It will come as destruction from the Almighty.

⁷ Therefore all hands will fall limp,
And every man's heart will melt.
⁸ They will be terrified,
Pains and anguish will take hold of them;
They will writhe like a woman in labor,
They will look at one another in astonishment,
Their faces aflame.

Conclusion: Jesus compared the first half of the seventieth week to a pregnant woman at the beginning of the birth pangs of labor. The second half will be like the hard labor which Jesus called the "great tribulation," so great that, according to Jesus in Matthew 24:21, it will be "such as has not occurred since the beginning of the world until now, nor ever shall." And the onset of the day of the Lord will be like a woman in travail, in intense labor prior to delivery.

If, as pretribulationism asserts, the wrath of the day of the Lord begins with the commencement of the seventieth week, then hard labor has to precede the beginning of birth pangs. That is not coherent. More importantly, it contradicts the words of Jesus Himself. Pillars 1 and 2 do not align with His teaching.

8. There will be no "peace and safety" in the day of the Lord

There are three additional points to be gleaned from the following passage in 1 Thessalonians that are fatal to pretribulationism:

<u>1 Thessalonians 5:1–11</u>

¹ Now as to the times and the epochs, brethren, you have no need of anything to be written to you. ² For you yourselves know full well that **the day of the Lord will come** just like a thief in the night. ³ **While they are saying, "Peace and safety!"** then destruction will come upon them suddenly like labor pains upon a woman with child; and they will not escape. ⁴ But you, brethren, are not in darkness, that the day would overtake you like a thief; ⁵ for you are all sons of light and sons of day. We are not of night nor of darkness; ⁶ so then let us not sleep as others do, but let us be alert and

sober. [7] For those who sleep do their sleeping at night, and those who get drunk get drunk at night. [8] But since we are of the day, let us be sober, having put on the breastplate of faith and love, and as a helmet, the hope of salvation. [9] **For God has not destined us for wrath, but for obtaining salvation through our Lord Jesus Christ,** [10] who died for us, so that whether we are awake or asleep, we may live together with Him. [11] Therefore encourage one another and build up one another, just as you also are doing. (emphasis added)

The first point is that this time of "peace and safety" must occur either

- before or
- within the seventieth week of Daniel.

If it occurs before, then the doctrine of imminence, pillar 4 of pretribulationism—which posits that there is no event that must yet occur before the rapture—fails because this event has not yet occurred in the world.

Conversely, if this "peace and safety" occurs within the seventieth week, then it must precede the onset of the day of the Lord (which the text clearly demonstrates). This means that the wrath of the day of the Lord cannot begin at the commencement of the seventieth week (which is pillar 2 of pretribulationism), because there will be no peace and no place of safety during the outpouring of God's final wrath in the great and terrible day of the Lord.

Conclusion: Whether the "peace and safety" occurs before the seventieth week or within it, either pillar 4 (imminence) is destroyed, or pillar 2 (that the whole of the seventieth week is the wrath of the day of the Lord) is destroyed. Either way, there can be no pretribulation rapture.

The second point from this passage follows.

9. THERE WILL BE SIGNS THAT PRECEDE THE ONSET OF THE DAY OF THE LORD

The second point from the same passage in 1 Thessalonians 5 derives from Paul's contrast of believers with unbelievers. Unlike unbelievers, who will be caught unawares when the day of the Lord comes upon them like a thief in the night, believers, having been forewarned, will not be surprised. But,

IF, as pretribulationism holds, the rapture must precede the commencement of the seventieth week because the entire week is God's wrath, a time period from which believers are spared (pillars 2 and 3, respectively), and

IF the rapture is imminent and could occur at any time, without any other intervening sign or event (pillar 4),

THEN the day of the Lord *will* overtake believers (as well as unbelievers) like a thief in the night.

Why, then, did Paul contrast unbelievers with unbelievers? Why did he write, "But you, brethren, are not in darkness, that the day would overtake you like a thief" (1 Thess. 5:4), if they will have no more warning than unbelievers?

Moreover, why would Paul, in 1 Thessalonians 5:6, warn believers to "be alert and sober" (KJV has "let us watch and be sober")?

The Greek word that is translated "be alert" or "let us watch" is *gregoreuo* (*Strong's* NT 1127) and it means "to keep awake, to watch."

Why was Paul warning believers to be alert, and what was he warning them to watch for, if not for signs that the day of the Lord is at hand, so that they will *not* be overtaken by that day in the same way that unbelievers will?

The fact is that Jesus promised that there would be signs that signal the onset of the day of the Lord:

Luke 21:25–28

[25] There will be signs in sun and moon and stars, and on the earth dismay among nations, in perplexity at the roaring of the sea and the waves, [26] men fainting from fear and the expectation of the things which are coming upon the world; for the powers of the heavens will be shaken. [27] Then they will see the Son of Man coming in a cloud with power and great glory. [28] But when these

things begin to take place, straighten up and lift up your heads, because your redemption is drawing near.

Paul's teaching, therefore, is, as we would hope and expect, consistent with his Lord's teaching. Believers will know to look for the signs. This contradicts and nullifies pillar 4, that the rapture is imminent.

> See also section IV.B above.

Conclusion: The rapture cannot precede the commencement of the seventieth week for the following reasons:

1. If the day of the Lord coincided with the beginning of the seventieth week, and if imminence were true, then believers would have no more warning of the upcoming day of the Lord than unbelievers, and Paul's letter to the Thessalonians would be incorrect (a choice we must discard immediately).

2. The Bible, both in the Old and New Testaments, clearly identifies specific signs that believers can recognize as the onset of the day of the Lord and thus recognize the time that they should "lift up [their] heads, because [their] redemption [*i.e.*, the rapture] is drawing near." Because there will be signs for believers to watch for, imminence is invalidated.

The third point follows in the next subsection.

10. THE RAPTURE WILL NOT OCCUR BEFORE THE APPEARANCE OF THE SIGNS OF THE ONSET OF THE DAY OF THE LORD

While the passage in 1 Thessalonians 5:1–11 addresses the day of the Lord expressly, it does not address whether believers will be raptured out just prior to the onset of that day or remain on earth, endure, and not be "overtaken" by it because they have been forewarned about it.

The fact that there is a question as to whether believers will be raptured out beforehand or remain on earth reveals something else, however. It shows that at the onset of the day of the Lord, *the rapture will not yet have occurred.* Several facts lead to this conclusion:

1. 1 Thessalonians 5:4 states that believers, having been forewarned that the day of the Lord will come as a thief in the night, will not be overtaken by that day.

2. That believers will not be overtaken means that they will still be on earth at that time.

3. The fact that the day of the Lord begins when Jesus cuts short the days of the great tribulation also shows that believers are still on earth during the great tribulation.

These facts also demonstrate that the rapture will not occur before the great tribulation begins at the midpoint of the seventieth week, a conclusion that is consistent with 2 Thessalonians 2:2–4, discussed in section IV.D.1.(b) above. At the earliest, believers will be raptured out when Jesus cuts short the days of the great tribulation and the cosmic disturbances signal the onset of the day of the Lord.

Conclusion: The rapture will not occur before the signs of the onset of the day of the Lord. The fact that there will be such signs beforehand abrogates imminence.

11. THE 144,000 JEWS ON EARTH ARE SEALED FOR PROTECTION FROM GOD'S WRATH JUST PRIOR TO ITS ONSET IN THE DAY OF THE LORD

Although the subject of the 144,000 Jews of Revelation 7 will be discussed at length in section V.A.1 below, I mention them here as well because it raises another question: If the wrath of the day of the Lord starts at the beginning of the seventieth week with the breaking of the first seal, why would the Lord wait until after the sixth seal to give these Jews on earth His seal of protection? It is more logical that He would seal them at the very time they would need it, which would be when He was about to unleash His fury on the world with the trumpets and bowl judgments of the day of the Lord.

Conclusion: God will seal the 144,000 Jews for their protection when it is needed, which is after the sixth seal, when the day of the Lord is about to begin.

12. Elijah must appear before the commencement of the day of the Lord

The Lord's last word to mankind before the intertestamental silence of approximately four hundred years was a promise given to Malachi:

Malachi 4:5–6

[5] Behold, I am going to send you Elijah the prophet before the coming of the great and terrible day of the Lord. [6] He will restore the hearts of the fathers to their children and the hearts of the children to their fathers, so that I will not come and smite the land with a curse.

Like the time of "peace and safety," discussed in section IV.D.8 above, the promised appearance of Elijah must occur either

- before the seventieth week of Daniel or
- within that seven-year period.

This presents the same problem for pretribulationism as the time of "peace and safety." That is, if Elijah appears before the onset of the seventieth week, then the rapture is no longer imminent (pillar 4) because there is another event that must occur. On the other hand, if Elijah appears during the seventieth week and his coming, according to the text itself, must occur "before the coming of the great and terrible day of the Lord," it means that the day of the Lord cannot begin at the commencement of the seventieth week (pillar 2).

It is probable that Elijah's coming will be within the seven years of the seventieth week, because Revelation 11:3 discloses that the ministry of the two witnesses will be 1,260 days, which is the same as three and a half years or half of the seven years. Most scholars have opined that the two witnesses will be Moses, who represents the Law, and Elijah, who represents the Prophets. Other scholars think they might be Enoch and Elijah because both of these men were taken up bodily into heaven without experiencing physical death.

Since, in either case, Elijah seems to be one of the two, whether he ministers in the first or second half is not relevant to this discussion.

What matters is that his ministry will be within the confines of the seventieth week, and since his coming will precede the day of the Lord, it means that the entire seventieth week cannot be the day of the Lord (pillar 2).

Conclusion:

IF Elijah appears before the commencement of the seventieth week,

THEN imminence (pillar 4) fails because there *is* another prophesied event occurring before the seventieth week.

On the other hand,

IF Elijah appears during the seventieth week, which is probable,

THEN because the prophecy in Malachi states that Elijah's appearance comes before the day of the Lord, the day of the Lord cannot start at the beginning of the seventieth week, and pillar 2 fails.

13. THE FUTURE FULFILLMENT OF JESUS'S PROPHECY OF THE END OF THE AGE PRECLUDES A PRETRIBULATION RAPTURE

There are several places in the Bible that signal the end of the age. They are the signs that herald the onset of the day of the Lord.

> See section IV.B above, as well as the passages regarding the day of the Lord in appendix E.

For the purposes of this subsection, the focus will begin with Matthew 13, where Jesus explained the parable of the tares of the field to His disciples:

Matthew 13:37–43 (emphasis added)

[37] And He said, "The one who sows the good seed is the Son of Man, [38] and the field is the world; and as for the good seed, these are the sons of the kingdom; and the tares are the sons of the evil one; [39] and the enemy who sowed them is the devil, and **the harvest is the end** [*Strong's* NT 4930 *sunteleia*] **of the age** [*Strong's* NT 165 *aion*]; and **the reapers are angels.** [40] So just as the tares are gathered up and burned with fire, **so shall it be at the end** [*sunteleia*] **of the**

age [*aion*]. ⁴¹ The Son of Man **will send forth His angels**, and they will gather out of His kingdom all stumbling blocks, and those who commit lawlessness, ⁴² and will throw them into the furnace of fire; in that place there will be weeping and gnashing of teeth. ⁴³ Then the righteous will shine forth as the sun in the kingdom of their Father. He who has ears, let him hear."

This passage clearly states that the end of the age will be the day of the Lord. In that day, His judgments (the trumpets and bowls of Revelation) will be administered by angels. This parable does not deal with the rapture explicitly, but verse 43 may indicate that it has just happened, because as the day of the Lord arrives, "*the righteous* will shine forth as the sun."

Another parable in the same teaching of Jesus, the parable of the dragnet cast into the sea, makes the same point, and its possible reference to the rapture has it immediately preceding the judgment of the wicked:

<u>Matthew 13:47–50</u> (emphasis added)

⁴⁷ Again, the kingdom of heaven is like a dragnet cast into the sea, and gathering fish of every kind; ⁴⁸ and when it was filled, they drew it up on the beach; and they sat down and **gathered the good fish into containers** [perhaps a reference to the rapture], but the bad they threw away. ⁴⁹ So it will be at the **end** [*sunteleia*] **of the age** [*aion*]; the angels will come forth and take out the wicked from among the righteous, ⁵⁰ and will throw them into the furnace of fire; in that place there will be weeping and gnashing of teeth.

The relevant point to be gleaned from these verses is that the end of the age is the same as the day of the Lord. Notice that there are "the righteous" and "good fish" present right up to the end of the age/day of the Lord.

Now let's shift the focus to Jesus's prophecy regarding the end of the age. These words of Jesus Christ Himself provide additional proof that the rapture cannot occur before the beginning of the seventieth week. This prophecy appears in Matthew 10 and 24 and is reinforced in His words of comfort at the end of the great commission in Matthew 28.

<u>**Matthew 10:21–22**</u> (emphasis added)

²¹ Brother will betray brother to death, and a father his child; and children will rise up against parents and cause them to be put to death. ²² You will be hated by all because of My name, but it is the one who has **endured to the end** [*Strong's* NT 5056 *telos*] who will be saved.

> Parallel passage in Mark 13:12–13.

<u>**Matthew 24:13–14**</u> (emphasis added)

¹³ But the one who **endures to the end** [*telos*], he will be saved. ¹⁴ This gospel of the kingdom shall be preached in the whole world as a testimony to all the nations, **and then the end** [*telos*] **will come.**

<u>**Matthew 28:18–20**</u> (emphasis added)

¹⁸ And Jesus came up and spoke to them, saying, "All authority has been given to Me in heaven and on earth. ¹⁹ Go therefore and **make disciples of all the nations**, baptizing them in the name of the Father and the Son and the Holy Spirit, ²⁰ teaching them to observe all that I commanded you; and lo, I am with you always, **even to the end** [*sunteleia*] **of the age** [*aion*]."

The risen Christ also delivered the same message to overcomers:

<u>**Revelation 2:26**</u> (emphasis added)

He who overcomes, and he who keeps My deeds **until the end** [*telos*], to him I will give authority over the nations.

Similar passages of encouragement (and inherent warning as well) appear in Hebrews:

<u>**Hebrews 3:14**</u> (emphasis added)

For we have become partakers of Christ, **if we hold fast the beginning of our assurance firm until the end** [*telos*].

<u>**Hebrews 6:11–12**</u> (emphasis added)

¹¹ And we desire that each one of you **show the same diligence so as to realize the full assurance of hope until the end** [*telos*], ¹² so that

you will not be sluggish, but imitators of those who through faith and patience inherit the promises.

The Greek word that is translated in Matthew 10:22; 24:13–14 and in Mark 13:13 as "end" is *telos* (*Strong's* NT 5056). *Vine's* states that "*telos* signifies 'the limit,' either at which a person or thing ceases to be what he or it was up to that point, or at which previous activities were ceased."[8]

In Matthew 28:20, a different Greek word is translated as "end." It is *sunteleia* (*Strong's* NT 4930). *Vine's* defines it as "a marking the 'completion' or consummation of the various parts of a scheme. ... The word does not denote a termination, but the heading up of events to the appointed climax."[9]

Why are different Greek words used? It could be just the use of synonyms or perhaps there may be some slightly nuanced difference. If the latter is the case, it seems logical to conclude that when *telos* is used, Jesus was referring to an event that will have a defined termination point.

Since the church will go into the great tribulation (because it cannot have been raptured out of the world prior to that time), Jesus is encouraging His followers to endure, knowing that the days of the great tribulation will come to a definite ending point when He cuts those days short and raptures them up to Himself in the clouds.

Conversely, when *sunteleia* is used, Jesus was referring to the completion of all the events over the course of human history that would culminate in the day of the Lord.

What is it that is ending or is being completed? It is the current age. The Greek word for "age" in Matthew 28:20 is *aion* (*Strong's* NT 165). This word does not mean "the world," as some English translations have instead of "age." *Aion* means, according to Vine's, "not the world, but a period or epoch or era in which events take place."[10]

---

8   Vine, Unger, and White, *Vine's Complete Expository Dictionary*, under "end, ending."

9   Ibid., under "end, ending."

10   Ibid., under "end, ending."

Jesus both encouraged and warned His followers to "endure to the end" (Matt. 24:13). Then He told them when the end would come—when "this gospel of the kingdom shall be preached in the whole world as a testimony to all the nations" (Matt. 24:14).

Does the Bible tell us when the last presentation of the gospel will be given? It does:

<u>Revelation 14:6–7</u> (emphasis added)

[6] And I saw another angel flying in midheaven, having an **eternal gospel to preach to those who live on the earth, and to every nation and tribe and tongue and people**; [7] and he said with a loud voice, "Fear God, and give Him glory, because the hour of His judgment has come; worship Him who made the heaven and the earth and sea and springs of waters."

This is the first of three angels in Revelation 14 with proclamations for all the world.

The second angel announces the fall of the world system (Babylon).

The third angel warns all people not to worship the beast or take his mark and then enumerates the consequences of doing so.

The dire warning of the third angel must occur during the time of the great tribulation, when all people are faced with the choice of taking the mark of the beast or being executed.

The second angel's proclamation seems to occur near the end of the great tribulation or at the onset of the day of the Lord, as he announces the imminent or ongoing fall of Babylon.

The first angel's presentation of the gospel to the world is the one last chance for people to repent of their sins and turn to the Lord, just before the great and terrible day of the Lord begins.

Note the following verses in Revelation 14. The Spirit blesses those who die in the Lord from then on, and then there are two reapings of the earth.

The first reaping is accomplished by the cloud rider, "like a son of man, having a golden crown on His head." This first reaping sounds like another description of the rapture. That this is so is confirmed (after the second reaping, which throws the "grapes" "into the great wine press of the wrath of God"—a description of the day of the Lord) in the opening verses of Revelation 15, which provide another view of the innumerable multitude of Revelation 7:12–17.

<u>Revelation 15:2–4</u> (emphasis added)

² And I saw something like a sea of glass mixed with fire, and **those who had been victorious over the beast and his image and the number of his name, standing on the sea of glass, holding harps of God**. ³ And they sang the song of Moses, the bond-servant of God, and the song of the Lamb, saying,
"Great and marvelous are Your works,
O Lord God, the Almighty;
Righteous and true are Your ways,
King of the nations!
⁴ "Who will not fear, O Lord, and glorify Your name?
For You alone are holy;
For all the nations will come and worship before You,
For Your righteous acts have been revealed."

Thus "the end of the age" will be the time when

- the gospel has been preached in the whole world for a witness to all the nations,

- the last opportunity for people to repent and to turn to the Lord has passed,

- the lights of the heavens are extinguished (this is the "sign of the end of the age" that the disciples asked about in Matt. 24:3 and is also described by Jesus in Matt. 24:29 and Rev. 6:12–17), and

- the sign of the Son of Man appears in the sky as the blinding light of His shekinah glory pierces the darkness, as

- Jesus descends from heaven to gather the dead and the living believers to Himself in the clouds, all signaling that

- the time for God's undiluted wrath to be poured out has arrived in the form of the day of the Lord.

Conclusion:

SINCE "the end of the age" will not come until the gospel has been preached to the whole world and

SINCE new believers will be coming to faith during the great tribulation, as a result of the testimony of the two witnesses, the church, and the evangelist angel of Revelation 14, and

> See section V.A.1.(f) below for further discussion on this point.

SINCE those new believers will also be part of the body of Christ, which is the church, and

SINCE there is no biblical support for the notion of two different raptures, and

> See section V.B.2.(b) below.

SINCE believers must "endure to the end" to be saved (*being saved* in this context means being saved from the wrath of God in the day of the Lord),

THEREFORE the rapture cannot occur and the dispensation of the church age cannot end at the beginning of the seventieth week, because the addition of new believers to the body of Christ during the great tribulation means that the gospel has not yet been preached to the whole world, and the end of the age (the commencement of the day of the Lord) has not yet arrived.

Section V

BELIEVERS ON EARTH DURING DANIEL'S 70TH WEEK

OTHER REASONS BELIEVERS WILL BE ON THE EARTH FOR AT LEAST A PORTION, IF NOT MOST, OF THE SEVENTIETH WEEK OF DANIEL

A. THE LORD HAS ALWAYS HAD WITNESSES ON THE EARTH

If all believers were to be raptured out before "the beginning of birth pangs" and the "great tribulation,"—that is, before the beginning of the seven years of the seventieth week—to whom will the lost turn in the time of the great tribulation? Would Jesus remove the light and the salt from the lost souls in the world in the time of their greatest need?

1. THE ASSUMPTION THAT THE 144,000 JEWS WILL BE WITNESSES TO GOD DURING THE GREAT TRIBULATION IS UNWARRANTED

Two groups are described in Revelation 7, both of which, if Revelation is read chronologically, appear during the interlude between the breaking of the sixth and seventh seals. The first is a group of 144,000 Jews; the second consists of an enormous throng of people. There are several contrasts between these groups that can be immediately spotted:

- The first group consists of an exact number of people—144,000, no more and no less. In contrast, the second group consists of a crowd so large that no one can count it.

- The first group is made up exclusively of Jews, whereas the second group includes people "from every nation and all tribes and peoples and tongues." (Rev. 7:9) Thus, the second group could also include Jews.

- The first group is on earth; the second is in heaven.

- The first group is in an imminent danger so great that it requires sealing for their protection, while the second group has successfully passed through their valley of the shadow of death (perhaps even death itself, as well as its shadow) and is joyfully in the presence of the Lord, safe from all adversity and danger.

Are these two groups related to one another in any way? Or is their appearance at the same time (between the breaking of the sixth and seventh seals) the result of some other reason? The answer to the first question is no—there is no causal relationship between the presence of both groups in this chapter. I will develop the argument further in this subsection.

The answer to the second question is derived from the text itself: The two groups appear together in this chapter because the last verses of Revelation 6 have announced the arrival of the wrath of the day of the Lord and posed the question, "Who is able to stand?" (Rev. 6:17). The arrival of the day of the Lord is the cause of both unrelated events:

- At this time of unparalleled danger to all human life, the 144,000 Jews must be sealed for God's protection.

- At the same time, the arrival of the day of the Lord is the reason that the Lord Himself cuts short the days of the great tribulation and that all believers (the church), both dead and those who "remain until the coming of the Lord" (1 Thess. 4:15), are raptured. It is they who compose the massive throng of people of all nations and ethnic groups.

Then, with one group sealed for protection on earth and the other group safely removed from the earth to heaven, the seventh seal is broken. After a silence of about thirty minutes, the seven angels appear and are given seven trumpets.

My answers to the two questions posed in the preceding paragraphs are necessarily different from the answers given by pretribulationists.

Many theologians who espouse pretribulationism teach that the 144,000 Jews who are sealed in the first part of Revelation 7 are evangelists. Some teachers go further, claiming that each of these 144,000 will be as effective as the apostle Paul in proclaiming the gospel and in leading lost people to the Light. Their reason for this conclusion is not based on the text itself, but on their apparent desire to be consistent with their position that all believers will have already been raptured off the earth prior to the beginning of the seven years of Daniel's seventieth week, before the first seal was broken.

In order to justify the existence of the second event that is recorded in Revelation 7, the appearance of a great multitude who come out of the great tribulation, these teachers have to answer the obvious question— How did this vast multitude of people come to faith when every last believer who might have led them to Christ has already departed the premises of earth? These teachers conclude that both events (the sealing of the 144,000 and the appearance of the multitude) must be related, because they appear to happen at the same time—that is, between the breaking of the sixth and seventh seals. Therefore the multitude, they assert, must be the fruit of the labors of the 144,000. This conclusion is insupportable, for the reasons that follow.

> **(a) THERE IS NOT ENOUGH TIME BETWEEN THE BREAKING OF THE SIXTH AND SEVENTH SEALS TO EVANGELIZE A HOST OF PEOPLE SO GREAT THAT IT CANNOT BE NUMBERED**

Most students of the Bible, including theologians and teachers, agree that, since the text itself tells us that the innumerable crowd came out of the great tribulation, these people were on earth during the great tribulation. Undoubtedly, the same Bible students, theologians, and teachers would concede that it would take some time to evangelize "a great multitude, which no one could count, from every nation and all tribes and peoples and tongues" (Rev. 7:9). While the three and a half years of the great tribulation (minus whatever number of days the Lord cuts off, according to Matt. 24:22) would probably be a sufficient length of time in today's world of technological advances to reach a large percentage of the globe's population, the same feat *could not* be accomplished in the space between the opening of the sixth and seventh seals.

The first four seals will fill the first half (three and a half years) of the seventieth week. The fifth seal is the great tribulation, which begins at the midpoint and lasts until Jesus cuts short its days with the cosmic disturbances of the sixth seal, at which point, the day of the Lord begins. The biblical text gives no indication of any significant time lapse at that point.

Instead, it moves immediately from the cosmic disturbances of the sixth seal (with the delay, perhaps, of the half hour of Rev. 8:1) to the onset of the Lord's wrath, which begins with the breaking of the seventh seal and the introduction of the seven trumpet judgments. The space of one half hour is by no means sufficient time to evangelize a throng of people.

(b) THERE IS NO TEXT FROM WHICH TO DRAW AN INFERENCE

More importantly, however, the connection between the two events of Revelation 7 is based on pure inference from something that is not implied in the text. An inference is a deduction drawn from given facts; an implication is a hint within the text.

There is plainly no biblical evidence to support the inference that the 144,000 Jews of Revelation 7:4–8 and 14:1–5 are witnesses/evangelists at all, much less 144,000 "Pauls." The passage in Revelation 7 simply describes the 144,000 as Jews from all the tribes (except Dan) being sealed as "bond-servants of our God on their foreheads" (7:3). *It neither describes any activity on their part nor any assignment given to them.* Even Revelation 14, which describes this group of faithful Jews more fully than Revelation 7, is also completely silent on this issue. That they are not evangelists is also supported by the next point regarding sealing.

(c) Sealing denotes ownership and protection

The seal was a sign of two things: ownership (the Lord knows who are His—Num. 16:5; Nah. 1:7; 2 Tim. 2:19) and protection. In the Old Testament, there was another time when the Lord sealed His own. Ezekiel records the following:

<u>Ezekiel 9:4–6</u> (emphasis added)

9 The LORD said to him, "Go through the midst of the city, even through the midst of Jerusalem, and **put a mark on the foreheads** of the men who sigh and groan over all the abominations which are being committed in its midst." 5 But to the others He said in my hearing, "Go through the city after him and strike; do not let your eye have pity and do not spare. 6 Utterly slay old men, young men, maidens, little children, and women, but **do not touch any man on whom is the mark**; and you shall start from My sanctuary." So they started with the elders who were before the temple.

> A side note is relevant at this point: Because Satan creates counterfeit parallels to the things of God, Satan's antichrist will also have a mark on the forehead or hands (Rev. 13:16) that is his counterpart to God's seal on His own. The mark of the beast will irrevocably seal Satan's ownership of those who take this mark. There will be no turning back for those souls once they do that (Rev. 14:9–11).

The context of this passage, as well as the passage itself, makes the purpose of the sealing clear: The Lord is putting His mark on those who are His (i.e., those who are faithful to Him) to protect them from His imminent judgment of the Jews' idolatry. This purpose has its parallel in Revelation 7:3. These Jews also belong to God, and He will therefore protect them from the horrors of the trumpet and bowl judgments as they are poured out on the earth in the coming day of the Lord.

Indeed, there is another parallel between the passages in Ezekiel 9 and Revelation 7. The act of sealing in both instances is followed by fire being cast onto the earth:

Ezekiel 10:2

And He spoke to the man clothed in linen and said, "Enter between the whirling wheels under the cherubim and fill your hands with coals of fire from between the cherubim and scatter them over the city."

Revelation 8:5

Then the angel took the censer and filled it with the fire of the altar, and threw it to the earth; and there followed peals of thunder and sounds and flashes of lightning and an earthquake.

The parallels of these two passages clearly indicate that the Lord was/will be sealing a remnant of His own to protect them from His impending wrath.

Another conclusion that can be drawn from the timing of God's sealing of these groups in Ezekiel and in Revelation follows in the next subsection.

(d) The 144,000 are sealed as the time for evangelizing closes out

The context of both Ezekiel 9–10 and Revelation 7–8 is the sealing of God's faithful remnant just before the outpouring of God's judgment. In the case of Revelation, the context is the launching of the day of the Lord. Because of the unique nature of this particular time period, there will be no new believers once it begins; the time for repentance will have passed.

See section IV.D.1.(a) above.

The time for evangelizing will also have passed, so the rapture of all believers off the earth at this time will leave behind only those for whom the time of possible repentance has passed as well as the sealed 144,000 Jews. As noted in the next subsection, Revelation 9:4 may be a reference to this select group.

(e) Other biblical references, whether direct or indirect, do not imply that the 144,000 will evangelize the world

There is an oblique reference to this same group of 144,000 in Revelation 9:4 that would confirm the dual purposes (ownership and protection) of their being sealed. In that verse, the evil creatures released from the bottomless pit are told that they should not hurt the grass, trees, or any green thing, "but only the men who do *not* have the seal of God on their foreheads." This verse implies that the 144,000 are still present on the earth but are immune from the torment of these creatures.

The dual purposes of the seal are also apparent in the next and only remaining explicit reference to the 144,000, which occurs in Revelation 14:1–5. In this passage, verse 1 describes the seal as the name of the Lamb and the name of His Father written on the foreheads of these 144,000. Having His seal, this group is marked as belonging to Him and under His protection.

While it appears at first that this group is still on earth (Mount Zion), the fact that Revelation 14:3 says that "they sang a new song before the throne and before the four living creatures and the elders" places them squarely in heaven. But what is the antecedent of the plural pronoun "they"? Since the rest of verse 3 tells us that no one could learn the song except the 144,000 who had been purchased from the earth, the clear implication is that the ones singing the new song in the throne room of heaven must be this group of the 144,000. Unfortunately, this passage provides no clue as to timing, so we cannot know when this group made the transition from earth to heaven.

An alternate interpretation is that the antecedent of the plural pronoun "they" is the "harpists playing on their harps" in Revelation 14:2. If this is the case, then the Lamb and the 144,000 (and John) are on the earthly Mount Zion, Jerusalem, and John hears the voice from heaven.

The problem with this alternate interpretation is that there were no literal harpists playing on their harps. The text of Revelation 14:2 says that the voice—singular—that John heard was

- *like* the sound of many waters and

- *like* the sound of loud thunder and

- *like* the sound of harpists playing on their harps.

This means that the only plural antecedent of "they" is the group of the 144,000.

There are a few additional bits of information that we can glean from Revelation 14 about this group of 144,000. As just noted above, verse 3 tells us that they are "purchased [or redeemed] from the earth." Verse 4 reiterates that these 144,000 Jews "have been purchased from among men." Clearly, what these verses are saying is that these are Jews who have become Christians, and they are among the nations and tribes and tongues and peoples of the earth (Rev. 7:9), whom Jesus Christ purchased with His blood.

Revelation 14:4 adds another detail: They "have not been defiled with women, for they have kept themselves chaste." Some commentators have interpreted this to mean that they never married or that they purposely remained celibate in their separation unto God. I think the more likely interpretation, however, based on 2 Corinthians 11:2 ("For I am jealous for you with a godly jealousy; for I betrothed you to one husband, so that to Christ I might present you as a pure virgin."), is that this is referring to the spiritual realm.

God often used the metaphor of marriage in describing His relationship with Israel; for this reason, their abandonment of God and their idolatry was described as adultery. Based on those facts, I believe that this description of the 144,000 indicates that they did not succumb to the spiritual seduction of the antichrist, and they did not commit spiritual adultery with the harlot of Revelation 17 by taking his mark on the foreheads or hands.

Revelation 14:4 also calls this group "first fruits to God and to the Lamb." They are the beginning of the harvest of the Jewish people, who will come to the Savior at the end of the seventieth week (see Rom. 11:25–32).

Finally, we are told in Revelation 14:5 that "no lie was found in their mouth; they are blameless." Clearly, by this point in chapter 14, these 144,000 Jews have acknowledged that Jesus Christ is their Savior. Verse 4 states that "these are the ones who follow the Lamb wherever He goes." Just as we are not told when this group made the transition from earth to heaven or when they received their imperishable bodies, we are also left uncertain as to *when* were they saved.

Were they saved at the time that they were sealed in Revelation 7, which was just before the onset of the day of the Lord? That is, after all, what sealing seems to indicate, because sealing is a sign of ownership. The problem, however, with interpreting the sealing as the time of their being saved is that one might logically conclude that they should then have been included among the believers who were raptured at that very same time. But if that were so, there would have been no need to seal them for protection from the horrors about to be unleashed upon the earth during the day of the Lord. The absence of any time clues in this passage leaves many questions unanswered.

As I stated earlier, however, there are no facts given in any of these passages from which a reasonable inference could be drawn that this group served as evangelists, especially since, as noted in the immediately preceding section, the time for evangelizing will have passed by the time they are sealed.

(f) THE BIBLE TELLS US THERE WILL BE WITNESSES TO GOD DURING THE GREAT TRIBULATION

If the 144,000 Jews are not witnesses to God, who will be? To begin with, there will be at least two—indeed, they are even called witnesses, and their impact will be worldwide. Revelation 11:7 contains the clause, "when they have finished their testimony." That's what witnesses do— they testify. Their ministry will take place in the second half of the seventieth week, when the great tribulation is in full swing and people are having to decide whether to take the mark of the beast or to commit their lives and deaths to Jesus Christ. They will need the ministry of these two powerful witnesses to turn away from the antichrist.

In addition, Revelation 14:6–7 depicts another worldwide evangelist:

> [6] And I saw another angel flying in midheaven, **having an eternal gospel to preach to those who live on the earth, and to every nation and tribe and tongue and people**; [7] and he said with a loud voice, "Fear God, and give Him glory, because the hour of His judgment has come; worship Him who made the heaven and the earth and sea and springs of waters." (emphasis added)

While it is not clear when this angel flies with his gospel message, it is safe to assume that it is at a time when it is still possible to repent and turn to the Lord. Thus it would be before the onset of the day of the Lord and most likely during the great tribulation, especially since another angel after him warns the people of the world of the eternal consequences of worshiping the beast and taking his mark.

In addition to the two witnesses and the evangelist angel, other witnesses of God will be faithful believers who are still on the earth during the great tribulation, obediently fulfilling the great commission on an individual basis. Indeed, if Revelation is read chronologically, the time that witnesses for Christ will be desperately needed will be the great tribulation, which begins at the fifth seal.

The fifth seal is unlike the first four seals, which

- may occur in rapid fire order,
- will together take up the first half of the seven years, and
- which, though horrifying, are described by Jesus as "merely the beginning of birth pangs," according to Matthew 24:8.

It is also unlike the short space between the sixth and seventh seals (maybe only as long as the half hour of Rev. 8:1). The fifth seal, which represents the great tribulation, begins at the midpoint of the seven years with the abomination of desolation (Dan. 9:27; Matt. 24:15; 2 Thess. 2:1–4) and continues for close to the entirety of the three and a half years of the second half of the seven years (Rev. 13:5–7; forty-two months = three and a half years).

The antichrist's dominion over the world will not last the full three and a half years, however, because the Lord will cut those days short (Matt. 24:22), probably near the end of that second half. At that point, the sixth seal (cosmic disturbances) will announce the arrival of the day of the Lord, the time when believers should look up, because their redemption/deliverance is at hand (Luke 21:28) in the rapture. It is this deliverance of God's people from the oncoming judgment that is depicted in the passage in Revelation 7:9–17.

Conclusion: The Bible does not tell us whether or not there will be a massive revival during the great tribulation. Undoubtedly, some people, perhaps even many, will finally have the satanically-imposed blinders (2 Cor. 4:4) divinely removed from their minds and will come to faith. Nevertheless, the mere proximity of the two events in Revelation 7—the sealing of the 144,000, and the appearance in heaven of the multitude—does not justify an inference that the first is the proximate cause of the second. Inferences are hardly the equivalent of biblical proof.

Instead, the Bible points us to the two witnesses, the evangelist angel, and the church—these are His witnesses during the great tribulation.

Before moving on to the next point, it is worth noting that other Bible verses in close proximity to one another have little or no relationship to each other in terms of time or causation. For example, in Isaiah 61, verse 1 and the first half of verse 2 refer to Jesus's first advent, but the second half of verse 2 refers to His second coming. Another example is in Revelation 12. The first five verses are an overview of Israel's history, up to and including, in verse 5, the birth, life, death, resurrection, and ascension of Jesus. But beginning with verse 6, the time frame jumps forward to the very end times, with a time reference (1,260 days) that equals one-half of the seventieth week.

2. ISRAEL AND THE CHURCH WERE MEANT TO BE THE WITNESSES OF GOD TO THE WORLD

The express purpose for which God created the nation of Israel was to be a kingdom of priests and a light to the gentiles. Priests serve as a mediator of God to mankind and of mankind to God. They stand between God and humans in spiritual matters; they represent the people before

God. If there are no priests, how will the lost hear the Word by which they must be saved? If there are no light-bearers, either in Israel or in the church, how will the lost find their way in this dark world?

After the scattering of the people at Babel in Genesis 11, God called Abram (later Abraham) and began the creation of His own special people (the Hebrews) and nation (Israel). At the outset, He promised that He would make Abraham into a great nation and that Israel was meant to be a light to the nations, a blessing to all the families of the earth:

Genesis 12:2–3 (emphasis added)

[2] And **I will make you a great nation**,
And I will bless you,
And make your name great;
And so you shall be a blessing;
[3] And I will bless those who bless you,
And the one who curses you I will curse.
And **in you all the families of the earth will be blessed**.

The promises and purposes of God are reiterated in many places in the Old Testament. Here are some of them:

Genesis 18:17–18 (emphasis added)

[17] The LORD said, "Shall I hide from Abraham what I am about to do, since Abraham will surely become a great and mighty nation, and **in him all the nations of the earth will be blessed?**"

Genesis 26:4 (emphasis added)

I will multiply your descendants as the stars of heaven, and will give your descendants all these lands; and **by your descendants all the nations of the earth shall be blessed**.

Exodus 19:5–6 (emphasis added)

[5] "Now then, if you will indeed obey My voice and keep My covenant, then you shall be My own possession among all the peoples, for all the earth is Mine; [6] and **you shall be to Me a kingdom of**

priests and a holy nation." These are the words that you shall speak to the sons of Israel.

<u>Deuteronomy 4:5–8</u> (emphasis added))

[5] See, I have taught you statutes and judgments just as the LORD my God commanded me, that you should do thus in the land where you are entering to possess it. [6] So keep and do them, for **that is your wisdom and your understanding in the sight of the peoples who will hear all these statutes and say, "Surely this great nation is a wise and understanding people."** [7] **For what great nation is there that has a god so near to it as is the LORD our God whenever we call on Him?** [8] **Or what great nation is there that has statutes and judgments as righteous as this whole law which I am setting before you today?**

<u>Isaiah 42:6</u> (emphasis added)

And I will appoint you as a covenant to the people,
As **a light to the nations.**

<u>Isaiah 49:6</u> (emphasis added)

I will also make You **a light of the nations**
So that My salvation may reach to the end of the earth.

The "light" pointed to and was ultimately fulfilled in Jesus the Messiah, as Simeon recognized when he saw Jesus as an infant in the temple:

<u>Luke 2:25–32</u> (emphasis added)

[25] And there was a man in Jerusalem whose name was Simeon; and this man was righteous and devout, looking for the consolation of Israel; and the Holy Spirit was upon him. [26] And it had been revealed to him by the Holy Spirit that **he would not see death before he had seen the Lord's Christ.** [27] And he came in the Spirit into the temple; and when the parents brought in the child Jesus, to carry out for Him the custom of the Law, [28] then he took Him into his arms, and blessed God, and said,

[29] "Now Lord, You are releasing Your bond-servant to depart in peace

According to Your word;
³⁰ **For my eyes have seen Your salvation,**
³¹ Which You have prepared in the presence of all peoples,
³² **A light of revelation to the Gentiles,
And the glory of Your people Israel."**

Moreover, the apostles understood that Israel's gifts and callings/purposes were and are irrevocable (Rom. 11:29) and that the gentiles shared in these as they, the church of Jewish and gentile believers, carried out the Great Commission:

<u>Acts 3:25</u> (emphasis added)

It is you who are the sons of the prophets and of the covenant which God made with your fathers, saying to Abraham, "And **in your seed all the families of the earth shall be blessed."**

<u>Galatians 3:8</u> (emphasis added)

The Scripture, foreseeing that God would justify the Gentiles by faith, preached the gospel beforehand to Abraham, saying, "**All the nations will be blessed in you."**

<u>Philippians 2:14–16</u> (emphasis added)

¹⁴ Do all things without grumbling or disputing; ¹⁵ so that you will prove yourselves to be blameless and innocent, children of God above reproach in the midst of a crooked and perverse generation, among whom **you appear as lights in the world,** ¹⁶ **holding fast the word of life.**

<u>Revelation 1:6</u> (emphasis added))

And **He has made us to be a kingdom, priests to His God and Father**—to Him be the glory and the dominion forever and ever. Amen.

<u>Revelation 5:10</u> (emphasis added)
**You have made them to be a
kingdom and priests to our God;**
and they will reign upon the earth.

Conclusion: The Lord will ensure that there are enough Christian Esthers and Mordecais on the earth who will have been born for "such a time as this" (Est. 4:14) and who will faithfully witness to God and lead the lost to the Light during the dark days of the great tribulation. They will be fellow laborers with the two witnesses of Revelation 11 and the evangelist/gospel angel of Revelation 14:6–7.

3. GOD HAS ALWAYS KEPT A REMNANT FOR HIMSELF, BOTH IN ISRAEL AND IN THE CHURCH

The following passages demonstrate that God has always preserved a remnant of His own faithful followers on the earth, even in the most dire of times.

(a) GOD PRESERVED WITNESSES TO HIMSELF AMONG THE JEWS

(1) 1 KINGS 18–19

This passage recounts the confrontation that Elijah had with the 450 prophets of Baal and the 400 prophets of the Asherah. The pagan prophets could not rouse their gods to consume their sacrifices, but the fire from the Lord consumed not only Elijah's sacrifice but also the water-saturated wood *and* the stones of the altar *and* the dust *and even* licked up the water that was in the trench surrounding the altar. When the people witnessed that staggering demonstration of God's power, they obeyed Elijah's command to kill all the pagan prophets—all in the presence of the evil King Ahab. When Ahab related the events of the day to his evil wife, Jezebel, she sent a message to Elijah in a rage and told him in no uncertain terms that his life was forfeit and that she would see to it that his own life would be as the lives of the prophets he had killed. Panicked, Elijah fled into the wilderness and asked God to take his life. Instead, the Lord sent an angel with food and water to fortify him, and he went to a cave on Mount Horeb. There he complained to the Lord that he alone was faithful and that Jezebel and her followers sought him to kill him. Among other things, the Lord assured Elijah that he was not alone, because He, the Lord, had preserved a remnant of "7,000 in Israel, all the knees that have not bowed to Baal and every mouth that has not kissed him" (1 Kings 19:18).

(2) Genesis 45

In this example, Joseph is speaking to his terrified brothers after they discovered that he was not only still alive but second in command to the pharaoh in Egypt:

<u>Genesis 45:4–7</u> (emphasis added)

[4] I am your brother Joseph, whom you sold into Egypt. [5] Now do not be grieved or angry with yourselves, because you sold me here, for God sent me before you to preserve life. [6] For the famine has been in the land these two years, and there are still five years in which there will be neither plowing nor harvesting. [7] **God sent me before you to preserve for you a remnant in the earth**, and to keep you alive by a great deliverance.

(3) Ezra 9

When the relatively few returned exiles began to intermarry with the pagan tribes in their land, Ezra grieved and prayed in fear and humiliation, acknowledging the faithfulness of God in returning them from captivity in Babylon to their land:

<u>Ezra 9:8, 13–15</u> (emphasis added)

[8] But now for a brief moment grace has been shown from the LORD our God, **to leave us an escaped remnant** and to give us a peg in His holy place, that our God may enlighten our eyes and grant us a little reviving in our bondage.

[13] After all that has come upon us for our evil deeds and our great guilt, since You our God have requited us less than our iniquities deserve, and have **given us an escaped remnant as this,** [14] shall we again break Your commandments and intermarry with the peoples who commit these abominations? Would You not be angry with us to the point of destruction, until there is no remnant nor any who escape? [15] O LORD God of Israel, You are righteous, for **we have been left an escaped remnant**, as it is this day; behold, we are

before You in our guilt, for no one can stand before You because of this.

(4) Isaiah 1 and 10

Through His prophet Isaiah, the Lord warned the southern kingdom of Judah that He was sending the Babylonians to judge them for their apostasy and idolatry. The judgment would be very severe, but effective in its purpose of cleansing and restoration, at least for a remnant:

<u>Isaiah 1:21–28</u> (emphasis added)

21 How **the faithful city has become a harlot,**
She who was full of justice!
Righteousness once lodged in her,
But now murderers.
22 Your silver has become dross,
Your drink diluted with water.
23 Your rulers are rebels
And companions of thieves;
Everyone loves a bribe
And chases after rewards.
They do not defend the orphan,
Nor does the widow's plea come before them.
24 Therefore the Lord God of hosts,
The Mighty One of Israel, declares,
"Ah, I will be relieved of My adversaries
And avenge Myself on My foes.
25 **"I will also turn My hand against you** [Israel as a whole, but Jerusalem in particular],
And will smelt away your dross as with lye
And will remove all your alloy.
26 **"Then I will restore your judges as at the first,**
And your counselors as at the beginning;
After that you will be called the city of righteousness,
A faithful city."
27 **Zion will be redeemed with justice**
And her repentant ones with righteousness.

²⁸ But transgressors and sinners will be crushed together,
And those who forsake the LORD will come to an end.

Isaiah 10:20–22 (emphasis added)

²⁰ Now in that day **the remnant of Israel, and those of the house of Jacob who have escaped**, will never again rely on the one who struck them, but will truly rely on the LORD, the Holy One of Israel. ²¹ **A remnant will return, the remnant of Jacob**, to the mighty God. ²² For though your people, O Israel, may be like the sand of the sea, **Only a remnant within them will return;**
A destruction is determined, overflowing with righteousness.

(5) ISAIAH 11

In the next chapter of Isaiah, the Lord provided a glimpse of the end times:

Isaiah 11:11–12 (emphasis added)

¹¹ Then it will happen on that day that **the Lord**
Will again recover the second time with His hand
The remnant of His people, who will remain,
From Assyria, Egypt, Pathros, Cush, Elam, Shinar, Hamath,
And from the islands of the sea.
¹² And He will lift up a standard for the nations
And assemble the banished ones of Israel,
And will gather the dispersed of Judah
From the four corners of the earth.

(6) JEREMIAH 23, 31, AND 50

A similar end-times promise is given several times through Jeremiah:

Jeremiah 23:3 (emphasis added)

Then I Myself will **gather the remnant of My flock** out of all the countries where I have driven them and bring them back to their pasture; and they will be fruitful and multiply.

<u>Jeremiah 31:7–8</u> (emphasis added)

[7] For thus says the LORD,
"Sing aloud with gladness for Jacob,
And shout among the chiefs of the nations;
Proclaim, give praise, and say,
'O Lord, save Your people,
The remnant of Israel.'
[8] "Behold, I am bringing them from the north country,
And I will gather them from the remote parts of the earth."

Later in the book of Jeremiah, the Lord addresses His people regarding the end of their time in captivity:

<u>Jeremiah 50:18–21</u> (emphasis added)

[18] Therefore thus says the LORD of hosts, the God of Israel: "Behold, I am going to punish the king of Babylon and his land, just as I punished the king of Assyria. [19] And I will bring Israel back to his pasture and he will graze on Carmel and Bashan, and his desire will be satisfied in the hill country of Ephraim and Gilead. [20] In those days and at that time," declares the LORD, "search will be made for the iniquity of Israel, but there will be none; and for the sins of Judah, but they will not be found; for **I will pardon those whom I leave as a remnant.**"

Other passages of judgment against Israel speak of *punishing all but leaving a remnant*, which God will save for Himself—see, for example, Isaiah 1:9; 6:13; Ezekiel 5:3, 10–13; 6:1–10; 9:1–11; Amos 5:1–15; Zechariah 13:8–9.

Other passages that contain the Lord's promise of the restoration of only a remnant of His people, either after the Babylonian captivity or in the end times, include Jeremiah 43:5; Micah 2:12; 5:7–8; 7:18–20; Zephaniah 3:13; Zechariah 8:6–15.

(7) Romans 9 and 11

In the New Testament, in his letter to the Romans, Paul quotes both Isaiah 10:22 (Rom. 9:27) and 1 Kings 19:10, 14 (Romans 11) regarding the salvation of a remnant:

<u>Romans 9:27</u> (emphasis added)

Isaiah cries out concerning Israel, "Though the number of the sons of Israel be like the sand of the sea, **it is the remnant that will be saved.**"

<u>Romans 11:2–5</u> (emphasis added)

² Or do you not know what the Scripture says in the passage about Elijah, how he pleads with God against Israel? ³ "Lord, they have killed Your prophets, they have torn down Your altars, and I alone am left, and they are seeking my life." ⁴ But what is the divine response to him? **"I have kept for Myself seven thousand men who have not bowed the knee to Baal."** ⁵ **In the same way then, there has also come to be at the present time a remnant according to God's gracious choice.**

(b) God also preserves witnesses to Himself in the church

While it is true that all the Old Testament passages cited in the preceding section deal with the Jews as a nation or as a distinct ethnic group, it is important to remember what Paul was teaching in Romans 9–11. In chapter 11, the Jews are pictured as the natural branches of a cultivated olive tree, the root of which represents either (1) the Jewish patriarchs, Abraham, Isaac, and Jacob, because they were the beginning of the Jewish nation; or (2) only Abraham, because in Romans 4:1, Paul referred to him as "our forefather according to the flesh."

Paul's point is that God has grafted branches from a wild olive tree (i.e., gentiles, non-Jews) into the root. While this practice is contrary to nature as we know it, God supernaturally has enabled even the branches of a wild olive tree to produce good fruit after He grafted them into the root of a cultivated olive tree.

The question is: What does the cultivated olive tree represent? The key to the answer is found in Romans 9:6, which is the crucial verse for the entirety of chapters 9–11. Romans 9:6 says that "they are not all Israel who are descended from Israel." Two nations came out of Abraham as the father and the root: one of them is a natural nation; the other is a spiritual nation and people. Just as Ishmael and Isaac were both the natural children of Abraham, only one of them, Isaac, was the spiritual child (see Gal. 4:22–31).

Similarly, the cultivated olive tree *as a whole* represents the spiritual (not natural) nation that grows from the root of Abraham; thus, it represents all the people of God, those who have believed in Him, whether Jew or gentile. Unbelieving Jews, though they are natural children of Abraham and are represented by the *natural* branches of the cultivated olive tree, are cut off because of their unbelief, and they do not really belong to the olive tree.

In contrast, believing gentiles, while they do not belong to the natural or physical nation of Israel, are grafted into the root of the cultivated olive tree and become Abraham's children. Galatians 3:29 states categorically that, "if you belong to Christ, then you are Abraham's descendants, heirs according to promise."

Having established that God's people are not the physical nation of Israel but rather that it is believers in Jesus Christ, whether Jew or gentile, who are Abraham's offspring by faith, we turn to Romans 4 to consider all the names and descriptions of Abraham.

<u>**Romans 4:9–13, 16–17**</u> (emphasis added)

[9] Is this blessing then on the circumcised, or upon the uncircumcised also? For we say, "Faith was credited to Abraham as righteousness." [10] How then was it credited? While he was circumcised, or uncircumcised? Not while circumcised, but while uncircumcised; [11] and he received the sign of circumcision, a seal of the righteousness of the faith which he had while uncircumcised, so that he might be **the father of all who believe without being circumcised, that righteousness might be credited to them,** [12] and **the father of circumcision to those who not only are of the**

circumcision, but who also follow in the steps of the faith of our father Abraham which he had while uncircumcised. [13] For the promise to Abraham or to his descendants that he would be heir of the world was not through the Law, but through the righteousness of faith.

[16] For this reason, it is by faith, in order that it may be in accordance with grace, so that the promise will be guaranteed to all the descendants, not only to those who are of the Law, but also to those who are of the faith of **Abraham, who is the father of us all,** [17] (as it is written, **"A father of many nations have I made you"**).

Conclusion: These passages, which tie together all believers by faith, whether Jew or gentile, whether before or after the cross, into "the people of God," clearly demonstrate that passages in the Old Testament about the remnant apply to the church today just as well as they apply to Israel. This biblical concept about what constitutes the people of God—also known as the body of Christ, also known as the spiritual sons of Abraham—is further developed next in section V.B.

B. The church is not absent from Revelation after chapter 3

1. The words *church* and *saints* are synonyms

The Greek word for *church* is *ekklesia* (*Strong's* NT 1577). It is a compound word consisting of the prefix *ek* (*Strong's* NT 1537), which means "out of, from," and the root word, *kaleo* (*Strong's* NT 2564), which means "to call." Thus, the church/*ekklesia* is made up of believers in Jesus who are called out of the world to follow Jesus. The word does not refer to any organized religious denomination or to a building.

The absence of the word *church* after the first three chapters of Revelation does not justify the conclusion that the rapture occurs at that point. Throughout the New Testament, *church* is not the only way that the body of believers is described. For example, Acts 9:13; Romans 15:25; 2 Corinthians 1:1; Ephesians 1:1, 15, 18; 2:19; 4:12; Philippians 1:1; Colossians 1:2; Hebrews 13:24; and Jude 3 all refer to groups of Christians—churches—as *saints*.

So it comes as no surprise that the same word, *saints* (from Greek *hagios*, *Strong's* NT 40), is used in Revelation twelve times after chapter 3 to refer to groups of believers, even if they are not associated with a particular church building or city grouping. Moreover, other descriptions of believers are used as well, which will appear in the passages below.

> As a sidebar, the Greek word *hagios* is also translated as "holy" thirteen times in Revelation.

The following passages from Revelation were not among the list of proof texts that believers will be raptured out of the world prior to Daniel's seventieth week. My purpose in including them here is to show the complete opposite—not only will believers *not* be raptured out of the world prior to Daniel's seventieth week but they will have to endure the great tribulation of the antichrist (his war against the saints), remaining faithful to the Lord, even unto death:

<u>Revelation 7:9, 13–14</u> (emphasis added)

⁹ After these things I looked, and behold, a great multitude which no one could count, **from every nation and all tribes and peoples and tongues**, standing before the throne and before the Lamb, clothed in white robes, and palm branches were in their hands.
¹³ Then one of the elders answered, saying to me, "These who are clothed in the white robes, who are they, and from where have they come?" ¹⁴ I said to him, "My lord, you know." And he said to me, "These are the ones who **come out of the great tribulation**, and they have washed their robes and made them white in the blood of the Lamb."

<u>Revelation 12:17</u> (emphasis added)

So the dragon was enraged with the woman, and went off to make war with the **rest of her children, who keep the commandments of God and hold to the testimony of Jesus.**

<u>Revelation 13:7–10</u> (emphasis added)

⁷ It was also given to him **to make war with the saints and to overcome them, and authority over every tribe and people and tongue**

and nation was given to him. [8] All who dwell on the earth will worship him, everyone whose name has not been written from the foundation of the world in the book of life of the Lamb who has been slain. [9] If anyone has an ear, let him hear. [10] **If anyone is destined for captivity, to captivity he goes; if anyone kills with the sword, with the sword he must be killed. Here is the perseverance and the faith of the saints.**

Revelation 14:12–13 (emphasis added)

[12] Here is the perseverance of **the saints who keep the commandments of God and their faith in Jesus.** [13] And I heard a voice from heaven, saying, "Write, 'Blessed are the dead who die in the Lord from now on!' " "Yes," says the Spirit, "so that they may rest from their labors, for their deeds follow with them."

Revelation 17:6 (emphasis added)

And I saw the woman drunk with **the blood of the saints, and with the blood of the witnesses of Jesus.**

The context of the passages in chapters 12, 13 and 14 indicates that these are references to the time of the great tribulation; chapter 17 looks back to the mass executions of the great tribulation.

Revelation 12:6–17 is a description of the second half of the seventieth week. This is apparent from the reference in verse 6 to 1,260 days, which is the same as three and a half years. Because all time references to three and a half years that are specific (i.e., 1,260 days; forty-two months; time, times, and half a time) apply only to the second half of the seventieth week, this is an obvious allusion to the great tribulation, which begins at the midpoint of the seventieth week.

Revelation 13 describes the first beast (the antichrist) and the second beast (his false prophet) and their activities, particularly in the second half of the seventieth week—that is, during the great tribulation. Since the beast/antichrist is allowed to make war and to *overcome* the saints, many, many believers will not survive the persecution of the antichrist. Faithful perseverance is called for and will be rewarded after death.

Revelation 14 is divided into three sections:

1. The first section, verses 1–5, documents the appearance of the 144,000 Jews in heaven.

2. The second section, beginning in verse 6, presents three angels in mid-heaven making announcements:

   - The first proclaims the gospel.

   - The second announces the fall of Babylon the great.

   - The third, in a loud voice, warns against worshiping the beast or taking the mark of the beast. Apparently, the mark is either a sign of allegiance to the beast or somehow actually causes those people who take the mark to worship the beast. Clearly, this is not a sin that can or will be forgiven.

3. The third section, beginning with verse 14, describes two reapings of the earth.

The chronology of events is established: After the appearance of the 144,000 in heaven in Revelation 14, there are three angelic announcements, the third of which is a warning against worshiping the beast or taking his mark. 2 Thessalonians 2 records that the antichrist will set himself up as God and demand that the world worship him as God. This is the abomination of desolation, spoken of by Daniel in Daniel 9:27 and by Jesus in Matthew 24:15. This triggers the onset of the great tribulation. During this time, all people are required to worship the beast and to take his mark—or be killed for failure or refusal to do so.

Therefore, it is logical to conclude that the third angel's warning in Revelation 14 occurs at the beginning of, or during, the great tribulation. Following *directly after the third angel's warning* are the verses about the perseverance of the saints and the blessing of the dead who would die in the Lord from then on. This indicates widespread persecution and execution of the saints during the great tribulation.

The final section of Revelation 14 describes the two reapings of the earth. The first appears to be a reference to the rapture, as Jesus cuts short the days of the great tribulation. The second is plainly a graphic description of the unbridled wrath of God in the day of the Lord.

Pretribulationists argue that all true believers have already been raptured out of the world and that therefore these passages must refer only to unbelievers who come to faith during the great tribulation. In response, I add to all prior arguments made in this book the following regarding *how* people come to faith, which is that the Lord has always had witnesses on the earth.

> This argument applies both to this subsection as well as to the entirety of section V.A. above.

In the previous section, I concluded that God will provide the two witnesses and the evangelist angel in the latter half of the seventieth week. But let's take that a step further.

SINCE

- the rapture cannot occur until the onset of the day of the Lord, which is the wrath from which believers are promised deliverance,

- the great tribulation cannot be characterized as God's wrath in the day of the Lord (see sections IV.D.1.(a) and 7 above), and

- the day of the Lord begins only when Jesus cuts short the days of the great tribulation,

THEN these facts lead to the conclusion that believers, also known as the church and as saints, will still be on the earth during the great tribulation. During that horrific time, the Lord will employ His people as His foot soldiers with evangelistic fervor.

After all, how do people become believers? The answer is that God the Holy Spirit regenerates the human spirit, but *human people* also play a critical role.

Romans 10:13–17 (emphasis added)

[13] For "Whoever will call upon the name of the Lord will be saved." [14] How then will they call upon Him in whom they have not believed? How will they believe in Him whom they have not heard? And **how will they hear without a preacher?** [15] How will they preach unless they are sent? Just as it is written, "How beautiful are

the feet of those who bring good news of good things!" [16] However, they did not all heed the good news; for Isaiah says, "Lord, who has believed our report?" [17] So **faith comes from hearing, and hearing by the word of Christ.**

Two final points counter the dispensational assertion that the absence of the word *church* after Revelation 3 is conclusive evidence of a rapture before the onset of the seventieth week:

1. **SINCE** dispensationalists contend that the great multitude in heaven of Revelation 7:9–17 as well as the "saints" of Revelation 13:7 and 17:6 cannot be the church because the church age ends with chapter 3 and the entire last section of the book of Revelation from chapter 4 to the end of the Bible is the resumption of the Jewish dispensation,

    THEN to be consistent with that position, dispensationalists must also conclude that the bride of Revelation 19:7–8 cannot be the church because that word (*church*) is absent from the text and therefore this chapter 19 is also only about the Jewish dispensation.

2. Actually, the word *church does* appear (in plural form) in Revelation after chapter 3:

    <u>Revelation 22:16</u> (emphasis added)

    I, Jesus, have sent My angel to testify to you these things for the **churches**. I am the root and the descendant of David, the bright morning star.

    Here at the end of Jesus's revelation to John, Jesus returns full circle to the beginning of Revelation, when He instructed John to record the vision. In the concluding verses of the entire revelation, He reminds John that He sent His angel to testify "these things *for the churches.*"

    Jesus did not give this instruction at the end of chapter 3 or even at the beginning of chapter 6, when the seals are broken, signaling the beginning of the seventieth week. The *entire vision* was for His church.

Conclusion: The Bible plainly portrays the church (the persecuted saints) as present on the earth during the great tribulation.

2.   THE CHURCH IS NOT AMONG THOSE WHO GREET THE MULTITUDE OF REVELATION 7 BECAUSE THE CHURCH *IS* THAT INNUMERABLE THRONG

When John sees the great multitude of people that no one could count in the throne room of heaven, he also describes the other occupants present. Besides the Most High God, seated on the throne, and the Lamb, they include:

- all the angels, who were standing around the throne and around

- the elders and

- the four living creatures. (Rev. 7:9)

Conspicuous by its absence is any mention of the church. If the church had been raptured prior to the beginning of the seventieth week, and if this throng of Revelation 7 comprises the believers who came to faith later, during the great tribulation, it is logical to look for the earlier raptured church to be among those who welcome this massive multitude to heaven.

Some pretribulationists have concluded that the twenty-four elders represent the earlier raptured church because of the song of redemption that they sang in Revelation 5:8–10:

[8] When He had taken the book, the four living creatures and the twenty-four elders fell down before the Lamb, each one holding a harp and golden bowls full of incense, which are the prayers of the saints.
[9] And they sang a new song, saying,
"Worthy art Thou to take the book
and to break its seals; for You were
slain, and purchased for God with

> Your blood men from every tribe
> and tongue and people and nation.
> [10] "You have made them to be a
> kingdom and priests to our God;
> and they will reign upon the earth."

It is clear from the text itself, however, that there are two problems with concluding that the twenty-four elders are representatives of the raptured church:

- The song is sung not only by the elders *but also by the four living creatures.*

- In every English translation except the KJV, verse 10 reads, "You have made **them** to be a kingdom and priests to our God; and **they** will reign upon the earth." (emphasis added). This indicates that the four living creatures and the elders are singing about someone other than themselves.

> Based on a textual variant in the Greek, the KJV changed the plural pronouns "them" and "they" of verse 10 to "us" and "we." The relevant Greek word is *autos* (*Strong's* NT 846). It is the reflexive pronoun, "self," *used of the third person.* Not only that but the verb, *reign*, at the end of verse 10, is also in the third person, plural, future, active, indicative, in the Greek.

The four living creatures and the twenty-four elders are not among those who were "purchased for God … from every tribe and tongue and people and nation" (Rev. 5:9), who will one day reign upon the earth. In Revelation 11:18, the elders again distinguish themselves from "the prophets and the saints," making it abundantly plain that they are a different group from those who are redeemed by the blood of the Lamb. Therefore, the twenty-four elders cannot represent the raptured church. And that takes us back to the conspicuous absence of the church in the group that welcomes this multitude of Revelation 7.

The only biblical conclusion is that the church is not present to greet those "from every nation and all tribes and peoples and tongues" (Rev. 7:9). This is because this throng represents *the church itself,* which has gone into the seventieth week, up to and through the great tribulation, adding new believers along the way, until the Lord cuts short the days of the great tribulation, raptures His church out of the world, and unleashes His wrath on the world in the day of the Lord.

This position is supported by the following five arguments.

(a) The passage in Revelation 4:1–2 does not describe a pretribulation rapture

Pretribulationists have appealed to Revelation 4:1–2 for support of their position regarding the rapture:

<u>Revelation 4:1–2</u> (emphasis added)

¹ After these things I looked, and behold, **a door standing open in heaven**, and the first voice which I had heard, like the sound of a trumpet speaking with me, said, "**Come up here**, and I will show you what must take place after these things." ² Immediately **I was in the Spirit**; and behold, a throne was standing in heaven, and One sitting on the throne.

The argument is that a voice which sounded like a trumpet calls John to heaven and he is immediately "in the Spirit." The argument continues with the assumption that John represents the church and that this must be a description of the rapture.

There are three problems with this line of argument:

1. 1 Thessalonians 4 and 1 Corinthians 15 include a trumpet in their descriptions of the rapture. But in Revelation 4:1, it was a voice that made the sound, not a trumpet. The voice sounded *like* a trumpet but was not itself a trumpet.

2. Rev. 4:2 is only one of four times that the phrase *in the Spirit* appears in Revelation. If this phrase describes a catching up of believers to heaven, what does the same phrase mean when it appears *earlier* in Revelation 1:10, while John is still literally on earth? Moreover, John employs the same phrase again in Revelation 17:3 and 21:10. How can *in the Spirit* refer to a rapture in those contexts?

3. John, as an observer and scribe, is often moved from earth to heaven and back again.

In Revelation 4, he is transported to the throne room/courtroom of God.

His viewpoint at the beginning of Revelation 10, however, appears to be back on earth, because he records seeing the strong angel "coming **down out of** heaven." The strong angel stands on the sea and on the land—of earth, presumably. Verse 8 continues, "Then the voice which I heard from heaven, I heard again speaking with me," which confirms that John's viewpoint is back on earth.

Chapter 11 describes activity on earth—the measuring of the temple and the activity of the two witnesses. But by verse 15, John's viewpoint is once more in heaven.

At the beginning of chapter 14, there is disagreement over the location of the 144,000 based on one's understanding of the antecedent of the pronoun "they." Nevertheless, it is clear that *John* is on earth because in verse 2, he "heard a voice from heaven." When in verse 6, John sees angels flying in midheaven, it is not clear what his positional perspective is. He could be looking up from earth, which makes sense, based on the immediately preceding verses, or he could be back up in heaven.

In chapter 15, it seems he is back in heaven, because he refers once more to the innumerable throng from chapter 7. In addition, he describes the temple in heaven being filled with smoke from the glory of God.

In Revelation 17:3, John is again carried away "in the Spirit into a wilderness." A wilderness sounds more like a description of earth than of heaven; one does not associate a wilderness with heaven. Moreover, the vision that John witnesses is on earth. In this context, the phrase *in the Spirit* could hardly describe a rapture.

In chapter 18, John appears to have remained on earth, because he sees another angel "coming down from heaven," and "the whole earth was illumined with his glory."

In chapter 19, all John's reports about the activity in heaven are a mix of things he heard (but apparently did not see) and of things he saw. In verse 10, he falls at the feet of his angelic guide, but even that is not necessarily proof of their location, because in verse 11, John writes, "And I saw heaven opened, and behold, a white horse, and He who sat on it," indicating he is outside heaven and presumably on earth.

In Revelation 20:1, John records seeing an angel "coming down from heaven," but by verse 4, he reports seeing thrones of judgment. Thus, his location may have changed again.

In Revelation 21:10, an angel carries John away "in the Spirit" to "a great and high mountain" to show him the new Jerusalem, "coming down out of heaven from God."

Where is the great and high mountain from which he views the new Jerusalem coming down out of heaven? A cogent argument could be made that this is on earth, since mountains are known to be on earth and since John saw the city "coming down" out of heaven. In any event, the use of the phrase *in the Spirit* in this context clearly has no relevance to the rapture.

Thus, three reasons prove that the argument that the opening verses of Revelation 4 are a description of the rapture is untenable:

1. There is no trumpet blast.

2. The phrase *in the Spirit* is employed three additional times in Revelation and cannot, in those contexts, relate to the rapture.

3. John cannot represent the raptured church because his position as observer and scribe changes from earth to heaven and back again throughout Revelation.

(b) THERE IS NO BIBLICAL SUPPORT FOR THE NOTION OF TWO RAPTURES

The problem with defining the multitude of Revelation 7 as a second group of believers who did not come to faith until during the great tribulation is that it requires two raptures:

- the first rapture, secret and silent, prior to the commencement of the seventieth week; and

- a second one at the end of the great tribulation—this is the one described in Revelation 7.

The notion that there is more than one rapture is not supported anywhere in the Bible. The passages in Matthew 24:30–31; 1 Corinthians 15:51–54; and 1 Thessalonians 4:13–17 are consistent in their varied descriptions of the same event:

- The dead in Christ will be raised imperishable.

- Those believers still alive will not sleep (experience physical death), but they will be gathered together from the four winds, from one end of the sky to the other, and caught up together with the dead in Christ in the clouds to meet the Lord in the air; and they will be changed—the perishable will have put on the imperishable.

No indication is given that this event will be secret and silent, leaving the rest of the world to wonder what happened. All three texts speak of

- a trumpet blast.

As well, two of the three, Matthew 24:30–31 and 1 Thessalonians 4:13–18, state

- that "the sign of the Son of Man **will appear in the sky**" (Matt. 24:30, emphasis added), as the Lord Himself descends "from heaven **with a shout** [and] with **the voice of the arch-angel**" (1 Thess. 4:16, emphasis added), and that "all the tribes of the earth will mourn, **and they will see** the Son of Man coming on the clouds of the sky with power and great glory" (Matt. 24:30, emphasis added); and

- that angels will be present.

Thus, all three texts describe events that can be heard and seen from the earth; there is no text that describes or even implies something secret and silent.

(c) THREE BIBLICAL TEXTS DISCUSS THE TIMING OF THE RAPTURE (SINGULAR)

Not only do all three passages describe the rapture in similar terms but they all also provide the same clue as to its timing, thus supplying additional proof that there will be only one:

- Matthew 24:31 says it will be "with a great trumpet"—note that Jesus also placed this event *after* the great tribulation in Matt. 24:9–21.)
- 1 Corinthians 15:52 says it will occur "at the last trumpet."
- 1 Thessalonians 4:16 says it will be "with the trumpet of God."

What do these phrases refer to? Matthew's gospel and both of Paul's letters were written decades before John received his revelation, so the original audience of Jesus and the initial recipients of Paul's letters could not have relied on Revelation as a frame of reference for understanding these clues about timing. Nevertheless, they had other Scriptural references to consult—what we know as the Old Testament.

At the beginning of the exodus, at Mount Sinai, God told Moses to prepare the Hebrews to be summoned to His presence. On the third day thereafter,

<u>**Exodus 16:16–19**</u> (emphasis added)

[16] there were thunder and lightning flashes and a thick cloud upon the mountain and a **very loud trumpet sound**, so that all the people who were in the camp trembled. [17] And **Moses brought the people out of the camp to meet God**, and they stood at the foot of the mountain. [18] Now Mount Sinai was all in smoke because the LORD descended upon it in fire; and its smoke ascended like the smoke of a furnace, and the whole mountain quaked violently. [19] When **the sound of the trumpet grew louder and louder**, Moses spoke and God answered him with thunder.

While the Hebrews were still encamped at Mount Sinai, God instructed Moses to make two silver trumpets (Num. 10:2–10) that would be used

- to summon the congregation to the presence of the Lord or
- to announce a call to war.

In addition to the silver trumpets, there were also trumpets made of rams' horns (Josh. 6:8). The trumpets were also blown on appointed feast days and on the first day of the month, which began with the new moon.

When an assembly was called, the people gathered at the tabernacle, which was considered the dwelling place of God. As an announcement of the call to war, trumpets were used regularly in the conquest of Canaan and by the judges.

Other references to the announcement of the arrival of the day of the Lord (the Lord's call to war) include trumpets:

<u>Joel 2:1</u> (emphasis added)
Blow a trumpet in Zion,
And sound an alarm on My holy mountain!
Let all the inhabitants of the land tremble,
For the day of the Lord is coming;
Surely it is near.

<u>Zephaniah 1:14–16</u> (emphasis added)
[14] **Near is the great day of the Lord,**
Near and coming very quickly;
Listen, the day of the Lord!
In it the warrior cries out bitterly.
[15] A day of wrath is that day,
A day of trouble and distress,
A day of destruction and desolation,
A day of darkness and gloom,
A day of clouds and thick darkness,
[16] **A day of trumpet** and battle cry.

Putting all these passages together, the great trumpet, the last trumpet, God's trumpet, will be sounded to accomplish both the primary purposes:

1. It will serve as the summons, the call to assembly, of the people of God to the place of God. This is the rapture of God's believing saints to meet with the Lord in the air and taken to His dwelling place.

2. It will serve as the announcement that the Lord Himself is going to war in the great and terrible day of the Lord.

Accordingly, the rapture will immediately precede the onset of the wrath of the day of the Lord, from which believers are exempted.

Still without reference to Revelation, what else could Jesus's listeners and Paul's readers have learned? If they were looking only for the last trumpet ever to be blown by *anyone*, the answer would have been found in Isaiah 27:12–13:

> ¹² In that day the LORD will start His threshing from the flowing stream of the Euphrates to the brook of Egypt, and you will be gathered up one by one, O sons of Israel. ¹³ It will come about also in that day that **a great trumpet will be blown**, and those who were perishing in the land of Assyria and who were scattered in the land of Egypt will come and worship the LORD in the holy mountain at Jerusalem. (emphasis added)

The context of these verses is the day of the Lord ("that day"), at the end of which the Lord will gather together His remnant of Israel from the lands that were then known as Assyria and Egypt. Thus, this trumpet sounds after Daniel's seventieth week, including the day of the Lord, is completed and the millennial kingdom is about to be inaugurated. Since Paul's readers knew, from his first letter to the Thessalonians, that they, as believers, were not destined for wrath (1 Thess. 5:9), they would have known that this was not the answer they sought.

From our perspective today, the events of Isaiah 27 would also come after the trumpets and bowls judgments of Revelation. Of course, pre-Revelation readers would not know about the trumpets and bowls of Revelation, but they would certainly know about Daniel's seventieth week and the day of the Lord.

But Jesus's audience and Paul's readers were not looking for the last trumpet ever to be blown by a Levite or an Aaronic priest or an angel, but by God. Where in the Old Testament is a trumpet blown by God? The answer comes from the prophet Zechariah:

Zechariah 9:8–15 (emphasis added)

> ⁸ But I will camp around My house because of an army,
> Because of him who passes by and returns;
> And no oppressor will pass over them anymore,

For now I have seen with My eyes.
⁹ Rejoice greatly, O daughter of Zion!
Shout in triumph, O daughter of Jerusalem!
Behold, your king is coming to you;
He is just and endowed with salvation,
Humble, and mounted on a donkey,
Even on a colt, the foal of a donkey.
¹⁰ I will cut off the chariot from Ephraim
And the horse from Jerusalem;
And the bow of war will be cut off.
And He will speak peace to the nations;
And His dominion will be from sea to sea,
And from the River to the ends of the earth.
¹¹ As for you also, because of the blood of My covenant with you,
I have set your prisoners free from the waterless pit.
¹² Return to the stronghold, O prisoners who have the hope;
This very day I am declaring that I will restore double to you.
¹³ For I will bend Judah as My bow,
I will fill the bow with Ephraim.
And I will stir up your sons, O Zion, against your sons, O Greece;
And I will make you like a warrior's sword.
¹⁴ Then the LORD will appear over them,
And His arrow will go forth like lightning;
And **the Lord GOD will blow the trumpet**,
And will march in the storm winds of the south.
¹⁵ The LORD of hosts will defend them.

The earlier verses of Zechariah 9 begin with prophecies against the neighboring nations of Israel. As with many prophecies, there are near and far fulfillments. The near fulfillment was most likely Greece's conquest of the region approximately two hundred years after Zechariah's prophecies. God used Greece to judge these nations, but He preserved Israel (v. 8).

Zechariah 9:9 is a prophecy of Christ's first coming; verse 10 relates to His second coming and the establishment of His millennial kingdom.

Beginning with Zechariah 9:11, God remembers His covenant with Abraham (Genesis 15) and promises to restore the exiles of Israel, as if they had been held captive in dry wells (as Joseph had been in Gen. 37:24). Not only does He promise to protect and empower them (vv. 13–15) but He also promises to "restore double" to them (v. 12).

The near fulfillment of the prophecy of Zechariah 9:11–15 occurred during the intertestamental period. The antichrist's foreshadower, Antiochus IV Epiphanes, had desecrated the temple (an abomination of desolation) in approximately 168 BC and had mercilessly persecuted the Jews, who refused to renounce their God and His commandments. The revolt of the faithful Jews against Antiochus is recorded in the books of the Maccabees in the Apocrypha. God Himself came to their defense (Zech. 9:14–15), and the result was the cleansing and restoration of the temple, with the attendant miracle of the lamp oil, resulting in what Jews today celebrate as Hanukkah.

Because Antiochus foreshadowed the antichrist, it is important to note that Jesus referred to his abomination of desolation (a fact of history that the Jews of Jesus's time knew) in His discourse on the end times recorded in Matthew 24:15 and Mark 13:14. That Jesus compared the coming great tribulation to the vicious persecution of the faithful Jews almost two hundred years earlier is noteworthy because it was, and will be, at these two times that God Himself blew and will blow the trumpet as He intervenes in human history.

This much Jesus's listeners and the recipients of Paul's letters in Thessalonica and in Corinth could understand without the benefit of Jesus's revelation to John.

The far fulfillment of this prophecy in Zechariah will occur when Jesus comes the second time to gather His own and to declare war in the day of the Lord. As in the near fulfillment with the antichrist's foreshadower, He Himself will blow the trumpet to proclaim His direct intervention to destroy the antichrist, who will have, like his predecessor, also defiled His temple.

Unlike Jesus's listeners and the recipients of Paul's letters in Thessalonica and Corinth, readers after the first century can include Revelation to bolster and confirm the earlier believers' understanding of the timing of the rapture. Here are the relevant questions to be asked in light of the revelation to John:

1. Do the phrases *the great trumpet, the last trumpet,* and *the trumpet of God* refer to the seventh trumpet of Revelation (which contains the seven bowl judgments)? Or

2. do they refer to all seven trumpet judgments (including the seventh, which contains the bowl judgments)? Or

3. do they refer to the seventh seal, which *contains all* seven trumpet judgments, *including all* seven bowl judgments, which are themselves contained within the seventh trumpet?

Recently, some pretribulationists theorized that there might be a space of some time (weeks, months, or even years) between the rapture and the onset of the day of the Lord. That theory was addressed and rejected as fallacious in section IV.D.6 above.

All other pretribulationists as well as those of all rapture positions (except posttribulationists) have agreed that the rapture will immediately precede the onset of the day of the Lord.

Thus, the only real issue (and point of departure among the various positions) is when the day of the Lord begins. Unfortunately for pretribulationists, an affirmative answer to any of the three questions listed above defeats the theory of a pretribulation rapture because

- we are looking for clues to "the great trumpet," "the last trumpet," and "the trumpet of God" *and*

- the seals precede the trumpets *and*

- the seals begin at the start of the seventieth week.

These facts preclude any possibility of the rapture occurring before the beginning of the seventieth week.

Posttribulationists answer that the seventh trumpet sounds at the end of the seventieth week (and the bowls are poured out in the seventy-five days thereafter), so the rapture and the day of the Lord occur at the end of the seventieth week.

Midtribulationists place the seventh trumpet at the midpoint, so that the rapture and the day of the Lord occur then.

The prewrath position is that all the trumpets and the bowls are contained in the seventh seal, so "the great trumpet" of Matthew 24:31, "the last trumpet" of 1 Corinthians 15:52, and "the trumpet of God" of 1 Thessalonians 4:16 will be sounded with the breaking of the seventh seal.

This position is consistent with the chronology of Revelation, which also parallels the chronology that Jesus presented according to Matthew 24 (and Mark 13). Note in particular that, when Jesus presented His chronology, He placed His trumpet call *after* the great tribulation and *after* the cosmic upheavals. Thus, any trumpet blown before then—for example, before the beginning of the seventieth week—could not, by definition, be "the last" trumpet, much less "the trumpet of God." Jesus's chronology given during His lifetime matches that of His later revelation to John:

- With the breaking of the sixth seal and the upheavals of heaven and earth, people recognize that the day of the Lord is at hand, and they attempt to flee or to hide.

- Immediately after that, the 144,000 Jews are sealed for protection during the oncoming day of the Lord, and at the same time, or immediately thereafter, the trumpet of God sounds (1 Cor. 15:52).

- The dead and living believers (1 Thess. 4:16–17), too many to count, are raptured up to heaven.

- The seventh seal is then broken, followed by silence.

- Then seven angels are given the seven trumpets, and the undiluted wrath of God in the day of the Lord begins to pour out.

(d) Jesus Himself provided a clue to the timing of His return to gather His people to Himself

In recent years, there has been renewed interest in the Christian community in the feasts of the Lord. These are not Jewish holidays like Hanukkah and Purim, which came later. The feasts of the Lord were established by God Himself in Leviticus 23.

<u>Leviticus 23:1-2</u> (emphasis added)

[1] The Lord spoke again to Moses, saying, [2] "Speak to the sons of Israel, and say to them, 'The Lord's appointed times which you shall proclaim as holy convocations — My appointed times are these: ...'"

Two Hebrew words are used that are translated into English as "feast" or "festival":

1. *Moed* or *mowed* (*Strong's* OT 4150), which means "an appointment, i.e., a fixed time or season; specifically, a festival ... by implication, an assembly (as convened for a definite purpose)."

2. *Chag* (*Strong's* OT 2282), which means a "festival." It derives from the root, *chagag* (*Strong's* OT 2287), which means "to move in a circle, i.e., specifically, to march in a sacred procession."

A third word used in connection with the feasts of the Lord is "convocation." The Hebrew word is *miqra* (*Strong's* OT 4744); it means "something called out, i.e., a public meeting (the act, the persons, or the place); also a rehearsal."

Thus, the feasts of the Lord are the Lord's appointed times, cycling around each year, to meet with His people.

The Lord embedded seven of His appointed times into the agricultural calendar of His people so that they would have regular reminders of His ultimate plan of redemption for Israel and, by extension, the gentiles, who would be blessed through Israel. For this reason, the appointed times were also called convocations as they rehearsed for what

God was planning for the future. God does His redemptive work at His "appointed times."

There are four spring feasts and three in the autumn. In His first coming, Jesus embodied and fulfilled all that the four spring feasts "rehearsed." He came as the Lamb Who would take away the sins of the world. For this reason, many Christians, including me, believe that He will embody and fulfill all that the fall feasts envision. He will return as Ruler and Judge. And this leads to the clue that Jesus gave as to the timing of His return:

Matthew 24:36 (emphasis added)

But of that **day and hour no one knows**, not even the angels of heaven, nor the Son, but the Father alone.

> Parallel verse in Mark 13:32.

Matthew 25:13 (emphasis added)

"Be on the alert then, for **you do not know the day nor the hour**."

Why is the unknown day and hour a clue?

Of the Lord's seven "appointed times," six begin after the first day of the month. Only one, the Feast of Trumpets, begins on the very first day of the month. It is the first of the fall feasts and is described in Leviticus 23 and in Numbers 29:

Leviticus 23:23–25

23 Again the LORD spoke to Moses, saying, 24 "Speak to the sons of Israel, saying, 'In the seventh month on the first of the month, you shall have a rest, a reminder by blowing of trumpets, a holy convocation. 25 You shall not do any laborious work, but you shall present an offering by fire to the LORD.'"

Numbers 29:1–6

1 Now in the seventh month, on the first day of the month, you shall also have a holy convocation; you shall do no laborious work. It will be to you a day for blowing trumpets. 2 You shall offer a burnt offering as a soothing aroma to the LORD: one bull, one ram,

and seven male lambs one year old without defect; [3] also their grain offering, fine flour mixed with oil: three-tenths of an ephah for the bull, two-tenths for the ram, [4] and one-tenth for each of the seven lambs. [5] Offer one male goat for a sin offering, to make atonement for you, [6] besides the burnt offering of the new moon and its grain offering, and the continual burnt offering and its grain offering, and their drink offerings, according to their ordinance, for a soothing aroma, an offering by fire to the Lord.

The Jewish calendar was lunar, and the beginning of each month began with the new moon. But they defined the new moon differently from today. Today the new moon is the phase at which the moon, viewed from earth, shows only the side that is not illuminated by the sun. Thus the moon appears to blend in with the night sky.

In contrast, the Jews defined the new moon as the phase when the first sliver of light appeared to different observers at different locations. When the observers made their report of the sighting of the first sliver of light, the head of the Sanhedrin, called the nasi, would declare the start of the new month.

Thus, the first day of each month was uncertain until this process of confirmation was concluded.

Because the Feast of Trumpets was the only one of the Lord's appointed times to occur on the first day of a month, it was known as *the hidden day* or *the day of concealment*. Until the nasi made the determination that there was a new moon, no one knew the day or the hour that the new month—and the Feast of Trumpets—would begin.

The first day of the Feast of Trumpets was also the start of the New Year of the civil calendar (as opposed to the religious calendar, in which the first month was in the spring); this day was and is known as Rosh Hashanah.

On this first day of the Feast of Trumpets, Rosh Hashanah, the ram's horn, the shofar, was blown one hundred times. The last blast was the longest and the loudest. It represented, in this rehearsal of God's plan of redemption, God's deliverance of His people and His intervention on their behalf to punish their enemies.

This takes us back to Jesus's time clue. Instead of the nasi, it will be God the Father who will determine the day of Jesus's return, but Jesus used an idiom that His listeners plainly understood as a reference to the Feast of Trumpets/Rosh Hashanah.

In addition to Jesus's idiomatic reference, there was an ancient Jewish belief that the resurrection of the dead would occur on the Feast of Trumpets. For this reason, many Jewish gravestones are engraved with a shofar, the ram's horn trumpet.

If it is correct that Jesus will return to gather to Himself all believers, dead and alive, in the rapture on Rosh Hashanah, the first day of the Feast of Trumpets, does this imply that we can look at the current Jewish calendar of any year and say, "Maybe this year, the rapture will occur on this day"? The answer is no, for two reasons:

1. Because of the uncertainty of the correct day of the new moon and because of the difficulty of communicating this information, once determined, to all of Israel, two days were observed as Rosh Hashanah. Moreover, because the determination of the new moon had to be made from locations within Jerusalem, the seventy years of captivity in Babylon made this determination impossible, and this further required a two-day celebration. The rabbis justified this practice by considering the two days as one long day.

2. The Jewish calendar used in Israel today began to be used in AD 360. It is called the Hillel II talmudic lunisolar calendar or the orthodox rabbinical calendar. Like the Western Gregorian calendar, which we observe today, this Jewish calendar is pre-calculated. It is no longer based on the observation of the phases of the moon and of the ripening barley crop in Jerusalem. Moreover, it is lunisolar, which means that the lunar calendar is adjusted to the solar seasonal year.

   The problem is that there is an error in the calculation of the Hillel II calendar that causes the new moon to be declared one to three days ahead of the observation of the sliver of crescent light from Jerusalem.

The significance of this error is that the Jewish calendar presently used is different from the calendar used in the days of Jesus. The Lord's seven appointed times or rehearsals listed on current calendars are not in sync with God's calendar.

(e) Because God is impartial, He would not arbitrarily treat one group of believers differently from another group of believers

The whole of the Bible demonstrates that, while God called Abraham, created the Jewish nation, and called them His people, His salvation is available to all mankind.

> As a side comment, I do not subscribe to the Calvinist and neo-Calvinist view that God the Father loves, and God the Son's death on the cross purchased, only "the predestined elect." That view contradicts the express and unequivocal language of John 3:16; 1 Tim. 2:4; and 2 Peter 3:9.

God told Abraham that all nations (meaning non-Jews/gentiles) would be blessed through him. After the conversion of Cornelius, Peter recognized that God was indeed saving gentiles. His statement is quoted below in Acts 10:34. Even the Herodians, in their attempt to trap Jesus, admitted that Jesus was impartial. Their false flattery spoke the truth and is quoted below in Matthew 22:16.

Plainly, impartiality is one of the characteristics of God:

Deuteronomy 10:17 (emphasis added)

For the LORD your God is the God of gods and the Lord of lords, the great, the mighty, and **the awesome God who does not show partiality** nor take a bribe.

2 Chronicles 19:7 (emphasis added)

Now then let the fear of the LORD be upon you; be very careful what you do, for **the LORD our God will have no part in unrighteousness or partiality or the taking of a bribe.**

<u>Matthew 22:15–16</u> (emphasis added))

[15] Then the Pharisees went and plotted together how they might trap Him in what He said. [16] And they sent their disciples to Him, along with the Herodians, saying, "Teacher, we know that You are truthful and teach the way of God in truth, and **defer to no one; for You are not partial to any.**"

<u>Acts 10:34</u> (emphasis added)

Opening his mouth, Peter said: "I most certainly understand now that **God is not one to show partiality.**"

<u>Romans 2:11</u> (emphasis added)

For **there is no partiality with God.**

<u>Galatians 2:6</u> (emphasis added)

But from those who were of high reputation (what they were makes no difference to me; **God shows no partiality**)—well, those who were of reputation contributed nothing to me.

<u>Ephesians 6:9</u> (emphasis added)

And masters, do the same things to them, and give up threatening, knowing that both their Master and yours is in heaven, and **there is no partiality with Him.**

<u>Colossians 3:25</u> (emphasis added)

For he who does wrong will receive the consequences of the wrong which he has done, and **that without partiality.**

IF all believers were raptured off the earth either before the beginning of the seventieth week (pretribulationism) or at the midpoint of the week, when the great tribulation begins (midtribulationism),

THEN there would be two classes of Christians:

1. Those who were spared the experience of the great tribulation and

2. Those who became Christians during the great tribulation.

The result of this would be that the first-class Christians would be taken to heaven for the marriage feast, but the second-class Christians would not be present to participate, simply because they came to faith later, during the great tribulation. They would be like the five virgins who didn't bring enough oil while they waited for the arrival of the bridegroom (Matt. 25:1–12). This would be so despite the fact that the second-class Christians were truly believers, in contrast to the five foolish virgins, who apparently were not.

But the time of conversion should not matter. Whether they come to faith at the beginning of the day or only at the last hour, the latter arrivals are just as truly believers as the first. This is seen in Matthew 20:1–16, the parable of the laborers in the vineyard.

This same parable also demonstrates the point that the owner of the vineyard (God) owes nothing to any person; He is free to do what He wishes with what is His own. He is free to treat the last as well as the first— or perhaps even better. The last sentence of the parable, Matthew 20:16, says, "Thus the last shall be first, and the first last." This indicates that sometimes people who are converted late in life produce more fruit than people who were converted earlier in their lives.

Conclusion: The church is not among those who welcome the multitude of Revelation 7 to heaven because the church itself has gone through the great tribulation and has been raptured into heaven when Jesus has cut short the days of the great tribulation to begin the day of the Lord:

- Revelation 4 does not describe a pretribulation rapture.

- The Bible describes only one rapture, not two, and it occurs between the breaking of the sixth and seventh seals.

- The seventh seal contains all the trumpet and bowl judgments, which are the final, eschatological outpouring of the wrath of God upon unrepentant unbelievers. Thus, "the great trumpet"/"the last trumpet"/"the trumpet of God" will sound between the sixth and seventh seals.

- While Jesus's warning about the unknown hour or day may be a clue that refers to the first day of the Feast of Trumpets, which is Rosh Hashanah, the Jewish calendar in use since the fourth century AD is not the same as the biblical calendar.

- While Christians will receive different rewards in heaven based on what they accomplished with the "talents" they were given in this life (Matt. 25:14–29), there is no indication that God will treat believers differently based upon the time when they were converted (see Matt. 20:1–16). Just as the means of salvation was and is the same both before and after the cross, those who come to faith during the great tribulation will not be treated as second-class citizens and excluded from the marriage feast.

3. GENTILES WERE ON EARTH FOR THE FIRST SIXTY-NINE WEEKS OF DANIEL

The argument that the seventy weeks of Daniel apply only to Israel and therefore believers/the church will be raptured out of the world before the seventieth week ignores the obvious fact that there were gentiles, both pagan and followers of Jesus (along with Jews), in the world during the first sixty-nine weeks and that they suffered right alongside Israel.

Did not pagan gentile nations also suffer at the hands of the Medo-Persians, the Greeks, and the Romans?

> The first sixty-nine weeks began with the decree of the Persian ruler Artaxerxes, so I have not included the earlier nations that oppressed the Jews and other pagan gentile nations.

Did not believers in Jesus (comprising both Jews and gentiles) exist during a portion of the first sixty-nine weeks? Since each "week" is a period of seven years and since Jesus was not crucified or "cut off" until *after* the sixty-ninth week (see Dan. 9:26), it means that there were believers, both Jew and gentile, who came to a saving faith during the first sixty-nine weeks.

Thus, because believers in Jesus (both Jews and gentiles) constitute the Body of Christ or "the church," it means that the church did exist in the sixty-ninth week. While the dispensationalist view is that the church was not born until Pentecost, the word *church* is synonymous with *saints* and *believers*, and those people, both Jews and gentiles, did live in the sixty-ninth week.

Moreover, as noted earlier, God's faithful remnant, including His own prophets, suffered along with the apostate majority whenever God judged Israel.

Conclusion: In order to keep believers out of the seventieth week, dispensationalism must also keep them out of the sixty-ninth week. For that reason, dispensationalism distinguishes and separates out believers who came to faith during Jesus's ministry from those who came to faith after Pentecost. The earlier believers are not considered part of the body of Christ, the church. This exclusion of earlier believers is required to justify the conclusion that the church age must end before the beginning of the seventieth week.

Unfortunately, this is an example of how the imposition of a man-made grid onto the text of the Bible results in distorted interpretive conclusions. In this case, it results in different treatment of believers, especially when it comes to the time of their resurrection. This violates the biblical principle of God's impartiality.

> See section VI.C below for related examples.

This leads to my next point, which is an expansion of my earlier discussion regarding the fact that gentile believers are also sons of Abraham.

> See section V.A.3.(b) above.

4. Gentile believers, as sons of Abraham, will also be on the earth for the seventieth week

What I am writing now is living proof that a believer's understanding of the Bible grows and changes as he or she continues to study the Word. When I wrote my first book, *In the Strength of His Might* (2014), I did not believe in a pretribulation rapture. I still do not today, but I had not considered the relationship between that position and Daniel 9:24–27. In the intervening years, I have studied the topic further, and the result is the need to expand on what I wrote in 2014.

The argument that the seventieth week applies only to Israel derives from Daniel 9:24:

> Seventy weeks have been decreed for ***your people*** and your holy city, to finish the transgression, to make an end of sin, to make atonement for iniquity, to bring in everlasting righteousness, to seal up vision and prophecy, and to anoint the most holy place. (emphasis added)

In my 2014 book, I stated,

> It is important to remember that Gabriel is speaking to Daniel about *his* people and *his* holy city. That means that this prophecy applies to the Jews and to Jerusalem. It is not a prophecy that applies to the Church, even though the Church is made up of Jews and gentiles, nor does it apply to the gentiles, at least not directly.[11]

No reader of that book pointed out to me the *apparent* inconsistency of those sentences with the position I was taking in the book—namely that believers will go into the seventieth week of Daniel.

While it is a principle of biblical hermeneutics (the principles of interpreting the Bible) that no one verse can be interpreted outside the context of the entire Bible, sometimes a student can get so focused on a particular passage that he or she does not consider other very familiar passages. And that is what happened to me. For that reason, I must add now what I failed to include in the 2014 book.

Let's begin with definitions. The Hebrew word in Daniel 9:24 that is translated into English as "people," is transliterated *am* (*Strong's* OT 5971), and it means "a people (as a congregated unit); specifically, a tribe (as those of Israel); hence (collectively) troops or attendants; figuratively, a flock." The word appears over eighteen hundred times in the Old Testament and is translated into English in the KJV translation as "folk, men, nation, people." Other Hebrew dictionaries go into more detail but do not add significant information relevant to my point here.

---

11   Susan E. Jeans, *In the Strength of His Might* (Master Design, 2014), 10–11.

Next, who, according to the Bible, are the people who constitute or make up Daniel's people? Is it only the Jews? The answer is no.

Throughout the Bible, the Most High God has made it plain that not all Jews are heirs of His promises. For example, He chose Isaac over his older half-brother, Ishmael, and He chose Jacob over his older twin brother, Esau. In the New Testament, in Romans 9:6–8, Paul states explicitly that being a physical descendant of Abraham does not automatically signify that one is saved.

> See also my discussion above, section V. A.3.(b).

Earlier in Romans 2, Paul defined a true Jew this way:

Romans 2:28–29

²⁸ For he is not a Jew who is one outwardly; nor is circumcision that which is outward in the flesh. ²⁹ But he is a Jew who is one inwardly; and circumcision is that which is of the heart, by the Spirit, not by the letter; and his praise is not from men, but from God.

Justification is and has always been by faith and not by works nor by the Mosaic law. Galatians 3:7 states, "Therefore, be sure that it is those who are of faith who are sons of Abraham."

> See also, e.g., Rom. 4:13; 5:1; 9:30–32; Gal. 2:16; 3:26, 29.

Since salvation/justification is not by one's ancestry or ethnic identification but by faith, the passages in appendix D make it plain that God has removed the dividing wall between Jews and gentiles and has joined them together in various metaphors such as *His body, a living building,* and *one spiritual house for a holy priesthood.*

Note that this is not about replacement theology. I am NOT saying that the church has replaced Israel. That is a Catholic and Calvinist/ neo-Calvinist position, with which I wholeheartedly disagree.

Nor am I saying that the Most High God has finished His dealings with Israel as a nation. In Isaiah 1:27, God Himself made this promise:

- Zion will be redeemed with justice,

- And her repentant ones with righteousness.

And it will be *Zion* (Jerusalem or Israel as a whole) that will be redeemed. This is not a promise to the church.

Centuries after Isaiah penned God's prophecies, Paul clarified in Romans 11:17–33 that, despite the unity of Jew and gentile in the natural olive root, God still has purposes for a Jewish remnant. In Romans 11:1, Paul asked rhetorically, "I say then, God has not rejected His people, has He? May it never be!" Under the inspiration of God the Holy Spirit, Paul explained that a partial hardening has happened to most of the Jews (clearly not all, because Paul was a Jew and the early church was predominantly Jewish) until the "fullness of the Gentiles" shall occur, and after that, whatever constitutes "all Israel" will be saved.

In the meantime, the church, the body of Christ, consists of both Jews and gentiles. Though they maintain their ethnic origins ("from every nation and all tribes and peoples and tongues" [Rev. 7:9]), they are not separate within the whole.

> See Eph. 2:11–3:12 regarding the unity of Jews and gentiles within the church.

The prior subsection (V.B.3) and this subsection (V.B.4) also refute the pretribulationist argument that since the church did not exist during the sixty-ninth week, it can have no part in the seventieth week, and therefore the rapture must occur before the seventieth week.

Conclusion: The seventy-week prophecy given to Daniel need not exclude the church because believers, by faith, have been "grafted" into the "rich root" and are also sons of Abraham. Therefore, just as gentiles who believed in Jesus were on the earth for the first sixty-nine weeks, they will also be on the earth for the major portion of the seventieth week.

C. The great tribulation will serve as God's cleansing, refining, and purifying of what is today's Laodicean/Thyatiran church, at least in America

1. New Testament believers need to learn about God's unchanging character from the Old Testament

Many, if not most, of the epistles of the New Testament were written, among other purposes,

- to contend earnestly for the faith, which was once for all delivered to the saints (Jude 3),

- to correct false teaching (this is the case for most of the epistles, e.g., 2 Thess. 2:1–5), and

- to encourage believers who were suffering (e.g., Heb. 10:23–25, 35–36; 1 Peter 1:6–7).

Because the New Testament was written in the decades following the life, death, resurrection, and ascension of Jesus, all references to the Scripture within those books necessarily referred to what we know as the Old Testament. The writers of the New Testament frequently incorporated citations from or paraphrases of Old Testament passages.

Since salvation by faith has been the only means of salvation both before and after the cross and since both Jews and gentiles compose the body of Christ, it means that believers after the cross have the greater advantage of the full and complete disclosure that God our Creator has given to us. In Romans 3, Paul wrote to the Jews,

> [1] Then what advantage has the Jew? Or what is the benefit of circumcision? [2] Great in every respect. First of all, that they were entrusted with the oracles of God. (Rom. 3:1–2)

Later, in Romans 9:4, Paul lists other advantages given to the Jews—"the covenants and the giving of the Law and the temple service and the promises."

What Paul was saying was that the Jews had advantages over the gentiles in coming to a saving faith because they had been previously given these things by God, including all the messianic prophecies in the Old Testament.

But believers today are in a much greater position of advantage than the Jews of the first century. Unfortunately, many of today's churches focus exclusively on learning the New Testament, and they do so to the detriment of their members. The writers of the New Testament remind believers of all times to learn from God's dealings with Israel, because His character does not change and therefore what applied to them then applies as well to us now—a point that goes against the very heart of the definition of dispensationalism, but not against progressive revelation:

<u>Romans 4:21–24</u> (emphasis added)

²¹ … and [Abraham] being fully assured that what God had promised, He was able also to perform. ²² Therefore also it was credited to him as righteousness. ²³ Now **not for his sake only was it written** that it was credited to him, ²⁴ **but for our sake also,** to whom it will be credited, as those who believe in Him who raised Jesus our Lord from the dead.

<u>Romans 15:4</u> (emphasis added)

For whatever was written in earlier times was **written for our instruction,** so that through perseverance and the encouragement of the Scriptures we might have hope.

<u>1 Corinthians 9:9–11</u> (emphasis added)

⁹ For it is written in the Law of Moses, "You shall not muzzle the ox while he is threshing." God is not concerned about oxen, is He? ¹⁰ Or is He speaking altogether for our sake? Yes, **for our sake it was written,** because the plowman ought to plow in hope, and the thresher to thresh in hope of sharing the crops. ¹¹ If we sowed spiritual things in you, is it too much if we reap material things from you?

<u>1 Corinthians 10:6, 11</u> (emphasis added)

⁶ Now these things [Israel's history, specifically the exodus] happened **as examples for us**, so that we would not crave evil things, as they also craved.

¹¹ Now these things happened to them as **an example**, and **they were written for our instruction**, upon whom the ends of the ages have come.

<u>2 Timothy 3:16–17</u> (emphasis added)

¹⁶ **All Scripture** is inspired by God and profitable for teaching, for reproof, for correction, for training in righteousness; ¹⁷ so that the man of God may be adequate, equipped for every good work.

The Bible also teaches that gentiles who believe in Jesus Christ are grafted into the "rich root of the olive tree" (Rom. 11:17) and "are Abraham's descendants, heirs according to promise." (Gal. 3:29; see section V.A.3 above).

For these reasons, all that was written to and for the Jews in the Old Testament regarding God's treatment of and dealings with His people was written for believing gentiles as well. I am *not* saying that the ceremonial sacrificial law and the dietary and other social restrictions still apply; it is only the moral law of God (that precedes even the Mosaic law) that applies for all time.

My focus here is on how God's character and plan of salvation do not change. Therefore, we can expect that God will deal with His people today in the same manner as He dealt with His people in Old Testament times. Thus, prophecies addressed to Israel could apply to His people today, especially considering that many prophecies had both near and far fulfillments. Consider, for example, the prophecy concerning Israel in Zechariah 13:

<u>Zechariah 13:7–9</u>

⁷ "Awake, O sword, against My Shepherd,
And against the man, My Associate,"
Declares the LORD of hosts.
"Strike the Shepherd that the sheep may be scattered;

And I will turn My hand against the little ones.
⁸ "It will come about in all the land,"
Declares the Lord,
"That two parts in it will be cut off and perish;
But the third will be left in it.
⁹ "And I will bring the third part through the fire,
Refine them as silver is refined,
And test them as gold is tested.
They will call on My name,
And I will answer them;
I will say, 'They are My people,'
And they will say, 'The Lord is my God.' "

What does "I will turn My hand against" mean? And who are the "little ones" of verse 7?

The phrase *turning His hand* in the Old Testament refers to both chastening and judgment. Here are just a few examples:

<u>**Psalm 81:11–14**</u> (emphasis added)
¹¹ But My people did not listen to My voice,
And Israel did not obey Me.
¹² So I gave them over to the stubbornness of their heart,
To walk in their own devices.
¹³ Oh that My people would listen to Me,
That Israel would walk in My ways!
¹⁴ I would quickly subdue their enemies
And **turn My hand against** their adversaries.

<u>**Isaiah 1:21–25**</u> (emphasis added)
²¹ How the faithful city has become a harlot,
She who was full of justice!
Righteousness once lodged in her,
But now murderers.
²² Your silver has become dross,
Your drink diluted with water.
²³ Your rulers are rebels

And companions of thieves;
Everyone loves a bribe
And chases after rewards.
They do not defend the orphan,
Nor does the widow's plea come before them.
²⁴ Therefore the Lord God of hosts,
The Mighty One of Israel declares,
"Ah, I will be relieved of My adversaries
And avenge Myself on My foes.
²⁵ I will also **turn My hand against** you,
And will smelt away your dross as with lye
And will remove all your alloy.

<u>Ezekiel 38:11–12</u> (emphasis added)

¹¹ And you [Gog] will say, "I will go up against the land of unwalled villages. I will go against those who are at rest, that live securely, all of them living without walls and having no bars or gates, ¹² to capture spoil and to seize plunder, **to turn your hand against** the waste places which are now inhabited, and against the people who are gathered from the nations, who have acquired cattle and goods, who live at the center of the world."

Returning to Zechariah 13, the "little ones" are the true believing remnant, the same group as the "afflicted of the flock" of Zechariah 11:11. There were Hebrews and then Jews in the Old Testament who were saved by faith as they looked forward to the promised Messiah (Abraham is a noted example); there were Jews (and gentiles, too) in Jesus's time who believed in Him, and there were many Jews (as well as gentiles) in the early church. There have always been some "little ones." And according to verse 13:7, these little ones, faithful believers, were afflicted, either because God sent the affliction or allowed the persecution. The early church suffered terrible persecution, which God used to refine, cleanse, and purify the believers.

This persecution should have been no surprise. After all, verse 7 first quotes the Lord as He awakens the sword against His Associate, the Shepherd. According to the eternal plan of the triune God, the Second

Person of the Trinity would be slain as the perfect and sufficient sacrifice for the sins of the world (not just for the sins of some). And His sheep would be scattered and suffer persecution, sent or allowed by the same triune God. Jesus warned His followers of this repeatedly. For example, in John 15:18, Jesus said: "If the world hates you, you know that it has hated Me before it hated you." And the consequence of that hatred appears in verse 20: "If they persecuted Me, they will also persecute you."

See appendixes A and B for other biblical passages.

Conclusion: The study of God's character as it is revealed in the Old Testament and of His manner of dealing with His people, Israel, is instructive and useful to New Testament believers because He does not change. Hebrews 13:8 says that "Jesus Christ is the same yesterday and today, and forever." Since God the Son is one with His Father, it means that the character of the trinitarian God does not change; moreover, His actions will always be consistent with His character.

As stated earlier in the comparison of progressive revelation with dispensationalism (see section I.B.3 above), God's revelation of Himself in His plan of the redemption of His creation was done in a progressive manner, in bits and pieces.

But in contrast to the gradual revelation of His plan of redemption, His dealings with mankind have been consistent throughout human history because His character, His perfection, His holiness, His mercy, His justice, and all His other attributes do not change. In other words, God's actions are based on His character; since His character has not and does not and will not change, His actions and interactions with mankind were, are, and will continue to be consistent.

Thus we are explicitly and repeatedly instructed in the New Testament to learn from what has gone before. The definition of dispensationalism—that God deals differently with people depending on the dispensation in which they lived—denies the clear instruction to the New Testament believers to learn from God's dealings with Israel and its enemies in the Old Testament.

2. GOD'S CONCERN FOR THE PURITY OF HIS PEOPLE HAS NOT CHANGED

Since a major portion of the New Testament demonstrates that the purity of the early church was so critical, why would that not apply even more so to the church in the last days before His return? Considering the worldly condition of most American churches today, is it any wonder that Jesus asked, "When the Son of Man comes, will He find faith on the earth?" (Luke 18:8)? Paul, too, was concerned that the church should be an appropriate bride for the Son of Man when He comes again:

<u>Ephesians 5:25–27</u> (emphasis added)

[25] Christ also loved the church and gave Himself up for her, [26] so that **He might sanctify her, having cleansed her by the washing of water with the word**, [27] that He might present to Himself the church in all **her glory, having no spot or wrinkle or any such thing; but that she would be holy and blameless.**

Peter shared Paul's concern about the condition of believers:

<u>**2 Peter 3:14**</u>

Therefore, beloved, since you look for these things, be diligent to be found by Him in peace, spotless and blameless.

Returning to Zechariah, the context of chapters 12–14 is the very last days. Gentile believers are also

- sons of Abraham,

- the wild branches grafted into the root of the olive tree, and

- members of Zechariah's "little ones."

Thus they should also expect severe persecution in the last days before Jesus's return. Just as God did with Israel and the early church, He still uses and will use the hatred and persecution of the world *to refine, cleanse, and purify His bride, sanctifying her*, that He might present her to Himself in all her glory, having no spot or wrinkle or any such thing, but that she should be holy and blameless.

And therein lies the problem that is the reason for the writing of this book.

IF the prevailing belief among American churches is that believers will be raptured out of the world before the beginning of the seventieth week, the breaking of the seals, and the time of the great tribulation, which begins at the midpoint of the seventieth week (this is pretribulationism), and

IF pretribulationism is wrong (the subject of this book),

THEN untold numbers of Christians will have been **DECEIVED** and will go into the seventieth week completely unprepared spiritually for the sanctifying work that will be accomplished in the believers who endure the great tribulation.

As Satan does his most effective work within the church and since believers are constantly admonished throughout the New Testament to be on guard for even slight deviations from the truth as well as blatantly unbiblical teaching, the danger of Christians being deceived is real in every age:

<u>1 Corinthians 6:9–10</u> (emphasis added)

⁹ Or do you not know that the unrighteous will not inherit the kingdom of God? **Do not be deceived**; neither fornicators, nor idolaters, nor adulterers, nor effeminate, nor homosexuals, ¹⁰ nor thieves, nor the covetous, nor drunkards, nor revilers, nor swindlers, will inherit the kingdom of God.

<u>1 Corinthians 15:33</u> (emphasis added)

Do not be deceived: "Bad company corrupts good morals."

<u>2 Corinthians 11:3</u> (emphasis added)

But I am afraid, that **as the serpent deceived Eve by his craftiness, your minds will be led astray from the simplicity and purity of devotion to Christ.**

<u>Galatians 6:3–4a</u> (emphasis added)

[3] For if anyone thinks he is something when he is nothing, **he deceives himself.** [4] But each one must examine his own work.

<u>Galatians 6:7–8</u> (emphasis added)

[7] **Do not be deceived**, God is not mocked; for whatever a man sows, this he will also reap. [8] For the one who sows to his own flesh will from the flesh reap corruption, but the one who sows to the Spirit will from the Spirit reap eternal life.

<u>Ephesians 5:5–6</u> (emphasis added)

[5] For this you know with certainty, that no immoral or impure person or covetous man, who is an idolater, has an inheritance in the kingdom of Christ and God. [6] **Let no one deceive you with empty words,** for because of these things the wrath of God comes upon the sons of disobedience.

<u>Colossians 2:8</u> (emphasis added)

See to it that no one takes you captive through philosophy and **empty deception, according to the tradition of men, according to the elementary principles of the world, rather than according to Christ.**

<u>1 Timothy 2:14</u> (emphasis added)

And it was not Adam who was deceived, **but the woman being deceived, fell into transgression.**

<u>2 Timothy 3:12–13</u> (emphasis added)

[12] Indeed, all who desire to live godly in Christ Jesus will be persecuted. [13] But evil men and impostors will proceed from bad to worse, **deceiving and being deceived.**

<u>Titus 3:3</u> (emphasis added)

For we also once were foolish ourselves, disobedient, **deceived,** enslaved to various lusts and pleasures, spending our life in malice and envy, hateful, hating one another.

<u>James 1:14–16</u> (emphasis added)

[14] But each one is tempted when he is carried away and enticed by his own lust. [15] Then when lust has conceived, it gives birth to sin; and when sin is accomplished, it brings forth death. [16] **Do not be deceived**, my beloved brethren.

<u>James 1:26</u> (emphasis added)

If anyone thinks himself to be religious, and yet does not bridle his tongue but **deceives his own heart,** this man's religion is worthless.

Cleverly worded false teaching that deceives and leads people astray from the pure Word will abound particularly in these last days. In His incarnation, Jesus repeatedly warned against the dangers of deception in the times surrounding the great tribulation. Further details regarding the level of deception that will prevail in the days of the antichrist appear in 2 Thessalonians and Revelation:

<u>2 Thessalonians 2:8–10</u> (emphasis added)

[8] Then that lawless one will be revealed …; [9] that is, **the one whose coming is in accord with the activity of Satan, with all power and signs and false wonders,** [10] **and with all the deception of wickedness** for those who perish, because they did not receive the love of the truth so as to be saved.

<u>Revelation 12:9</u> (emphasis added)

And the great dragon was thrown down, the serpent of old who is called the devil and **Satan, who deceives the whole world**; he was thrown down to the earth, and his angels were thrown down with him.

<u>Revelation 13:14</u> (emphasis added)

And **he** [the false prophet] **deceives** those who dwell on the earth because of the signs which it was given him to perform in the presence of the beast, telling those who dwell on the earth to make an image to the beast who had the wound of the sword and has come to life.

<u>Revelation 18:23–24</u> (emphasis added)

[23] **All the nations were deceived by your sorcery.** [24] And in her was found the blood of prophets and of saints and of all who have been slain on the earth.

<u>Revelation 19:20</u> (emphasis added)

And the beast was seized, and with him the false prophet who performed the signs in his presence, by which **he deceived those who had received the mark of the beast and those who worshiped his image**; these two were thrown alive into the lake of fire which burns with brimstone.

<u>Revelation 20:7–10</u> (emphasis added)

[7] When the thousand years are completed, Satan will be released from his prison, [8] and will come out **to deceive the nations which are in the four corners of the earth**, Gog and Magog, to gather them together for the war; the number of them is like the sand of the seashore. [9] And they came up on the broad plain of the earth and surrounded the camp of the saints and the beloved city, and fire came down from heaven and devoured them. [10] And **the devil who deceived them** was thrown into the lake of fire and brimstone, where the beast and the false prophet are also; and they will be tormented day and night forever and ever.

Returning to the warnings of Jesus Himself, the most dire description of deception appears in Matthew 24:24:

For false Christs and false prophets will arise and will show great signs and wonders, **so as to mislead, if possible, even the elect.**

> Parallel in Mark 13:22.

Any Christian who thinks he or she doesn't have to take that warning to heart simply because of the phrase "if possible," *deceives* himself or herself. Consider the following:

- the fact that the false prophet will perform the same signs and wonders that Moses and Elijah worked, such as calling down fire from heaven,

- the breakneck speed of technology and AI, allegedly all for the purpose of making our lives simpler, easier, and "safer,"
- the intense governmental and social pressure, including the loss of jobs and social isolation, that was placed on every American to take the COVID-19 shot because it was "safe and effective" but proved to be neither,
- the vanishing of all privacy in the home as well as in public spaces,
- the tracking of the movements of people through closed-circuit television (CCTV) cameras on street corners, Ring® doorbells on homes, Real ID drivers' licenses, and all purchases not made with cash.

This short list, hardly exhaustive, should be enough to send Christians scurrying to their Bibles to saturate themselves in the Word in order to learn to discern direction and guidance from God the Holy Spirit. The coming times are going to be beyond dangerous to our souls as well as our bodies. We are in no fit condition to deal with the level of deception that is well on its way. We need to

- stop being "children, tossed here and there by waves and carried about by every wind of doctrine, by the trickery of men, by craftiness in deceitful scheming" (Eph. 4:14),
- "grow up in all aspects into Him, who is the head, even Christ" (Eph. 4:15),
- learn how "to stand firm against the schemes of the devil" (Eph. 6:11), and
- "take up the full armor of God," so that we "will be able to resist in the evil day" (Eph. 6:13).

Conclusion: As world and national events accelerate toward the fulfillment of the prophecies of the very last days, we Christians need to grow in sanctification. We cannot afford the luxury of watching the exponential growth of tracking devices and the increasing violence, antisemitism, and—before long—anti-Christian movements, thinking that these are all just signs that we will be "out of here" very soon. We cannot afford to be deceived.

3. The purpose of sanctification/purification is to make the believer more Christlike

Sanctification is the ongoing work of God the Holy Spirit in the life of the believer. Some examples of His work include the following:

- He convicts the believer when he or she sins.

- He brings to the believer's remembrance a verse or doctrine to guide him or her when necessary.

- He illuminates the Scripture when the believer reads or studies.

- He intercedes for the believer and guides his or her prayers.

- He calls to the believer's mind the name or circumstances of another in need.

The sanctifying work of God the Holy Spirit requires the full cooperation of the believer. One who consistently tunes out or ignores His "still small voice" (1 Kings 19:12 KJV) will find it more difficult to sense His direction. Conversely, one who invests time in Bible study and prayer will find that he or she is more sensitive to His voice.

Just as Paul, at the end of his life, called himself "the chief sinner" (1 Tim. 1:15 KJV), we can become more and more aware of our sins, even as we (hopefully) sin less often.

Often sanctification makes the most progress when the believer undergoes trials and testing of various sorts. It is an unfortunate fact that we humans rarely learn life's lessons from others' mistakes; we learn better in the school of hard knocks. Our spiritual muscles must be exercised and tested regularly in order for us to grow stronger spiritually. Indeed, resisting temptation and enduring trials require both spiritual discipline and dependent reliance upon the inexhaustible resources of God.

Believers who are spiritually lazy and undisciplined remain weak and are thus unprepared to deal with troubles when they come. Such people think they are self-sufficient but find out otherwise when they have not disciplined themselves to invest in Bible study and prayer—not only are they unable to discern direction from the Holy Spirit but they also don't know how to lean on the Lord for His strength.

The goal of spiritual growth and maturity is undoubtedly one of the reasons we are admonished to rejoice when we are tried:

James 1:2–4

² Consider it all joy, my brethren, when you encounter various trials, ³ knowing that the testing of your faith produces endurance. ⁴ And let endurance have its perfect result, so that you may be perfect and complete, lacking in nothing.

In short, the process of sanctification, the purifying of believers, is a work of God the Holy Spirit; the role of the believer is to submit to the sanctifying trials and disciplines with the proper attitude of submission and cooperation—and, perhaps, even with rejoicing.

The following verses from both the Old and New Testaments testify to the purposes of God in either sending trials or allowing persecution at the hands of the world:

Deuteronomy 8:5 (emphasis added)

Thus you are to know in your heart that the Lord your **God was disciplining you just as a man disciplines his son.**

Psalm 94:12 (emphasis added)

Blessed is the man **whom You chasten**, O Lord, and whom You teach out of Your law.

Proverbs 3:11–13 (emphasis added)

¹¹ My son, do not reject the discipline of the Lord
Or loathe His reproof,
¹² For **whom the Lord loves He reproves,**
Even as a father corrects the son in whom he delights.

Jeremiah 30:11 (emphasis added)

"For I am with you," declares the LORD, "to save you;
For I will destroy completely all the nations where I have scattered you,
Only I will not destroy you completely.
But I will chasten you justly
And will by no means leave you unpunished."

John 15:1–2 (emphasis added)

¹ I am the true vine, and My Father is the vinedresser. ² Every branch in Me that does not bear fruit, He takes away; and **every branch that bears fruit, He prunes it so that it may bear more fruit.**

Romans 8:16–18 (emphasis added)

¹⁶ The Spirit Himself testifies with our spirit that we are children of God, ¹⁷ and if children, heirs also, heirs of God and fellow heirs with Christ, **if indeed we suffer with Him so that we may also be glorified with Him.** ¹⁸ **For I consider that the sufferings of this present time are not worthy to be compared with the glory that is to be revealed to us.**

Romans 8:29 (emphasis added)

For those whom He foreknew, He also predestined to **become conformed to the image of His Son,** so that He would be the firstborn among many brethren.

1 Corinthians 11:32 (emphasis added)

But when we are judged, **we are disciplined by the Lord so that we will not be condemned along with the world.**

2 Corinthians 3:18 (emphasis added)

But we all, with unveiled face, beholding as in a mirror the glory of the Lord, are being **transformed into the same image** from glory to glory, just as from the Lord, the Spirit.

<u>2 Corinthians 4:16–17</u> (emphasis added)

[16] Therefore we do not lose heart, but though our outer man is decaying, yet **our inner man is being renewed day by day.** [17] **For momentary, light affliction is producing for us an eternal weight of glory far beyond all comparison.**

<u>Hebrews 12:5–11</u> (emphasis added)

[5] And you have forgotten the exhortation which is addressed to you as sons,

"My son, do not regard lightly the discipline of the Lord,

Nor faint when you are reproved by Him;

[6] For **those whom the Lord loves He disciplines,**

And He scourges every son whom He receives."

[7] **It is for discipline that you endure; God deals with you as with sons; for what son is there whom his father does not discipline?** [8] But if you are without discipline, of which all have become partakers, then you are illegitimate children and not sons. [9] Furthermore, we had earthly fathers to discipline us, and we respected them; shall we not much rather be subject to the Father of spirits, and live? [10] For they disciplined us for a short time as seemed best to them, but **He disciplines us for our good, so that we may share His holiness.** [11] **All discipline for the moment seems not to be joyful, but sorrowful; yet to those who have been trained by it, afterwards it yields the peaceful fruit of righteousness.**

<u>Revelation 3:19</u> (church of Laodicea, emphasis added)

Those whom I love, I reprove and discipline; therefore be zealous and repent.

Conclusion: Many Christians believe that the church will not need to go into the seventieth week of Daniel and suffer the unprecedented horrors of the great tribulation because, as Christians, we are already being sanctified. But who is worthy to decide what trials and what level of suffering are sufficient to cleanse the believer individually and the church corporately? Surely not the believer! We ignore the Bible's warnings at our own peril.

4. The American church is not even close to being a pure bride who has "no spot or wrinkle or any such thing" but is "holy and blameless" (Eph. 5:27)

Consider the current condition of the church in America. I am not knowledgeable enough to comment on the condition of the church elsewhere, beyond knowing that most countries in Europe are slightly further along the path of apostasy than America and hearing that the persecuted church in China is exploding. But I can comment on American churches. As a general rule (there are always a few exceptions), most churches in America are, at best, lukewarm. Their members are wealthy (by the world's standards) and utterly self-sufficient, with no need for or dependence upon God for anything.

Many mainstream denominations are so worldly that they are not even identifiable as Christian. They have utterly abandoned the Bible as the authoritative Word of God and are making up their own rules for their new "religion," which for some perverse reason, they insist on continuing to identify as Christian.

Most churches in America could at best be considered like the church in Laodicea, and many could be seen as comparable to the churches in Sardis and Thyatira. Jesus described these three churches:

1. Laodicea: Revelation 3:15–19 (emphasis added)

> [15] I know your deeds, that you are neither cold nor hot; I would that you were cold or hot. [16] So because **you are lukewarm**, and neither hot nor cold, I will spit you out of My mouth. [17] Because you say, "I am rich, and have become wealthy, and have need of nothing," and **you do not know that you are wretched and miserable and poor and blind and naked,** [18] I advise you to buy from Me gold refined by fire so that you may become rich, and white garments so that you may clothe yourself, and that the shame of your nakedness may not be revealed; and eye salve to anoint your eyes so that you may see. [19] Those whom I love, I reprove and discipline; therefore be zealous and repent.

2. Sardis: Revelation 3:1–3 (emphasis added)

    [1] I know your deeds, that you have a name that you are alive, but **you are dead**. [2] Wake up, and strengthen the things that remain, which were about to die; for **I have not found your deeds completed in the sight of My God**. [3] So remember what you have received and heard; and keep it, and repent. **Therefore if you do not wake up, I will come like a thief, and you will not know at what hour I will come to you.**

3. Thyatira: Revelation 2:20–23 (emphasis added)

    [20] But I have this against you, that you **tolerate the woman Jezebel, who calls herself a prophetess, and she teaches and leads My bond-servants astray so that they commit acts of immorality and eat things sacrificed to idols**. [21] I gave her time to repent, and she does not want to repent of her immorality. [22] Behold, **I will throw her on a bed of sickness, and those who commit adultery with her into great tribulation,** unless they repent of her deeds. [23] And **I will kill her children with pestilence**, and all the churches will know that I am He who searches the minds and hearts; and **I will give to each one of you according to your deeds**.

Many American churches are simply dead, like the church in Sardis. The members go through the motions, but their work is not the fruit of salvation, not "good works, which God prepared beforehand so that we would walk in them" (Eph. 2:10). Instead, their works are human in origin and in execution. They have "programs" for all ages and modern music bands—complete with light shows—that perform and entertain, but God the Holy Spirit is not there.

Other churches in America, like the church in Thyatira, have allowed the spirit of Jezebel to overtake and overpower the few true believers present. Sexual immorality among the leaders and teachers is common and accepted as normal. The gospel is focused on human desires rather than on God's commandments. God is love, the members are told, so He wants you to have your heart's desire (a complete misreading of

Ps. 37:4, "Delight yourself in the Lord / And He will give you the desires of your heart").

Despite the presence of the characteristics of the churches at Sardis and Thyatira, I think the Laodicean church comes closest to the condition of the majority of so-called Christian churches in America today. As a general rule, American Christians are well-off financially. Compared to the vast majority of the rest of the world, they are rich. And even if American Christians are not really wealthy, we live as if we were, spending on credit as if there were no tomorrow. Whatever we desire, we get, one way or another. We ignore the wisdom of Agur, the writer of Proverbs 30:

Proverbs 30:7–9

⁷ Two things I asked of You,
Do not refuse me before I die:
⁸ Keep deception and lies far from me,
Give me neither poverty nor riches;
Feed me with the food that is my portion,
⁹ That I not be full and deny You and say, "Who is the Lord?"
Or that I not be in want and steal,
And profane the name of my God.

Conclusion: In this state, is the American church a bride fit for Christ by any stretch of the imagination?

5. Judgment begins with the household of God

In the context of how Christians ought to respond to trials, Peter wrote of the judgment of the household of God:

1 Peter 4:12–19 (emphasis added)

¹² Beloved, do not be surprised at the **fiery ordeal** among you, which comes upon you **for your testing**, as though some strange thing were happening to you; ¹³ but **to the degree that you share the sufferings of Christ, keep on rejoicing**, so that also at the revelation of His glory you may rejoice with exultation. ¹⁴ **If you are

reviled for the name of Christ, you are blessed, because the Spirit of glory and of God rests on you. [15] Make sure that none of you suffers as a murderer, or thief, or evildoer, or a troublesome meddler; [16] **but if anyone suffers as a Christian, he is not to be ashamed, but is to glorify God in this name.** [17] *For it is time for judgment to begin with the household of God; and if it begins with us first, what will be the outcome for those who do not obey the gospel of God*? [18] And if it is with difficulty that the righteous is saved, what will become of the godless man and the sinner? [19] Therefore, **those also who suffer according to the will of God shall entrust their souls to a faithful Creator in doing what is right.**

The prewrath position holds that the great tribulation (the fifth seal of Revelation 6) is the Lord's judgment of His household. Indeed, it is probable that all of the first five seals are final tests sent by God through human agency. While tyrannical dictators, war, famine, and pestilence (or death by any of the above means) are truly terrible, God has allowed them or sent them throughout human history. But His tests, including this final judgment of His household in the great tribulation, serve opposing purposes.

Just as the same sun that melts the wax also hardens the clay, so the same destructive events of the great tribulation will have two opposite outcomes, based on people's responses. Some will soften their hearts in repentance, learn to rely solely upon God, and be purified. Others will harden their hearts in anger, hostility, and rebellion against God; for them, the effect of the same destructive events will be punitive. One's character as wheat or tare will be manifested. Thus God will allow the trials of the great tribulation to serve two purposes at the same time: (1) to purify and cleanse the maturing wheat and (2) to expose the tares that were disguised as wheat.

Ezekiel 14 provides an example of the same sort of judgment, one in which all Israel was going to suffer persecution because of widespread idolatry. God's purpose was to punish the majority of the nation and, at the same time, to purify the righteous by testing their faith.

Beginning in Ezekiel 14:6, the Lord calls upon the people of Israel to "repent and turn away from your idols and turn your faces away from all your abominations." Then, in the passage below, the Lord lists the sword, famine, wild beasts, and plague as his judgments:

Ezekiel 14:21–23

[21] For thus says the Lord GOD, "How much more when I send My four severe judgments against Jerusalem: sword, famine, wild beasts and plague to cut off man and beast from it! [22] Yet, behold, survivors will be left in it who will be brought out, both sons and daughters. Behold, they are going to come forth to you and you will see their conduct and actions; then you will be comforted for the calamity which I have brought against Jerusalem for everything which I have brought upon it. [23] Then they will comfort you when you see their conduct and actions, for you will know that I have not done in vain whatever I did to it," declares the Lord GOD.

Notice the parallels between the four types of judgment listed here in Ezekiel and the first four seals of Revelation 6:

- The rider of the first horse (Rev. 6:1–2) represents the antichrist, who is called a "beast" in Revelation 13; this parallels the wild beasts of Ezekiel 14.

- The second horse (Rev. 6:3–4) represents war; the sword is mentioned both here and in Ezekiel 14.

- The third horse (Rev. 6:5–6) represents food shortages; this is the famine of Ezekiel 14.

- The fourth horse (Rev. 6:7–8) represents death. Pestilence or plague is mentioned in Luke 21:11, which parallels the seals of Revelation, and plague is listed in Ezekiel 14 as well.

But, after listing the terrifying judgments that He is going to impose upon Israel, the Lord reassures Ezekiel that He will preserve a remnant of survivors who will have been purified through the judgments. That purification will be apparent from "their conduct and actions."

Conclusion: As God has done with His people in past times, He will use the great tribulation to cleanse and purify His church. This intense time of extreme testing will have two outcomes: For some it will be purifying and redemptive; for others, it will be judicial and punitive. While both the righteous and the unrighteous will suffer during the breaking and opening of the seals, their response to the hardship represented by each of the seals will determine the outcome. For those who belong to Christ, the unprecedented trial will bring to their minds passages such as those listed in appendix A on expected tribulation. They will recognize that their faith is being tested, and they will prove that their faith, "being more precious than gold which is perishable, even though tested by fire, may be found to result in praise and glory and honor at the revelation of Jesus Christ" (1 Peter 1:7). These believers will not "be overcome by evil but [will] overcome evil with good" (Rom. 12:21).

D. The prewrath rapture position is based upon the belief that the rapture will occur just prior to the commencement of the day of the Lord

The prewrath rapture position holds that the wrath from which believers are spared is not only the eternal wrath that comes at physical death to unbelievers but is also the final outpouring of God's wrath on the nations in the day of the Lord.

According to the prewrath position, the day of the Lord not only does *not* fill the entire seven years of the seventieth week but consists of a time period that begins *toward the end* of the seventieth week when, according to Matthew 24:22, the Lord will cut short the days of the great tribulation for the sake of the elect. At that point, He will gather His own together in the rapture, and the day of the Lord will commence immediately thereafter.

The chronology presented in both Matthew 24 and Revelation 6:9–8:2 is the same:

- Beginning with the abomination of desolation by the antichrist at the midpoint of the seven years of Daniel's seventieth week, the antichrist will initiate the great tribulation.

- The days of the great tribulation will be cut short by the Lord. (Note that the days of *the seventieth week* continue to the end; all that is cut short are the days of *the great tribulation*.)

- At that point, right after the sixth seal (cosmic disturbances), He will gather His people from the four winds (meaning from all over the world) and take them—both the many who have died and the few who lived until His arrival—to heaven.

- According to Revelation 8, when He breaks the seventh seal, there will be silence in heaven for a while, and then the trumpet judgments of the great day of the Lord will herald the onset of the pouring out of God's wrath upon the unrepentant nations.

1. THERE ARE DIFFERENCES AND SIMILARITIES BETWEEN PRETRIBULATIONISM AND THE PREWRATH POSITION

The chart below conveniently compares the views of pretribulationism and the prewrath position.

Pretribulationism	Prewrath Position
Pillar 1: All seven years are tribulation.	The first three and a half years are "the beginning of birth pangs." The second three and a half years are the "great tribulation."
Pillar 2: All seven years are also the wrath of the day of the Lord (i.e., tribulation = wrath).	The day of the Lord does not begin until Jesus cuts short the days of the great tribulation sometime in the second half.
Pillar 3: Believers are spared from the wrath of the day of the Lord.	Believers are spared from the wrath of the day of the Lord.
Pillar 4: The rapture is imminent.	The rapture will be preceded by signs.

2. There are problems even with the prewrath position

(a) If the rapture is modelled on Jewish betrothal and marriage, the pattern is not followed

When a Jewish father gave his daughter in marriage, the process began with a betrothal of approximately a year. At the time of the betrothal, the couple was considered legally married, and if the groom wanted out of the deal before the actual wedding, he was required to get a divorce. During that year of betrothal, the young woman stayed a virgin in her father's house while the young man built a house for the couple. When the groom's father deemed the house completed, the groom led a procession of his family and friends at the end of the day to the house of his bride to collect her, her family, and her friends. The whole procession would then set out to the couple's new home for the marriage supper. The path would be lit with oil lamps held by the wedding guests. After that, the couple was allowed to consummate the marriage and live together. During the betrothal and for the first year of their marriage, the new husband was to focus on establishing his marriage:

Deuteronomy 20:7

And who is the man that is engaged to a woman and has not married her? Let him depart and return to his house, otherwise he might die in the battle and another man would marry her.

Deuteronomy 24:5

When a man takes a new wife, he shall not go out with the army nor be charged with any duty; he shall be free at home one year and shall give happiness to his wife whom he has taken.

Many Christians have likened the rapture to the groom's procession to collect his bride. Before His crucifixion, resurrection, and ascension, Jesus told His followers:

<u>John 14:2–3</u> (emphasis added)

² In My Father's house are many dwelling places; if it were not so, I would have told you; for **I go to prepare a place for you**. ³ **If I go and prepare a place for you, I will come again and receive you to Myself; that where I am, there you may be also.**

This sounds very much like the period of the betrothal in which the groom would build the house for the couple. Then 1 Thessalonians 4:16–17 describes His procession to claim His bride:

¹⁶ For the Lord Himself will descend from heaven with a shout, with the voice of the archangel and with the trumpet of God, and the dead in Christ will rise first. ¹⁷ Then we who are alive and remain will be caught up together with them in the clouds to meet the Lord in the air, and **so we shall always be with the Lord**. (emphasis added)

In both of these passages, believers are assured that where Jesus is, there believers will also be, and "so we shall always be with the Lord."

What's wrong with this picture? In pretribulationism, midtribulationism, *and even* the prewrath rapture position, as soon as Jesus has collected His bride and taken her home to heaven, He immediately leaves her to go to war against the nations in the day of the Lord—in direct contravention of the passages in Deuteronomy!

Some have dealt with this obvious problem by concluding that the actual marriage feast does not occur directly after the rapture but later, after the day of the Lord. But if Revelation 19 is read chronologically, verse 7 ("the marriage of the Lamb has come and His bride has made herself ready") precedes His eruption out of heaven on the white horse (v. 11), with the "sharp sword, so that with it He may strike down the nations" (v. 15).

Others have concluded that the rapture will occur on the first day of the Feast of Trumpets—that is, on Rosh Hashanah (a day known only to God, since the current Jewish calendar is not the same as the one used in Jesus's day). On that day, after the rapture, the day of the Lord will begin and will last for one year and ten days, at the end of which time—on Yom Kippur—the seventieth week will end. That allows God the Son to have His allotted year with His bride while God the Father is pouring out His wrath in the day of the Lord.

Then at the end of that year, God the Son will erupt out of heaven on His white horse (Rev. 19:11–21) for the final battle. The only problem I have with this possible explanation is that Revelation 6:16 speaks of "the wrath of the Lamb," which indicates that His role is instrumental in the entire day of the Lord, not in just the final battle.

(b) Some Bible verses indicate that the church will be present even in the day of the Lord

Like pretribulationism (as well as midtribulationism), the prewrath position is overshadowed by verses that do not fit into the paradigm, such as those below.

(1) Isaiah 26:19–21

[19] Your dead will live;
Their corpses will rise.
You who lie in the dust, awake and shout for joy,
For your dew is as the dew of the dawn,
And the earth will give birth to the departed spirits.
[20] Come, my people, enter into your rooms
And close your doors behind you;
Hide for a little while
Until **indignation** runs its course.
[21] For behold, the Lord is about to come out from His place
To punish the inhabitants of the earth for their iniquity;
And the earth will reveal her bloodshed
And will no longer cover her slain. (emphasis added)

The operative question here is whether "indignation" refers to the great tribulation or to the day of the Lord.

Isaiah 26:19 sounds like a description of the rapture, particularly since verse 21 describes the day of the Lord.

If the intervening verse 20 is about the great tribulation, during which believers will have to hide to avoid persecution and execution at the hands of the antichrist, then the order of events is rapture, great tribulation, and the day of the Lord. The problem is that then there must be two raptures: (1) pretribulation and (2) at the end of the great tribulation, as described in Revelation 7:9–17.

> Section V.B.2 above addresses that impossibility.

But in order to support the prewrath position, the order of verses 19 and 20 should be reversed.

A counterargument could be advanced, however, that the indignation refers to God's wrath in the day of the Lord, but that He will supernaturally provide His own people divine protection during that time, as exemplified by the sealing of the 144,000 Jews just prior to the onset of the day of the Lord.

(2) Psalm 30:4–5

⁴ Sing praise to the LORD, you His godly ones
And give thanks to His holy name.
⁵ For **His anger** is but for a moment,
His favor is for a lifetime;
Weeping may last for the night,
But a shout of joy comes in the morning. (emphasis added)

Once more, the question here is whether "His anger" refers to the final wrath of the day of the Lord or only to the great tribulation. A third option is that the answer is neither of the above, but rather that it refers only to His chastening or discipline or temporal punishment in this lifetime.

(3) Ezekiel 9:4–6

⁴ The LORD said to him, "Go through the midst of the city, even through the midst of Jerusalem, and put a mark on the foreheads of the men who sigh and groan over all the abominations which are being committed in its midst." ⁵ But to the others He said in my hearing, "Go through the city after him and strike; do not let your

eye have pity and do not spare. ⁶ Utterly slay old men, young men, maidens, little children, and women, but do not touch any man on whom is the mark; and you shall start from My sanctuary." So they started with the elders who were before the temple.

This is clearly a passage of judgment. No indication is given in this passage that those who were not slain were spared the horror of watching unbelieving friends and even family members being struck down. They seem to have been present.

(4) Zephaniah 2:3

Seek the Lord,
All you humble of the earth
Who have carried out His ordinances;
Seek righteousness, seek humility.
Perhaps you will be hidden
In the day of the Lord's anger.

Once more, the question is whether "the Lord's anger" is the final wrath. A stronger argument can be made in this case that the day of the Lord is indeed indicated because the text itself says, "in *the day of the Lord's anger*" (emphasis added).

I am also including in this category of passages with unclear timing a New Testament passage that I discussed earlier:

(5) 1 Thessalonians 5:1–4

¹ Now as to the times and the epochs, brethren, you have no need of anything to be written to you. ² For you yourselves know full well that the day of the Lord will come just like a thief in the night. ³ While they are saying, "Peace and safety!" then destruction will come upon them suddenly like labor pains upon a woman with child, and they will not escape. ⁴ But you, brethren, are not in darkness, **that the day should overtake you like a thief.** (emphasis added)

To reemphasize what I said above in section IV.D.10, this passage in 1 Thessalonians 5 leaves open the possibility that believers, having been forewarned about the day of the Lord, may still be present on earth during that time but will endure and overcome, with God's protection and provision. The point of the open question, however, is that the rapture will not have yet occurred.

(6) OTHER BIBLICAL EXAMPLES

Finally, I would reiterate three points made earlier:

1. Although Noah and his family were sheltered from the terrifying wrath of God during the flood, they had to live through it. They were not spared the experience.

2. The first Passover is another example of God's people being present but protected in the midst of the outpouring of God's divine wrath:

   <u>Exodus 12:22–23</u> (emphasis added)

   ²² You shall take a bunch of hyssop and dip it in the blood which is in the basin, and apply some of the blood that is in the basin to the lintel and the two doorposts; and none of you shall go outside the door of his house until morning. ²³ For the LORD will pass through to smite the Egyptians; and **when He sees the blood on the lintel and on the two doorposts, the LORD will pass over the door and will not allow the destroyer to come in to your houses to smite you.**

3. The day of the Lord is the period of time at or near the end of human history when God judges *the nations*, and since nations are made up of people, it is the people of the nations who will suffer.

   > See appendix E for biblical passages showing that the day of the Lord is a time when the Lord will judge the nations.

Conclusion: The point of this section is to point out that, of the current positions on the timing of the rapture—pretribulation, midtribulation, posttribulation, and prewrath—not one can claim that there are no verses in the Bible that contradict its position. While I have taken the prewrath position, I am compelled to acknowledge that there are verses in the Bible that I cannot reconcile with it. Nevertheless, my purpose in writing this book was to warn Christians about the dangers associated with pretribulationism, because I am convinced that the church will go into the great tribulation.

Section VI

"THE LAST DAY"

IS "THE LAST DAY" THE MILLENNIUM?

The last day is different from the *day of the Lord*, and it is also different from *the last days*.

The day of the Lord is a period of time in which God will execute His final judgment of the nations and unrepentant sinners.

The phrase *the last days* (plural) refers to the period of time between the first and second comings of Jesus Christ. We have been in the last days for approximately two thousand years now. The writers of the New Testament called the time in which they were writing "the last days." An example appears in Hebrews 1:1–2 (emphasis added):

> [1] God, after He spoke long ago to the fathers in the prophets in many portions and in many ways, [2] **in these last days** has spoken to us in His Son, whom He appointed heir of all things, through whom also He made the world.

The phrase *the last day* (singular) appears four times in John 6 and once each in John 11 and 12. (It also appears in John 7, but the context there is the last day of the Feast of Tabernacles.)

An examination of these verses from John follows.

A. The resurrection of the dead is associated with "the last day"

John 6:39 (emphasis added)

This is the will of Him who sent Me, that of all that He has given Me I lose nothing, but **raise it up on the last day.**"

John 6:40 (emphasis added)

For this is the will of My Father, that everyone who beholds the Son and believes in Him will have eternal life, and **I Myself will raise him up on the last day.**

John 6:44 (emphasis added)

No one can come to Me unless the Father who sent Me draws him; and **I will raise him up on the last day.**

John 6:54 (emphasis added)

He who eats My flesh and drinks My blood has eternal life, and **I will raise him up on the last day.**

John 11:24 (emphasis added)

Martha said to Him, "**I know that he will rise again in the resurrection on the last day.**"

John 12:48 (emphasis added)

He who rejects Me and does not receive My sayings, has one who judges him; **the word I spoke is what will judge him at the last day.**"

The focus in these passages in John is on the resurrection of all those who have believed in Jesus and on the judgment of those who have rejected Him. It appears that those who rejected Him are also resurrected and then judged. In John 5:28–29, Jesus said,

[28] An hour is coming, in which all who are in the tombs will hear His voice, [29] and will come forth; those who did the good deeds

to **a resurrection of life**, those who committed the evil deeds to **a resurrection of judgment**. (emphasis added)

If the resurrection of the dead is associated with this "last day," is it a literal twenty-four-hour day? Or is it a period of time, like the day of the Lord? Or is it the full one thousand years of the millennium?

Several New Testament passages rule out a literal twenty-four-hour day by indicating that there will be stages of resurrection:

<u>1 Corinthians 15:20–26</u> (emphasis added)

[20] But now **Christ has been raised from the dead, the first fruits of those who are asleep.** [21] For since by a man came death, by a man also came the resurrection of the dead. [22] For as in Adam all die, so also in Christ all will be made alive. [23] But **each in his own order: Christ the first fruits, after that those who are Christ's at His coming,** [24] then comes the end, when He hands over the kingdom to the God and Father, when He has abolished all rule and all authority and power. [25] For He must reign until He has put all His enemies under His feet. [26] The last enemy that will be abolished is death.

<u>Revelation 20:4–6</u> (emphasis added)

[4] Then I saw thrones, and they sat on them, and judgment was given to them. And I saw the souls of those who had been beheaded because of their testimony of Jesus and because of the word of God, and those who had not worshiped the beast or his image, and had not received the mark on their forehead and on their hand; and **they came to life and reigned with Christ for a thousand years. [5] The rest of the dead did not come to life until the thousand years were completed. This is the first resurrection. [6] Blessed and holy is the one who has a part in the first resurrection;** over these the second death has no power, but they will be priests of God and of Christ and **will reign with Him for a thousand years.**

<u>Revelation 20:7, 11–15</u> (emphasis added)

[7] **When the thousand years are completed,** …

> [11] I saw a great white throne and Him who sat upon it, from whose presence earth and heaven fled away, and no place was found for them. [12] And **I saw the dead, the great and the small, standing before the throne,** and books were opened; and another book was opened, which is the book of life; and the **dead were judged from the things which were written in the books, according to their deeds.** [13] **And the sea gave up the dead which were in it, and death and Hades gave up the dead which were in them; and they were judged, every one of them according to their deeds.** [14] Then death and Hades were thrown into the lake of fire. This is the second death, the lake of fire. [15] And if anyone's name was not found written in the book of life, he was thrown into the lake of fire.

Since these passages describe resurrections at varying times, including the beginning and the end of the millennium, does that mean that "the last day" could span the entire one thousand years of the millennium? It is possible.

One of the purposes of the millennium might be the final and complete fulfillment of all of God's commands. Because the Bible tells us that not one jot or tittle of God's word will fail, all His commands will be fulfilled—and if not by the first Adam, then by the second. According to Matthew 5:17–18, Jesus declared,

> [17] Do not think that I came to abolish the Law or the Prophets; I did not come to abolish, but to fulfill. [18] For truly I say to you, until heaven and earth pass away, not the smallest letter or stroke shall pass from the Law until all is accomplished.

The KJV reads,

> [17] Think not that I am come to destroy the law, or the prophets: I am not come to destroy, but to fulfil. [18] For verily I say unto you, Till heaven and earth pass, one jot or one tittle shall in no wise pass from the law, till all be fulfilled.

The first Adam did not obey God's command to replenish the earth and subdue it (Gen. 1:26–28), but the second Adam will, during His millennial reign.

Conclusion: Since the Bible describes the resurrection of the dead happening at varying times, it is clear that "the last day" must be more than a twenty-four-hour day. Because Revelation 20 delineates resurrections both at the beginning and at the end of the millennium, some Christians have concluded that "the last day" is a reference to the millennium.

B. There are differing opinions regarding the age of the creation

Because the Bible records that God created the earth in six days and rested on the seventh day, some Christians believe that it means that God has a six-thousand-year plan for mankind that will be followed by a one-thousand-year reign of Christ.

Most timeline charts based on biblical genealogies suggest the following spans of time:

- Two thousand years from Adam to Abraham
- Two thousand years from Abraham to Jesus
- Two thousand years since Jesus
- One-thousand-year millennium

Obviously, this timeline conflicts with today's science, which projects a creation date back billions of years rather than mere thousands.

Those who espouse the six-thousand-year plan for mankind, followed by the millennial reign of Christ, point to two verses in particular for support:

Psalm 90:4

For a thousand years in Your sight
Are like yesterday when it passes by,
Or as a watch in the night.

2 Peter 3:8

But do not let this one fact escape your notice, beloved, that with the Lord one day is like a thousand years, and a thousand years like one day.

In addition, the author of Hebrews 3–4 discusses entering into God's "rest." The first generation of Hebrews to come out of Egypt in the Exodus failed to enter into God's rest—represented by the promised land—because of their unbelief and disobedience at the threshold of entering. And yet even the second generation, which did enter into the promised land under the leadership of Joshua, also did not enter into that "rest":

Hebrews 4:8–11

[8] For if Joshua had given them rest, He would not have spoken of another day after that. [9] So there remains a Sabbath rest for the people of God. [10] For the one who has entered His rest has himself also rested from his works, as God did from His. [11] Therefore, let us be diligent to enter that rest, so that no one will fall, through following the same example of disobedience.

These verses depict a future seventh-day rest, just as God rested after the six days of creation. If "the last *day*" of human history, before the new heavens and the new earth are inaugurated, will be Jesus's millennial kingdom, it follows that the prior six "days" were six thousand years of fallen mankind's governance of the earth (under the oversight of the "prince of the power of the air," according to Eph. 2:2). The Bible paints a chiaroscuro that juxtaposes the darkness of Satan's rule with the light of the millennial kingdom under the rule of the risen Christ.

Since the time of the fall of Adam, even the created order suffers:

Romans 8:19–22 (emphasis added)

[19] For the anxious longing of the creation waits eagerly for the revealing of the sons of God. [20] For **the creation was subjected to futility**, not willingly, but because of Him who subjected it, **in hope** [21] **that the creation itself also will be set free from its slavery to corruption into the freedom of the glory of the children of God.** [22] For we know that **the whole creation groans and suffers the pains of childbirth together until now.**

In stark contrast, Isaiah describes the golden life of people in the millennial kingdom in several passages. Most of these also depict, in one way or another, the created order set free from its slavery to corruption, rejoicing, and at rest.

Isaiah 11:1–10 depicts Jesus Christ ruling with righteousness, the wolf lying down with the lamb, and the nursing child playing by the hole of the cobra. The passage culminates with these verses:

Isaiah 11:9–10

⁹ They [the predatory animals] will not hurt or destroy in all My holy mountain,
For the earth will be full of the knowledge of the LORD
As the waters cover the sea.
¹⁰ Then in that day
The nations will resort to the root of Jesse,
Who will stand as a signal for the peoples;
And His resting place will be glorious.

Isaiah 14:7, regarding the Lord's victory over the "king of Babylon" [and Satan], adds,

The whole earth is at rest and is quiet;
They break forth into shouts of joy.

At the Lord's redemption of Israel, the earth and the heavens will celebrate:

Isaiah 44:23

Shout for joy, O heavens, for the LORD has done it!
Shout joyfully, you lower parts of the earth;
Break forth into a shout of joy, you mountains,
O forest, and every tree in it;
For the LORD has redeemed Jacob
And in Israel He shows forth His glory.

In chapter 49, Isaiah describes the land of Israel so full of families and children that there is hardly space for everyone. Israel's redemption and restoration will be as beautiful as a jewel-bedecked bride. Once more, the creation rejoices:

Isaiah 49:13

Shout for joy, O heavens! And rejoice, O earth!
Break forth into joyful shouting, O mountains!
For the LORD has comforted His people
And will have compassion on His afflicted.

Finally, in Isaiah 54–55, the Lord comforts Israel, as if she were a forsaken wife who has been restored. He invites all to seek Him, and His word will not return to Him empty. And again, the people and the created order will rejoice:

Isaiah 55:12–13

[12] For you will go out with joy
And be led forth with peace;
The mountains and the hills will break forth into shouts of joy before you,
And all the trees of the field will clap their hands.
[13] Instead of the thorn bush the cypress will come up,
And instead of the nettle the myrtle will come up,
And it will be a memorial to the LORD,
For an everlasting sign which will not be cut off.

Conclusion: These biblical portrayals of the golden life in the millennial kingdom are considered by many Christians to be the "seventh day" of human history, the time that Jesus designated "the last day."

There are two caveats, however:

1. It can be difficult to discern whether some of Isaiah's descriptions concern the millennium or the eternal state in the new heavens and earth.

2. One must consider the following:

   IF the millennium is "the last day," and

   IF all resurrections of the dead occur at varying times within that one thousand years,

THEN all rapture positions, except posttribulationism, are nullified.

C. What is the dispensationalist view of "the last day"?

Although not all dispensationalists espouse the young-earth view, many do affirm this shorter timeline of mankind's history because of the genealogical records in Genesis 5, 10, and 11, as well as those traced through 1 Chronicles, Matthew, and Luke. Equally important, dispensationalists understand that a belief in a young earth is consistent with a belief in the literal integrity of the Bible.

Based on the biblical references and the seven-thousand-year timeline listed above, many Christians, dispensationalist or not, have concluded that "the last day" is indeed the millennium and that there will be resurrections both at the beginning of that last day and at the end of that same time period.

There are, however, conflicts between this view and dispensational pretribulationism, which is the subject of this book:

IF the millennium, and the seventieth week which precedes it, are part of *Israel's* dispensation; and

IF the millennium is "the last day"; and

IF all resurrections occur at some point on this "last day," whether at the beginning or the end;

THEN this means that

- the rapture cannot occur prior to the onset of the millennium, much less prior to the seventieth week (the seven years preceding the millennium) because all resurrections must occur during the millennial "last day," and thus

- the church must go through the entire seven years of the seventieth week to get to the millennial "last day," when believers can be raptured and resurrected, and thus

- Christians (i.e., the church) will be raptured and resurrected during Israel's dispensation, and thus
- the church's dispensation has bled over into Israel's dispensation, and thus
- the church's dispensation cannot end until, at a minimum, the beginning of the millennium.

Note that this also nullifies the midtribulation and prewrath rapture positions; only the posttribulation view would fit. Thus, dispensationalists are left with these choices:

EITHER the millennium is *not* part of Israel's dispensation but is an extension of the church's dispensation (which means the prior seventieth week is also still the church's dispensation),

OR the millennium is *not* "the last day," when all resurrections occur,

OR the rapture is *not* a resurrection of the body; in other words, the rapture is something different from what Jesus was promising in John 6.

All three premises—the "if" statements listed earlier—cannot be true at the same time. The contradictions are addressed in different ways in the next two subsections.

1. SOME DISPENSATIONALISTS DISTINGUISH BETWEEN DIFFERENT CLASSES OF SAINTS, ASSIGNING THEM DIFFERENT RESURRECTION DATES

While advocates of the view that the millennium is "the last day" agree that the Bible indicates resurrections at various time, dispensationalists go further, distinguishing between which saints are resurrected at which times, based on which dispensation they lived in:

- Believers of the church age dispensation are the only recipients of Jesus's promise of John 6, and these are therefore the only ones resurrected at the rapture, which is prior to the beginning of the seventieth week, seven full years before the millennium ("the last day") begins.

- All Old Testament saints are resurrected at the end of the seventieth week (which is the beginning of the millennium, "the last day") along with the so-called tribulation saints—that is, people who will come to a saving faith during the seven years of the misnamed "tribulation period."

- All the unbelievers of all ages are raised at the end of the millennium—that is, at the end of "the last day."

In addition to the internal conflicts listed earlier, there are these inconsistencies:

- The problem with limiting the promise of John 6 to believers of the church age dispensation is that Jesus promised to raise them on "the last day,"—that is, the millennium—but dispensationalism has this very group of believers raptured out seven years *before* "the last day" begins.

- According to dispensationalism, the church age dispensation does not begin during Jesus's lifetime but goes only from Pentecost onward. This excludes from the rapture Mary and Martha and Lazarus and all other Jews and gentiles who came to faith during Jesus's lifetime, believers who actually heard His promise about resurrection on "the last day."

- Setting *the end* of the seventieth week as the time of the resurrection of those who come to faith ostensibly only during the seventieth week flatly contradicts Revelation 7:9–17, which explicitly depicts their resurrection *during* the seventieth week, just prior to the day of the Lord.

- Believers from the church age dispensation are treated differently from the believers from other so-called dispensations, a contradiction of the character of God, who shows no partiality.

  See section V.B.2.[e] above.

I could not find any dispensationalist who discussed what happens to all the humans who are born, live, and die during the millennium, whether they are believers or unbelievers.

2. THERE IS YET ANOTHER, VERY LIMITED, DISPENSATIONALIST VIEW OF "THE LAST DAY"

It should be noted that other dispensationalists redefine "the last day" to limit it to the *rapture only*, which would be seven years before the millennium. This limitation is based on the interpretation, mentioned above, that Jesus's promise of John 6 was made only to people who came to faith during the dispensation called the church age.

This adds another layer of contradiction: To be consistent with the limitation of the "last day" to the rapture only, these dispensationalists must conclude that the "last day" does not include the seventieth week or the millennium, directly contradicting, in the case of the millennium, the explicit language in Revelation 20 describing resurrections both at the beginning and at the end of the millennium.

3. DISPENSATIONALISTS OFFER A SOLUTION TO THE CONTRADICTIONS

Dispensationalism deals with most of these contradictions by expanding "the last day" to include the rapture of believers prior to the seventieth week, thus adding seven years—before the millennium even begins—to "the last day." This results in the following:

- "The last day" consists of both the entirety of the seven years of the seventieth week plus the one thousand years of the millennium, for a total of 1,007 years.

- The rapture and resurrection of those who came to faith in the church age still occurs at the very earliest hour of "the last day."

This solution does not address other problems that remain:

- Limiting the rapture to those of the church age, as defined by dispensationalism, means that Mary and Martha and Lazarus and all others who came to faith in Jesus during His ministry—but before Pentecost—would be excluded, despite the fact that they are the very ones to whom Jesus made the promise.

- The problem of different treatment for believers of all ages has not been addressed.

Conclusion: The problems associated with dispensationalism began with a man-made grid of dispensations placed over the Bible, with the accompanying requirement that all interpretations had to pass through the lens of that grid. The ramifications of imposing this overlying grid—specifically, the arbitrary division between the church age and the Jewish age—required further fabrications of new concepts to reconcile the dispensational view with contradictory language in the Bible.

Once the grid placed the end of the church age at the beginning of the seventieth week, dispensationalists had to logically place the rapture of the church before the seventieth week began. This is the misnamed pretribulational rapture position.

When some Christians began to equate "the last day" with the millennium, dispensationalists had to make adjustments in order to maintain their placement of the end of the church age and its necessary adjunct, the rapture of the church, prior to the seventieth week. They adjusted by arbitrarily stretching "the last day" backward past the one thousand years of the millennium to include also the preceding seven years of the seventieth week.

The internally contradictory explanations discussed in this subsection on "the last day" are examples of the problems caused by the dispensational grid.

And all these convoluted explanations were contrived even though the Bible is not absolutely clear that when Jesus referred to "the last day," He was referring to the millennium. What if He was referring to the day of the Lord when He spoke of "the last day"?

D. There are other problems with limiting "the last day" to the millennium

While it is clear from Revelation 20 that bodily resurrections will occur at different times during the millennium, one cannot conveniently overlook other passages that indicate other resurrections at other times or at unknown times. For example, Revelation 7 plainly described the resurrection of saints who have come out of the great tribulation:

<u>Revelation 7:9, 14–17</u> (emphasis added)

9 After these things I looked, and behold, **a great multitude** which no one could count, from every nation and all tribes and peoples and tongues, **standing before the throne and before the Lamb, clothed in white robes**, and palm branches were in their hands. 14 And he said to me, "These are the ones who come out of the great tribulation, and **they have washed their robes and made them white in the blood of the Lamb.** 15 For this reason, **they are before the throne of God; and they serve Him day and night in His temple; and He who sits on the throne will spread His tabernacle over them.** 16 They will hunger no longer, nor thirst anymore; nor will the sun beat down on them, nor any heat; 17 for the Lamb in the center of the throne will be their shepherd, and will guide them to springs of the water of life; and God will wipe every tear from their eyes.

If Revelation is read chronologically, this appearance of the saints who come out of the great tribulation occurs between the breaking of the sixth and seventh seals. With the breaking of the seventh seal in Revelation 8, the wrath of the day of the Lord begins.

But the day of the Lord is still within the seventieth week, though near the end; it is not within the one thousand years of the millennium. Since this resurrection of chapter 7 precedes the day of the Lord, it is also a resurrection *before* the millennium/last day.

And there are two other resurrections described in Revelation before chapter 20 (which discusses the millennium):

<u>Revelation 14:1–3</u> (emphasis added)

¹ Then I looked, and behold, the Lamb was standing on Mount Zion, and with Him **one hundred and forty-four thousand, having His name and the name of His Father written on their foreheads.** ² And I heard a voice from heaven, like the sound of many waters and like the sound of loud thunder, and the voice which I heard was like the sound of harpists playing on their harps. ³ And they sang a new song **before the throne and before the four living creatures and the elders;** and no one could learn the song except the one hundred and forty-four thousand who had been purchased from the earth.

This scene appears to take place between the trumpets and the bowls. The point is that the 144,000 Jews who were sealed on the earth just before the beginning of the day of the Lord are now in heaven, before the throne of God. Since the bowl judgments have yet to be poured out, it means the time frame is still within the day of the Lord and still not yet into the millennium.

<u>Revelation 15:2–3</u> (emphasis added)

² And I saw something like a sea of glass mixed with fire, and **those who had been victorious over the beast and his image and the number of his name, standing on the sea of glass,** holding harps of God. ³ And they sang the song of Moses, the bond-servant of God, and the song of the Lamb.

Like the prior passage from chapter 14, this passage appears just before the bowl judgments. It is unlikely that the people described here are the fifth-seal martyrs who were under the altar (Rev. 6:9–11) because the description of the group in Revelation 20:4 seems to match the fifth-seal martyrs closely, down to calling them "souls."

Instead, this Revelation 15 group matches the description of the saints resurrected (they have bodies, because John observes that they are *standing*) in Revelation 7:9–17:

- The scene is the same in both passages—the throne room/ courtroom of God the Father and the Lamb.

- In both passages, the resurrected saints are praising God and the Lamb.

- In both passages, they are described as overcomers in the time of the great tribulation:

Revelation 7:14

These are the ones who come out of the great tribulation, and they have washed their robes and made them white in the blood of the Lamb.

Revelation 15:2

And I saw … those who had been victorious over the beast and his image and the number of his name, standing on the sea of glass.

This passage in Revelation 15 appears to be either a flashback to Revelation 7:9–17, or it is the fulfillment of the promises enumerated by the elder in Revelation 7:

Revelation 7:15–17

[15] For this reason, they are before the throne of God; and they serve Him day and night in His temple; and He who sits on the throne will spread His tabernacle over them. [16] They will hunger no longer, nor thirst anymore; nor will the sun beat down on them, nor any heat; [17] for the Lamb in the center of the throne will be their shepherd, and will guide them to springs of the water of life; and God will wipe every tear from their eyes.

In either event, this passage in Revelation 15 occurs toward the end of the seventieth week but is still within it and thus not within the millennium.

Conclusion: Whether one espouses the young-earth view or not, many Christians view the millennium as "the last day." The problem arises with confining all the various resurrections to that one thousand years. Certainly Revelation 20 indicates that there are at least two during the thousand years.

Because one cannot ignore contradicting passages, it must be openly acknowledged that there are at least three other passages in Revelation that describe resurrected people in heaven before the beginning of the millennium. That means that, besides Jesus, there will be other resurrections before "the last day."

If we consider the possibility that Jesus might have been referring to the day of the Lord when He promised resurrection on "the last day," then the description in Revelation 7:7–17 of the saints' resurrection immediately prior to the onset of the day of the Lord would fit. This group appears again in Revelation 15, but these people are safely home in heaven during the ongoing day of the Lord.

While the 144,000 Jews of Revelation 7:1–8 are sealed to remain on earth through at least the fifth trumpet (Rev. 9:4) of the day of the Lord, the seal protects them from the Lord's wrath. By Revelation 14, they are resurrected and in heaven, but we are not given any time clues apart from the fact that this chapter is placed between the trumpets and the bowls of the day of the Lord.

Whether one defines "the last day" as the day of the Lord or the millennium, it is safe to say that *after* the millennium, there will be no more resurrection.

Conclusion

Believers cannot be complacent about deception

Ultimately, no one knows, or can know, exactly when the rapture will occur. But Jesus charged us

- with knowing the general season—that is, during the latter days of the great tribulation and

- with watching for the signs of His coming.

Thus we ignore the Lord's warnings at our peril. Part and parcel of being ready for our Master's return is preparing spiritually for persecution and hardship. If we have not exercised our spiritual muscles to strengthen them through the disciplines of Bible study, prayer, and practice in listening to discern His voice over the noise of the world, we will be ill-prepared to endure the final testing and trials of our lives.

He may come for us sooner than we anticipate, or He may delay much longer than we can envisage. This means that we must be ready at all times. See, for example, the parable of the ten virgins (Matt. 25:1–13) and the parable of the slave in charge of the household (Matt. 24:44–51). Let us not be distracted from our preparation, however, by allowing differing interpretations to be a source of division amongst believers.

As I stated at the beginning of this book, my purpose in writing is to expose some of the flaws in the foundational pillars of pretribulationism and to show that unthinking adherence to this position can lead to *deception and being led astray* if the Lord does not come as expected. Even highly respected theologians, pastors, and teachers, who are spot-on regarding the elements of the gospel, can be mistaken on this rapture issue for two reasons:

- The first is the semantics problem—that is, imprecise terms, if followed to their logical end, can lead to the wrong conclusion.
- The second is that the grid of dispensationalism, superimposed onto the text of the Bible, is a man-made construct and, like the semantics problem, can lead to the wrong conclusion.

It is sheer folly to place your eternal destiny in the hands of another human being, regardless of how well educated, how well-spoken, and how persuasive that person may be. You will die by yourself, alone, and no other human being will go with you to take the responsibility for your thoughts, words, and actions. You alone will taste the fruits of your decisions, whether they are "sweeter than honey" (Pss. 19:9–11; 119:103) or unutterably bitter. You alone will be responsible for the choices you have made in this life.

A. Each believer will be accountable to God

Each believer will stand before the Lord and be accountable for what he or she did with the light they had available and with the talents/gifts God gave him or her. This is not an eternal judgment issue but one of rewards or losses:

1 Corinthians 3:10–15

[10] According to the grace of God which was given to me, like a wise master builder I laid a foundation, and another is building on it. But each man must be careful how he builds on it. [11] For no man can lay a foundation other than the one which is laid, which is Jesus Christ. [12] Now if any man builds on the foundation with gold, silver, precious stones, wood, hay, straw, [13] each man's work will become evident; for the day will show it because it is to be revealed with fire, and the fire itself will test the quality of each man's work. [14] If any man's work which he has built on it remains, he will receive a reward. [15] If any man's work is burned up, he will suffer loss; but he himself will be saved, yet so as through fire.

<u>2 Corinthians 5:10</u>

For we must all appear before the judgment seat of Christ, so that each one may be recompensed for his deeds in the body, according to what he has done, whether good or bad.

The only foundation is Jesus Christ, the corner stone (Eph. 2:20). Upon this foundation, all Christians build. This is so because it is through Christ alone that God is reconciling a sinful world to Himself:

<u>2 Corinthians 5:18–19</u> (emphasis added)

[18] Now all these things are from **God, who reconciled us to Himself through Christ** and gave us the ministry of reconciliation, [19] namely, that **God was in Christ reconciling the world to Himself**, not counting their trespasses against them, and He has committed to us the word of reconciliation.

To build one's hopes of heaven on any other foundation is to build on sand:

<u>Matthew 7:24–27</u> (emphasis added)

[24] Therefore everyone who hears these words of Mine and acts on them, may be compared to a wise man who built his house on the rock. [25] And the rain fell, and the floods came, and the winds blew and slammed against that house; and yet it did not fall, for it had been founded on the rock. [26] **Everyone who hears these words of Mine and does not act on them, will be like a foolish man who built his house on the sand.** [27] **The rain fell, and the floods came, and the winds blew and slammed against that house; and it fell— and great was its fall.**

But even among those who build upon the foundation of Christ, there are two kinds: (1) those who build with gold, silver, and precious stones; and (2) those who build with wood, hay, and straw. The former group has learned to depend upon the illumination and guidance and teaching of God the Holy Spirit, as He leads them to Christ and molds them into His image. They submit (with joy, we hope) to the work of the triune God, as He remodels them into His image by permitting trials of all sorts. As anyone who has endured a remodeling project at home knows, this is—especially during the demolition phase—very messy work.

The latter group, though they have not departed from the foundation of faith, have substituted their own thinking and inventions and standards (which are usually those of the world) for the sound doctrines in which they are meant to walk. Each person's life's work will be laid open to view before God, and I daresay most of us will be ashamed of our poor utilization of the gifts/talents God gave us (Matt. 25:15–30), when we had all the advantages of the full revelation of God available to us for our edification and spiritual growth.

B. To avoid being deceived, each believer should study the Bible thoroughly, as the end of days draws ever closer

Deception will be the hallmark, the defining characteristic of the reign of the Satan-empowered, and possibly even Satan-possessed, antichrist. Jesus warned that the deception will be so thick that even the elect would be deceived, if it were possible:

Matthew 24:24–25

[24] For false Christs and false prophets will arise and will show great signs and wonders, so as to mislead, if possible, even the elect. [25] Behold, I have told you in advance.

The King James Version says it even more graphically:

Matthew 24:24

For there shall arise false Christs, and false prophets, and shall shew great signs and wonders; insomuch that, if it were possible, they shall deceive the very elect.

It is dangerous to assume that you are one of the "very elect" and thus assured of not being deceived. The consequences of being deceived are too great; indeed, they will be eternal. Jesus did not issue this warning lightly.

And that was not Jesus's only warning. The entire passages in Matthew, Mark, and Luke regarding the seventieth week of Daniel are replete with warnings not to be deceived/misled. Here are some from Matthew:

<u>Matthew 24:4–33</u> (emphasis added)

[4] And Jesus answered and said to them, "**See to it that no one misleads you**. [5] For many will come in My name, saying, 'I am the Christ,' and **will mislead many**. [6] You will be hearing of wars and rumors of wars. **See that you are not frightened, for those things must take place, but that is not yet the end**. ...

[11] Many false prophets will arise and **will mislead many**. [12] Because lawlessness is increased, **most people's love will grow cold**. ...

[15] Therefore when you see the abomination of desolation which was spoken of through Daniel the prophet, standing in the holy place (let the reader understand), [16] then those who are in Judea must flee to the mountains. [17] Whoever is on the housetop must not go down to get the things out that are in his house. [18] Whoever is in the field must not turn back to get his cloak. [19] But woe to those who are pregnant and to those who are nursing babies in those days! [20] But pray that your flight will not be in the winter, or on a Sabbath. [21] For then there will be a great tribulation, such as has not occurred since the beginning of the world until now, nor ever will. [22] Unless those days had been cut short, no life would have been saved; but for the sake of the elect those days will be cut short. [23] Then if anyone says to you, 'Behold, here is the Christ,' or 'There He is,' **do not believe him**. [24] For false Christs and false prophets will arise and will show great signs and wonders, **so as to mislead, if possible, even the elect**. [25] **Behold, I have told you in advance**. [26] So if they say to you, 'Behold, He is in the wilderness,' **do not go out**, or, 'Behold, He is in the inner rooms,' **do not believe them**. [27] For just as the lightning comes from the east and flashes even to the west, so will the coming of the Son of Man be. [28] Wherever the corpse is, there the vultures will gather. [29] But immediately after the tribulation of those days the sun will be darkened, and the moon will not give its light, and the stars will fall from the sky, and the powers of the heavens will be shaken. [30] And then the sign of the Son of Man will appear in the sky, and then all the tribes

of the earth will mourn, and they will see the Son of Man coming on the clouds of the sky with power and great glory. [31] And He will send forth His angels with a great trumpet and they will gather together His elect from the four winds, from one end of the sky to the other. [32] Now **learn the parable from the fig tree: when its branch has already become tender and puts forth its leaves, you know that summer is near; [33] so, you too, when you see all these things, recognize that He is near, right at the door.**"

And the warnings against deception (and, by extension, false teachers) came not only from Jesus Himself but are also contained in every single letter in the New Testament, except Philemon.

1. Spiritual deception occurs gradually

The essence of deception is that the one being deceived does not know that he or she is being deceived. To deceive is to make someone believe something is true that is actually false.

SINCE

- the very nature of deception is insidious, subtle, and cumulative, and

- the biblical evidence presented in this book militates against a rapture prior to the seventieth week,

THEN it is important for the believers who go into the great tribulation as well as those who come to a saving faith during the great tribulation, to understand how easily they can be deceived into taking the mark of the beast when he (the beast, the antichrist) declares himself to be God and demands the worship of the world.

Many Christians think that the mark of the beast will be something technological, like a microchip. For that reason, they think they will recognize the mark when it is required, and therefore they will know to avoid it. While it is undoubtedly true that the mark will be something technological, that is only part of what is involved.

The beast will require the worship of the world (Rev. 13:8, 12, 14–15). Worship means allegiance and believing loyalty. At the exponential rate technology and AI are progressing, it is anyone's guess what the physical mark will be. It may indeed be a microchip inserted under the skin of the right hand or the forehead (or into the brain: think NEURALINK), but it is more important to recognize *what the head and the hand represent*:

- The head/forehead/mind represents thought and beliefs.
- The hand represents action, which is based on those thoughts and beliefs.

In Exodus 13, Moses, relaying the Lord's command to observe the Feast of Unleavened Bread (which begins with Passover), told the Israelites to teach their sons the history of the exodus and its importance:

<u>Exodus 13:9</u> (emphasis added)

It shall serve as **a sign to you on your hand, and as a reminder on your forehead,** that the law of the Lord may be in your mouth; for with a powerful hand the Lord brought you out of Egypt."

A few verses later, he reiterated the command:

<u>Exodus 13:16</u> (emphasis added)

So it shall serve as **a sign on your hand and as phylacteries on your forehead,** for with a powerful hand the Lord brought us out of Egypt.

In Deuteronomy, Moses repeated God's commands to the second generation of the Hebrews before they entered the promised land (under Joshua's leadership). Chapter 6 contains the *Shema*:

<u>Deuteronomy 6:4–9</u> (emphasis added)

4 Hear, O Israel! The Lord is our God, the Lord is one! 5 You shall love the Lord your God with all your heart and with all your soul and with all your might. 6 These words, which I am commanding you today, shall be on your heart; 7 You shall teach them diligently to your sons and shall talk of them when you sit in your house and when you walk by the way and when you lie down and when you rise up. 8 **You shall bind them as a sign on your hand and they**

shall be as frontals on your forehead. [9] You shall write them on the doorposts of your house and on your gates.

The Israelites took these commands literally and made phylacteries (also called tefillin), tying them with ribbons to their foreheads and left arms. The phylacteries were leather boxes inscribed with scriptural passages, often the *Shema* quoted above. They were a visible expression of the wearer's covenantal relationship with and loyalty to the Most High. Whether the phylacteries actually helped them to remember the Lord and His commands and to live out what they remembered is another question altogether.

But God's point was that worship of Him involved both the head and the hands. The minds of His people were to be continually directed toward Him, because He was their God, and His laws and His commands were to be lived out in the daily activities of their lives. If their minds were focused on Him and His commands, their lives would reflect their belief and loyalty to Him and their rejection of all other gods/idols.

As I have noted earlier in this book, God "marks" His own, as demonstrated in Ezekiel 9:4–7 and in Revelation 7:1–8, 9:4. In addition, the indwelling of God the Holy Spirit could also be considered His mark—see, for example, 2 Corinthians 1:21–22; 5:5; Ephesians 1:13–14; 4:30. Finally, Revelation 22:4 declares that God's people will serve Him in the eternal state, and "His name will be on their foreheads."

Always the counterfeiter, Satan also will have a mark, which the antichrist will require. Like the true mark of God's people, his counterfeit mark will consist of something that engages the mind (the forehead) and is consequently lived out by action (the hand). The belief will come first, and the action (taking the beast's mark, in whatever form it may be) will follow naturally.

And here is where deception plays its leading role. Through patient, very gradual (at least at first) but very deliberate, multi-decades-long processes, entire societies are being conditioned to trade biblical truth for compromise, comfort, and convenience. These processes include:

- "law-fare" (removing prayer from schools, removing the Ten Commandments from the public square),

- the replacement of biblical thinking with unthinking acceptance of the world system in the K–12 public schools, with intense concentration in most universities, public or private,

- requiring Christians first to tolerate ("live and let live"), then to accept as normal, then to approve, and finally even to participate in behavior that is explicitly forbidden in the Bible (e.g., Rom. 1:18–32),

- desensitizing adults, then teens, and then children to violence in word and action, through television, movies, and video games,

- encouraging, legalizing, and enabling addictions of all kinds, whether to video games, pornography, alcohol, or mind-altering drugs,

- conditioning people to stop thinking for themselves so that they will willingly accept whatever the government decrees, even to the point of reporting their noncompliant neighbors to the authorities,

- sexualizing children and ruining their mental and physical health with "gender-affirming" surgeries that permanently mutilate their bodies,

- replacing absolute truth with "my" truth and "your" truth, lest offense be taken by someone who believes something different.

This conditioning is akin to the fable of the frog that if thrown into a pot of boiling water, would immediately sense the threat to its life and do all in its power to get out. But if it were gently placed in a pot of cool water, it would swim happily about, oblivious to the gradual increase in the temperature of the water until it was too late.

The water temperature in America has reached the boiling point, but at least half or more of the country (I'm probably too optimistic) is oblivious to the mortal threat to their eternal souls. Consider how polarized America has become in the last couple of decades; there is no middle ground anymore. Even families are divided by politics now, though political issues are just the symptoms of the true, underlying problem. And that leads to the second point about deception.

2. SPIRITUAL DECEPTION MAKES ONE FEEL SAFE

In the last subsection, I said that people are already being conditioned to trade biblical truth for compromise, comfort, and convenience. But they are also being conditioned to trade their freedoms—of religion, speech, movement, and even thought—out of fear. History has proved that Americans will willingly trade their freedoms for perceived safety and security.

The COVID-19 lockdowns are a prime example. The word from "authorities" was that the only way to stop this new disease from killing off untold millions of people was to

- stay at home, and work from home, if possible,
- keep a distance of six feet from other people when it was necessary to be out in public,
- wear a mask at all times in public places, and
- take the "safe and effective," relatively untested vaccine.

Although there were already UN studies that had proved that the first three of these strategies were ineffective at retarding the spread of infection, American authorities implemented them all. There was one official narrative, and any and all dissent was suppressed. Those who did dissent were silenced in various ways:

- They lost their jobs.
- They lost their professional licenses.
- They were barred or removed from public platforms like Twitter® (now X®) and Facebook®. Those in control of all social media quickly removed dissenting comments and posted only those in favor of the approved narrative.
- They were treated as outcasts of society.

Five years later, it is now widely known what the earlier UN studies had already proved: All of the strategies to limit the spread of the disease were worthless, including and especially the vaccine, which neither prevented the recipient from getting the disease nor prevented them from spreading the disease to others. Moreover, untold thousands (probably a lot more) of recipients suffered neurological, cardiological, vascular, and other bodily injuries from the vaccine, up to and including death.

Nevertheless, during the years of the lockdowns, the damage to American society was incalculable:

- Families split over whether family members did or did not take "the shot."

- Untold numbers of children suffered physical and mental illnesses from the masks and the long period of social isolation and fell behind in academic progress in ways that are, in many cases, impossible to recover.

- The pressure from peers and friends to take the vaccine was so intense that friendships were irrevocably lost.

- Those who declined or refused to take the vaccine were ostracized, publicly ridiculed, and humiliated.

And all this damage was caused because of the *fear* generated by those in power and amplified by all forms of media. People gave up their freedoms, their jobs, their friendships—all out of fear. Their compliance with unreasonable and ineffective authoritarian demands made them feel safe; the failure or refusal of others to comply provoked extreme outrage because it undermined their illusory safety.

If this COVID-19 experience was a test to see how American Christians would react to the demands of the antichrist at the midpoint of the seventieth week, it is no understatement to aver that the vast majority failed. It demonstrated in vivid living color the truth that, when the antichrist makes his demands for worship, allegiance will have been given to him long before any mark is received. That is because people have now been trained to trust in man-made systems and global consensus.

Truth is no longer the compass.

The spiritual lives of most people today are marked by compromise, unbelief, and idolatry.

Christians think that they are safe because they are not openly denying Christ, but they deny Him with every compromise with the world's culture. As a result of decades of deceptions,

- truth is now considered hateful or hate speech,

- sound doctrine is considered intolerant, and

- what God defines as sin is openly celebrated.

Despite the recent election, the world still promotes equity (of outcomes), tolerance (of everything except Christ and Christians), progress, and ultimately acceptance of, approval of, and participation in the world system. Lacking intact, functioning thinking skills due to years of nonuse, many people have forgotten that *truth, by its very nature, is exclusive.*

Christians who are worried about the offensiveness to unbelievers of John 14:6 ("I am the way, and the truth, and the life; no one comes to the Father, but through Me") have forgotten that 2 + 2 still = 4 and that any and all other numbers are not the correct answer. Similarly, in exams of all subjects administered in school, there are correct answers, and all others are marked as wrong.

For example, in science, you can claim that the law of gravity may be "true" for others, but it isn't "your truth." But just try walking off the top of a skyscraper—you will discover that gravity applies to you as well as to everyone else and is universally true, regardless of what you think or believe.

If you are worried about the people in the world who have not heard the gospel of Jesus Christ, the most unreasonable response is to reject the gospel yourself. Why would you cut off your nose to spite your face? A more reasonable response is to join the body of Christ and work to reach those outside.

A thinking person will adjust his or her behavior in accordance with what is true. If you compromise with the world system, where "truth" is fluid and unstable, you will find that you have built your eternity upon the sand (Matt. 7:24–27).

This is so because the world system is, at its core, rebellion against the authority of Jesus Christ:

James 4:4 ESV (emphasis added)

You adulterous people! **Do you not know that friendship with the world is enmity with God? Therefore whoever wishes to be a friend of the world makes himself an enemy of God.**

1 John 2:15–17 (emphasis added)

[15] **Do not love the world nor the things in the world. If anyone loves the world, the love of the Father is not in him.** [16] For **all that is in the world,** the lust of the flesh and the lust of the eyes and the boastful pride of life, **is not from the Father, but is from the world.** [17] The world is passing away, and also its lusts; but the one who does the will of God lives forever.

2 John 7 (emphasis added)

For many deceivers have gone out into the world, those who do not acknowledge Jesus Christ as coming in the flesh. This is the deceiver and the antichrist.

The problem is that most American Christians have reversed the order of Romans 12:1–2:

[1] Therefore I urge you, brethren, by the mercies of God, to present your bodies a living and holy sacrifice, acceptable to God, which is your spiritual service of worship. [2] And do not be conformed to this world, but be transformed by the renewing of your mind, so that you may prove what the will of God is, that which is good and acceptable and perfect.

Most believers today do not want to inconvenience themselves by learning what their spiritual gifts are and exercising them for their own growth and that of their fellow believers. That would entail sacrifice, a living sacrifice. So, instead of being "transformed by the renewing" of the mind, most Christians today are already "conformed to this world." With headsets or earbuds that fill the ears with the noise of the world, people are drifting downstream, deaf to the rushing, thundering sounds that would warn them of the coming rapids and the precipice after:

Hebrews 2:1–3

[1] We must pay much closer attention to what we have heard, so that we do not drift away from it. [2] For if the word spoken through angels proved unalterable, and every transgression and disobedience received a just penalty, [3] how will we escape if we neglect so great a salvation?

The danger of the mark of the beast is not so much what external form it takes but the internal spiritual alignment and submission in the heart that precedes the requirement to take the mark. Your internal loyalty and allegiance will determine your response to the antichrist's demand. This is about whom/Whom you worship now.

This is about who owns your soul now.

We humans were created to worship. It is in our very nature, and we will either worship our Creator, or we will rebel and worship idols of all varieties that all tie back to the "ruler of this world" (John 12:31; 16:11). When the time comes to choose, those who already belong to this world will readily take the mark. Indeed, they will see the mark as a natural, most reasonable next step, and they will consider those who refuse to take the mark to be not just foolish but also dangerous to the rest of society.

Sound familiar?

The most dangerous spiritual deception makes you feel safe.

The danger is the spiritual blindness, the *deception*, that makes a person think their choices will make them safe when they are already compromised. The more truth is ignored or pushed aside, the more deception fills the void. Deception is Satan's most useful tool; he plays upon people's fear, their pride, and their instinctive desire for self-preservation. Those three characteristics will make people think that what they are doing will make them safe, but they will be *deceived*.

The only way to avoid deception is to be so steeped in the truth that you instinctively recognize the false. Decades ago, I was told that bank tellers learn how to recognize counterfeit money from the hours, days, and years that their hands handle and their eyes see the real thing.

The point of this book is to encourage readers to invest as much time as possible in reading, studying, and learning the Bible so that they will instantly sense the move of God the Holy Spirit, warning them of whatever falsity is before them. Even for those readers who have followed Jesus as their Lord for decades, this reminder is given: All people need to

- acknowledge their sins and their failure and inability to reach God on their own,

- repent, turning away from their sins, and turning to Jesus Christ as Savior and Lord,

- learn the truths of the Bible and stand firm in them by investing time, thought, and prayer as they study, and

- allow God the Holy Spirit to transform their minds (Rom. 12:2) and conform them to the image of God the Son (Rom. 8:29), as they set their minds on things above, not on the things that are on earth (Col. 3:2).

- BE NOT DECEIVED.

Jude 24–25

24 Now to Him who is able to keep you from stumbling, and to make you stand in the presence of His glory blameless with great joy, 25 to the only God our Savior, through Jesus Christ our Lord, be glory, majesty, dominion, and authority, before all time and now and forever. Amen.

Afterword

Throughout the Bible, God employed His prophets to warn anyone with ears to hear of a coming judgment. In His mercy, He never sent His judgment without giving prior warning:

<u>Amos 3:7</u>
Surely the Lord God does nothing
Unless He reveals His secret counsel
To His servants the prophets.

While I am by no means a prophet, my prayer is that this book can serve as a warning to my fellow Christians. Because so many of them believe in a pretribulation rapture, they do not concern themselves with spiritual preparation for persecution. I fear that, when the time of the great tribulation comes, they will be caught unprepared.

Giving Christians the first half of the seventieth week and the warnings about what will happen during the great tribulation of the second half are demonstrations of God's mercy. The time period we are in now—however short—before the onset of the seventieth week, is also a period of His long-suffering mercy. He is providing believers a strategic opportunity to prepare and to bring more unbelievers into the fold.

May we all use this time of mercy wisely, so that we will be like the five prudent virgins (Matthew 25), who were ready when the bridegroom did finally arrive.

Appendix A

Biblical Texts Regarding
Expected Tribulation in This World

Matthew 10:38

And he who does not take his cross and follow after Me is not worthy of Me.

Matthew 16:24 (parallel passages Mark 8:34; Luke 9:23)

Then Jesus said to His disciples, "If anyone wishes to come after Me, he must deny himself, and take up his cross, and follow Me."

Luke 6:22

Blessed are you when men hate you, and ostracize you, and insult you, and scorn your name as evil, for the sake of the Son of Man.

John 15:18–20

[18] If the world hates you, you know that it has hated Me before it hated you. [19] If you were of the world, the world would love its own; but because you are not of the world, but I chose you out of the world, because of this the world hates you. [20] Remember the word that I said to you, "A slave is not greater than his master." If they persecuted Me, they will also persecute you; if they kept My word, they will keep yours also.

John 16:33

In the world you have tribulation, but take courage; I have overcome the world.

Acts 14:22

… strengthening the souls of the disciples, encouraging them to continue in the faith, and saying, "Through many tribulations we must enter the kingdom of God."

Romans 5:3

And not only this, but we also exult in our tribulations, knowing that tribulation brings about perseverance.

Romans 8:16–18

[16] The Spirit Himself testifies with our spirit that we are children of God, [17] and if children, heirs also, heirs of God and fellow heirs with Christ, if indeed we suffer with Him so that we may also be glorified with Him. [18] For I consider that the sufferings of this present time are not worthy to be compared with the glory that is to be revealed to us.

Romans 8:35–37

[35] Who will separate us from the love of Christ? Will tribulation, or distress, or persecution, or famine, or nakedness, or peril, or sword? [36] Just as it is written,
"For Your sake we are being put to death all day long;
We were considered as sheep to be slaughtered."
[37] But in all these things we overwhelmingly conquer through Him who loved us.

Romans 12:10–12

[10] Be devoted to one another in brotherly love; give preference to one another in honor; [11] not lagging behind in diligence, fervent in spirit, serving the Lord; [12] rejoicing in hope, persevering in tribulation, devoted to prayer.

2 Corinthians 4:17–18

[17] For momentary, light affliction is producing for us an eternal weight of glory far beyond all comparison, [18] while we look not at the things which are seen, but at the things which are not seen; for the things which are seen are temporal, but the things which are not seen are eternal.

Philippians 1:29

For to you it has been granted for Christ's sake, not only to believe in Him, but also to suffer for His sake.

1 Thessalonians 1:6

You also became imitators of us and of the Lord, having received the word in much tribulation with the joy of the Holy Spirit.

2 Timothy 3:12

Indeed, all who desire to live godly in Christ Jesus will be persecuted.

Hebrews 10:32–33

But remember the former days, when, after being enlightened, you endured a great conflict of sufferings, [33] partly by being made a public spectacle through reproaches and tribulations, and partly by becoming sharers with those who were so treated.

James 1:2–3

[2] Consider it all joy, my brethren, when you encounter various trials, [3] knowing that the testing of your faith produces endurance.

James 1:12

Blessed is a man who perseveres under trial; for once he has been approved, he will receive the crown of life, which the Lord has promised to those who love Him.

1 Peter 2:20–21

[20] But if when you do what is right and suffer for it you patiently endure it, this finds favor with God. [21] For you have been called for this purpose, since Christ also suffered for you, leaving you an example for you to follow in His steps.

1 Peter 4:12–19

[12] Beloved, do not be surprised at the fiery ordeal among you, which comes upon you for your testing, as though some strange thing were happening to you; [13] but to the degree that you share the sufferings of Christ, keep on rejoicing, so that also at the revelation of His glory you may rejoice with exultation. [14] If you are reviled for the name of Christ, you are blessed, because the Spirit of glory and of God rests on you. [15] Make sure that none of you suffers as a murderer, or thief, or evildoer, or a troublesome meddler; [16] but if anyone suffers as a Christian, he is not to be ashamed, but is to glorify God in this name. [17] For it is time for judgment to begin with the household of God; and if it begins with us first, what will be the outcome for those who do not obey the gospel of God? [18] And if it is with difficulty that the righteous is saved, what will become of the godless man and the sinner? [19] Therefore, those also who suffer according to the will of God shall entrust their souls to a faithful Creator in doing what is right.

1 Peter 5:8–10

[8] Be of sober spirit, be on the alert. Your adversary, the devil, prowls about like a roaring lion, seeking someone to devour. [9] But resist him, firm in your faith, knowing that the same experiences of suffering are being accomplished by your brethren who are in the world. [10] After you have suffered for a little while, the God of all grace, who called you to His eternal glory in Christ, will Himself perfect, confirm, strengthen and establish you.

1 John 3:13

Do not be surprised, brethren, if the world hates you.

Revelation 1:9

I, John, your brother and fellow partaker in the tribulation and kingdom and perseverance which are in Jesus, was on the island called Patmos, because of the word of God and the testimony of Jesus.

Revelation 2:8–10

[8] And to the angel of the church in Smyrna write: The first and the last, who was dead, and has come to life, says this: [9] "I know your tribulation and your poverty (but you are rich), and the blasphemy by those who say they are Jews and are not, but are a synagogue of Satan. [10] Do not fear what you are about to suffer. Behold, the devil is about to cast some of you into prison, so that you will be tested, and you will have tribulation for ten days. Be faithful until death, and I will give you the crown of life."

Appendix B

Biblical Texts Regarding God's Testing of His People and in Afflicting Them as Punishment

Genesis 22:1, 12

[1] Now it came about after these things, that God tested Abraham.

> vv. 2–11: God commands Abraham to sacrifice Isaac, and the sacrifice is prepared.

[12] He said, "Do not stretch out your hand against the lad, and do nothing to him; for now I know that you fear God, since you have not withheld your son, your only son, from Me."

Exodus 15:25–26

[25] Then he [Moses] cried out to the Lord, and the Lord showed him a tree; and he threw it into the waters, and the waters became sweet. There He made for them a statute and regulation, and there He tested them. [26] And He said, "If you will give earnest heed to the voice of the Lord your God, and do what is right in His sight, and give ear to His commandments, and keep all His statutes, I will put none of the diseases on you which I have put on the Egyptians; for I, the Lord, am your healer."

Exodus 16:4

Then the Lord said to Moses, "Behold, I will rain bread from heaven for you; and the people shall go out and gather a day's portion every day, that I may test them, whether or not they will walk in My instruction."

Exodus 20:20

Moses said to the people, "Do not be afraid; for God has come in order to test you, and in order that the fear of Him may remain with you, so that you may not sin."

Deuteronomy 8:2–3

[2] You shall remember all the way which the Lord your God has led you in the wilderness these forty years, that He might humble you, testing you, to know what was in your heart, whether you would keep His commandments or not. [3] He humbled you and let you be hungry, and fed you with manna which you did not know.

Deuteronomy 8:16

In the wilderness He fed you manna which your fathers did not know, that He might humble you and that He might test you, to do good for you in the end.

Deuteronomy 13:3–4

[3] You shall not listen to the words of that prophet or that dreamer of dreams; for the Lord your God is testing you to find out if you love the Lord your God with all your heart and with all your soul. [4] You shall follow the Lord your God and fear Him; and you shall keep His commandments, listen to His voice, serve Him, and cling to Him.

Judges 2:20–22

[20] So the anger of the Lord burned against Israel, and He said, "Because this nation has transgressed My covenant which I commanded their fathers and has not listened to My voice, [21] I also will no longer drive out before them any of the nations which Joshua left when he died, [22] in order to test Israel by them, whether they will keep the way of the Lord to walk in it as their fathers did, or not."

Judges 3:1, 4

[1] Now these are the nations which the LORD left, to test Israel by them (that is, all who had not experienced any of the wars of Canaan.)
[4] They were for testing Israel, to find out if they would obey the commandments of the LORD, which He had commanded their fathers through Moses.

2 Chronicles 32:31

Even in the matter of the envoys of the rulers of Babylon, who sent to him [Hezekiah] to inquire of the wonder that had happened in the land, God left him alone only to test him, that He might know all that was in his heart.

Psalm 11:4–5

[4] The LORD is in His holy temple; the LORD's throne is in heaven;
His eyes behold, His eyelids test the sons of men.
[5] The LORD tests the righteous and the wicked,
And the one who loves violence His soul hates.

Psalm 105:17–19

[17] He sent a man before them,
Joseph, who was sold as a slave.
[18] They afflicted his feet with fetters,
He himself was laid in irons;
[19] Until the time that His word came to pass.
The word of the LORD tested him.

Psalm 119:67, 71, 75

[67] Before I was afflicted I went astray,
But now I keep Your word.
[71] It is good for me that I was afflicted,
That I may learn Your statutes.
[75] I know, O LORD, that Your judgments are righteous,
And that in faithfulness You have afflicted me.

Proverbs 17:3

The refining pot is for silver and the furnace for gold,
But the LORD tests hearts.

Proverbs 27:21

The crucible is for silver and the furnace for gold,
And each is tested by the praise accorded him.

Isaiah 6:8–13

[8] Then I heard the voice of the Lord, saying, "Whom shall I send,
and who will go for Us?" Then I said, "Here am I. Send me!"
[9] He said, "Go, and tell this people:
'Keep on listening, but do not perceive;
Keep on looking, but do not understand.'
[10] "Render the hearts of this people insensitive,
Their ears dull,
And their eyes dim,
Otherwise they might see with their eyes,
Hear with their ears,
Understand with their hearts,
And return and be healed."
[11] Then I said, "Lord, how long?" And He answered,
"Until cities are devastated and without inhabitant,
Houses are without people
And the land is utterly desolate,
[12] The LORD has removed men far away,
And the forsaken places are many in the midst of the land.
[13] "Yet there will be a tenth portion in it,
And it will again be subject to burning,
Like a terebinth or an oak
Whose stump remains when it is felled.
The holy seed is its stump."

Isaiah 48:10

Behold, I have refined you, but not as silver;
I have tested you in the furnace of affliction.

Isaiah 64:11–12

¹¹ Our holy and beautiful house,
Where our fathers praised You,
Has been burned by fire;
And all our precious things have become a ruin.
¹² Will You restrain Yourself at these things, O Lord?
Will You keep silent and afflict us beyond measure?

Jeremiah 17:9–10

⁹ The heart is more deceitful than all else
And is desperately sick;
Who can understand it?
¹⁰ I, the Lord, search the heart,
I test the mind,
Even to give to each man according to his ways,
According to the results of his deeds.

Jeremiah 20:12

Yet, O Lord of hosts, You who test the righteous,
Who see the mind and the heart;
Let me see Your vengeance on them;
For to You I have set forth my cause.

Amos 6:14

"For behold, I am going to raise up a nation against you,
O house of Israel," declares the Lord God of hosts,
"And they will afflict you from the entrance of Hamath
 To the brook of the Arabah."

Zechariah 13:8–9

⁸ "It will come about in all the land,"
Declares the Lord,
"That two parts in it will be cut off and perish;
But the third will be left in it.
⁹ "And I will bring the third part through the fire,
Refine them as silver is refined,

And test them as gold is tested.
They will call on My name,
And I will answer them;
I will say, 'They are My people,'
And they will say, 'The LORD is my God.' "

1 Thessalonians 2:4

But just as we have been approved by God to be entrusted with the gospel, so we speak, not as pleasing men, but God who examines our hearts.

Hebrews 11:17

By faith Abraham, when he was tested, offered up Isaac, and he who had received the promises was offering up his only begotten son.

Hebrews 12:5–11

[5] And you have forgotten the exhortation which is addressed to you as sons,
"My son, do not regard lightly the discipline of the Lord,
Nor faint when you are reproved by Him;
[6] For those whom the Lord loves He disciplines,
And He scourges every son whom He receives."
[7] It is for discipline that you endure; God deals with you as with sons; for what son is there whom his father does not discipline? [8] But if you are without discipline, of which all have become partakers, then you are illegitimate children and not sons. [9] Furthermore, we had earthly fathers to discipline us, and we respected them; shall we not much rather be subject to the Father of spirits, and live? [10] For they disciplined us for a short time as seemed best to them, but He disciplines us for our good, that we may share His holiness. [11] All discipline for the moment seems not to be joyful, but sorrowful; yet to those who have been trained by it, afterwards it yields the peaceful fruit of righteousness.

James 1:2–3

[2] Consider it all joy, my brethren, when you encounter various trials, [3] knowing that the testing of your faith produces endurance.

1 Peter 1:6–7

[6] In this you greatly rejoice, even though now for a little while, if necessary, you have been distressed by various trials, [7] so that the proof of your faith, being more precious than gold which is perishable, even though tested by fire, may be found to result in praise and glory and honor at the revelation of Jesus Christ.

1 Peter 4:12

Beloved, do not be surprised at the fiery ordeal among you, which comes upon you for your testing, as though some strange thing were happening to you.

Revelation 2:10

Do not fear what you are about to suffer. Behold, the devil is about to cast some of you into prison, that you will be tested, and you will have tribulation for ten days. Be faithful until death, and I will give you the crown of life.

Revelation 3:19

Those whom I love, I reprove and discipline; therefore be zealous and repent.

Appendix C

Biblical Texts Regarding God's Corrective Discipline and His Provision in Times of Testing

Deuteronomy 8:2–3, 5–6

[2] You shall remember all the way which the LORD your God has led you in the wilderness these forty years, that He might humble you, testing you, to know what was in your heart, whether you would keep His commandments or not. [3] He humbled you and let you be hungry, and fed you with manna.

[5] Thus you are to know in your heart that the LORD your God was disciplining you just as a man disciplines his son. [6] Therefore, you shall keep the commandments of the LORD your God, to walk in His ways and to fear Him.

2 Samuel 7:14

[God's word to King David regarding Solomon] I will be a father to him and he will be a son to Me; when he commits iniquity, I will correct him with the rod of men and the strokes of the sons of men.

1 Kings 8:35–36

[35] When the heavens are shut up and there is no rain, because they have sinned against You, and they pray toward this place and confess Your name and turn from their sin when You afflict them,

[36] then hear in heaven and forgive the sin of Your servants and of Your people Israel, indeed, teach them the good way in which they should walk. And send rain on Your land, which You have given Your people for an inheritance.

2 Kings 17:13

Yet the Lord warned Israel and Judah through all His prophets and every seer, saying, "Turn from your evil ways and keep My commandments, My statutes according to all the law which I commanded your fathers, and which I sent to you through My servants the prophets."

Job 5:17–18

[17] Behold, how happy is the man whom God reproves,
So do not despise the discipline of the Almighty.
[18] For He inflicts pain, and gives relief;
He wounds, and His hands also heal.

Psalm 119:75–77

[75] I know, O Lord, that Your judgments are righteous,
And that in faithfulness You have afflicted me.
[76] O may Your lovingkindness comfort me,
According to Your word to Your servant.
[77] May Your compassion come to me that I may live,
For Your law is my delight.

Proverbs 3:11–12

[11] My son, do not reject the discipline of the Lord
Or loathe His reproof,
[12] For whom the Lord loves He reproves,
Even as a father corrects the son in whom he delights.

Proverbs 13:24

He who withholds his rod hates his son,
But he who loves him disciplines him diligently.

1 Corinthians 10:13

No temptation has overtaken you but such as is common to man; and God is faithful, who will not allow you to be tempted beyond what you are able, but with the temptation will provide the way of escape also, so that you may be able to endure it.

1 Corinthians 11:31–32

[31] But if we judged ourselves rightly, we would not be judged. [32] But when we are judged, we are disciplined by the Lord so that we will not be condemned along with the world.

Hebrews 2:18

For since He Himself was tempted in that which He has suffered, He is able to come to the aid of those who are tempted.

Hebrews 4:15–16

[15] For we do not have a high priest who cannot sympathize with our weaknesses, but One who has been tempted in all things as we are, yet without sin. [16] Therefore let us draw near with confidence to the throne of grace, so that we may receive mercy and find grace to help in time of need.

Hebrews 11:35–40

[35] And others were tortured, not accepting their release, so that they might obtain a better resurrection; [36] and others experienced mockings and scourgings, yes, also chains and imprisonment. [37] They were stoned, they were sawn in two, they were tempted, they were put to death with the sword; they went about in sheepskins, in goatskins, being destitute, afflicted, ill-treated [38] (men of whom the world was not worthy), wandering in deserts and mountains and caves and holes in the ground. [39] And all these, having gained approval through their faith, did not receive what was promised, [40] because God had provided something better for us, so that apart from us they would not be made perfect.

Hebrews 12:1–4

[1] Therefore, since we have so great a cloud of witnesses surrounding us, let us also lay aside every encumbrance and the sin which so easily entangles us, and let us run with endurance the race that is set before us, [2] fixing our eyes on Jesus, the author and perfecter of faith, who for the joy set before Him endured the cross, despising the shame, and has sat down at the right hand of the throne of God. [3] For consider Him who has endured such hostility by sinners against Himself, so that you will not grow weary and lose heart. [4] You have not yet resisted to the point of shedding blood in your striving against sin.

Hebrews 12:5–11

[5] And you have forgotten the exhortation which is addressed to you as sons, "My son, do not regard lightly the discipline of the Lord, Nor faint when you are reproved by Him;
[6] For those whom the Lord loves He disciplines,
And He scourges every son whom He receives."
[7] It is for discipline that you endure; God deals with you as with sons; for what son is there whom his father does not discipline? [8] But if you are without discipline, of which all have become partakers, then you are illegitimate children and not sons. [9] Furthermore, we had earthly fathers to discipline us, and we respected them; shall we not much rather be subject to the Father of spirits, and live? [10] For they disciplined us for a short time as seemed best to them, but He disciplines us for our good, so that we may share His holiness. [11] All discipline for the moment seems not to be joyful, but sorrowful; yet to those who have been trained by it, afterwards it yields the peaceful fruit of righteousness.

Revelation 3:19

Those whom I love, I reprove and discipline; therefore be zealous and repent.

Appendix D

Biblical Texts Regarding
the Identity of Daniel's People, Israel

Exodus 19:5-6

[5] Now then, if you will indeed obey My voice and keep My covenant, then you shall be My own possession among all the peoples, for all the earth is Mine; [6] and you shall be to Me a kingdom of priests and a holy nation.' These are the words that you shall speak to the sons of Israel.

Romans 2:28-29

[28] For he is not a Jew who is one outwardly; neither is circumcision that which is outward in the flesh. [29] But he is a Jew who is one inwardly; and circumcision is that which is of the heart, by the Spirit, not by the letter; and his praise is not from men, but from God.

Romans 3:29–30

[29] Or is God the God of Jews only? Is He not the God of Gentiles also? Yes, of Gentiles also, [30] since indeed God who will justify the circumcised by faith and the uncircumcised through faith is one.

Romans 9:6–8

[6] For they are not all Israel who are descended from Israel; [7] nor are they all children because they are Abraham's descendants, but: "through Isaac your descendants will be named." [8] That is, it is not

the children of the flesh who are children of God, but the children of the promise are regarded as descendants.

Romans 11:17-32

[17] But if some of the branches were broken off, and you, being a wild olive, were grafted in among them and became partaker with them of the rich root of the olive tree, [18] do not be arrogant toward the branches; but if you are arrogant, remember that it is not you who supports the root, but the root supports you. [19] You will say then, "Branches were broken off so that I might be grafted in." [20] Quite right, they were broken off for their unbelief, but you stand by your faith. Do not be conceited, but fear; [21] for if God did not spare the natural branches, neither will He spare you. [22] Behold then the kindness and severity of God; to those who fell, severity, but to you, God's kindness, if you continue in His kindness; otherwise you also will be cut off. [23] And they also, if they do not continue in their unbelief, will be grafted in; for God is able to graft them in again. [24] For if you were cut off from what is by nature a wild olive tree, and were grafted contrary to nature into a cultivated olive tree, how much more shall these who are the natural branches be grafted into their own olive tree? [25] For I do not want you, brethren, to be uninformed of this mystery, lest you be wise in your own estimation, just as it is written, "The Deliverer will come from Zion, He will remove ungodliness from Jacob." [27] "And this is My covenant with them, When I take away their sins." [28] From the standpoint of the gospel they are enemies for your sake, but from the standpoint of God's choice they are beloved for the sake of the fathers; [29] for the gifts and the calling of God are irrevocable. [30] For just as you once were disobedient to God, but now have been shown mercy because of their disobedience, [31] so these also now have been disobedient, in order that because of the mercy shown to you they also may now be shown mercy. [32] For God has shut up all in disobedience that He might show mercy to all.

Galatians 3:6–9

[6] Even so Abraham believed God, and it was reckoned to him as righteousness. [7] Therefore, be sure that it is those who are of faith who are sons of Abraham. [8] The Scripture, foreseeing that God would justify the Gentiles by faith, preached the gospel beforehand to Abraham, saying, "All the nations will be blessed in you." [9] So then those who are of faith are blessed with Abraham, the believer.

Ephesians 2:11–19

[11] Therefore remember that formerly you, the Gentiles in the flesh, who are called "Uncircumcision" by the so-called "Circumcision," which is performed in the flesh by human hands—[12] remember that you were at that time separate from Christ, excluded from the commonwealth of Israel, and strangers to the covenants of promise, having no hope and without God in the world. [13] But now in Christ Jesus you who formerly were far off have been brought near by the blood of Christ. [14] For He Himself is our peace, who made both groups into one, and broke down the barrier of the dividing wall, [15] by abolishing in His flesh the enmity, which is the Law of commandments contained in ordinances, so that in Himself He might make the two into one new man, thus establishing peace, [16] and might reconcile them both in one body to God through the cross, by it having put to death the enmity. [17] And He came and preached peace to you who were far away, and peace to those who were near; [18] for through Him we both have our access in one Spirit to the Father. [19] So then you are no longer strangers and aliens, but you are fellow citizens with the saints, and are of God's household.

Ephesians 3:4–12

[4] By referring to this, when you read you can understand my insight into the mystery of Christ, [5] which in other generations was not made known to the sons of men, as it has now been revealed to His holy apostles and prophets in the Spirit; [6] to be specific, that the Gentiles are fellow heirs and fellow members of the body, and fellow partakers of the promise in Christ Jesus through the

gospel, [7] of which I was made a minister, according to the gift of God's grace which was given to me according to the working of His power. [8] To me, the very least of all saints, this grace was given, to preach to the Gentiles the unfathomable riches of Christ, [9] and to bring to light what is the administration of the mystery which for ages has been hidden in God who created all things; [10] so that the manifold wisdom of God might now be made known through the church to the rulers and the authorities in the heavenly places. [11] This was in accordance with the eternal purpose which He carried out in Christ Jesus our Lord, [12] in whom we have boldness and confident access through faith in Him.

I Peter 2:5

You also, as living stones, are being built up as a spiritual house for a holy priesthood, to offer up spiritual sacrifices acceptable to God through Jesus Christ.

Revelation 1:4, 6

[4] John to the seven churches that are in Asia: …
[6] He has made us to be a kingdom, priests to His God and Father—to Him be the glory and the dominion forever and ever. Amen.

Appendix E

Biblical Texts Regarding the Day of the Lord

- Establishing that the day of the Lord is the time at or near the end of the age,

- establishing that the day of the Lord will be the time when the Lord will render His final judgment of the nations,

- establishing that in the day of the Lord, the Lord alone will be exalted, and

- establishing that the signs of the commencement of the day of the Lord are cosmic upheavals followed by silence.

Psalm 110:5–6

5 The Lord is at Your right hand;
He will shatter kings in the day of His wrath.
6 He will judge among the nations,
He will fill them with corpses,
He will shatter the chief men over a broad country.

Isaiah 2:2–4

2 Now it will come about that
In the last days
The mountain of the house of the Lord
Will be established as the chief of the mountains,
And will be raised above the hills;
And all the nations will stream to it.

³ And many peoples will come and say,
"Come, let us go up to the mountain of the Lord,
To the house of the God of Jacob;
That He may teach us concerning His ways
And that we may walk in His paths."
For the law will go forth from Zion
And the word of the Lord from Jerusalem.
⁴ And He will judge between the nations,
And will render decisions for many peoples;
And they will hammer their swords into plowshares and their spears into pruning hooks.
Nation will not lift up sword against nation,
And never again will they learn war.

Isaiah 2:10–12, 17, 19–21

¹⁰ Enter the rock and hide in the dust
From the terror of the Lord and from the splendor of His majesty.
¹¹ The proud look of man will be abased
And the loftiness of man will be humbled,
And the Lord alone will be exalted in that day.
¹² For the Lord of hosts will have a day of reckoning
Against everyone who is proud and lofty
And against everyone who is lifted up,
That he may be abased.
¹⁷ The pride of man will be humbled
And the loftiness of men will be abased;
And the Lord alone will be exalted in that day.
¹⁹ Men will go into caves of the rocks
And into holes of the ground
Before the terror of the Lord
And the splendor of His majesty,
When He arises to make the earth tremble.
²⁰ In that day men will cast away to the moles and the bats
Their idols of silver and their idols of gold,
Which they made for themselves to worship,
²¹ In order to go into the caverns of the rocks and the clefts of the cliffs

Before the terror of the Lord and the splendor of His majesty,
When He arises to make the earth tremble.

Isaiah 13:4–6

[4] A sound of tumult on the mountains,
Like that of many people!
A sound of the uproar of kingdoms,
Of nations gathered together!
The Lord of hosts is mustering the army for battle.
[5] They are coming from a far country,
From the farthest horizons,
The Lord and His instruments of indignation,
To destroy the whole land.
[6] Wail, for the day of the Lord is near!
It will come as destruction from the Almighty.

Isaiah 13:9–13

[9] Behold, the day of the Lord is coming,
Cruel, with fury and burning anger,
To make the land a desolation;
And He will exterminate its sinners from it.
[10] For the stars of heaven and their constellations
Will not flash forth their light;
The sun will be dark when it rises
And the moon will not shed its light.
[11] Thus I will punish the world for its evil
And the wicked for their iniquity;
I will also put an end to the arrogance of the proud
And abase the haughtiness of the ruthless.
[12] I will make mortal man scarcer than pure gold
And mankind than the gold of Ophir.
[13] Therefore I will make the heavens tremble,
And the earth will be shaken from its place
At the fury of the Lord of hosts
In the day of His burning anger.

Isaiah 24:1–6

[1] Behold, the LORD lays the earth waste, devastates it, distorts its surface and scatters its inhabitants. [2] And the people will be like the priest, the servant like his master, the maid like her mistress, the buyer like the seller, the lender like the borrower, the creditor like the debtor. [3] The earth will be completely laid waste and completely despoiled, for the LORD has spoken this word. [4] The earth mourns and withers, the world fades and withers, the exalted of the people of the earth fade away. [5] The earth is also polluted by its inhabitants, for they transgressed laws, violated statutes, broke the everlasting covenant. [6] Therefore, a curse devours the earth, and those who live in it are held guilty. Therefore, the inhabitants of the earth are burned, and few men are left.

Isaiah 24:17–23

[17] Terror and pit and snare
Confront you, O inhabitant of the earth.
[18] Then it will be that he who flees the report of disaster will fall into the pit,
And he who climbs out of the pit will be caught in the snare;
For the windows above are opened, and the foundations of the earth shake.
[19] The earth is broken asunder,
The earth is split through,
The earth is shaken violently.
[20] The earth reels to and fro like a drunkard
And it totters like a shack,
For its transgression is heavy upon it,
And it will fall, never to rise again.
[21] So it will happen in that day,
That the LORD will punish the host of heaven, on high,
And the kings of the earth on earth.
[22] They will be gathered together
Like prisoners in the dungeon,
And will be confined in prison;
And after many days they will be punished.

[23] Then the moon will be abashed and the sun ashamed,
For the Lord of hosts will reign on Mount Zion and in Jerusalem,
And His glory will be before His elders.

Isaiah 29:5–7

[5] But the multitude of your enemies will become like fine dust,
And the multitude of the ruthless ones like the chaff which blows away;
And it will happen instantly, suddenly.
[6] From the Lord of hosts you will be punished with thunder and earthquake and loud noise,
With whirlwind and tempest and the flame of a consuming fire.
[7] And the multitude of all the nations who wage war against Ariel [Jerusalem],
Even all who wage war against her and her stronghold, and who distress her,
Will be like a dream, a vision of the night.

Isaiah 30:27–28, 30

[27] Behold, the name of the Lord comes from a remote place;
Burning is His anger, and dense is His smoke;
His lips are filled with indignation
And His tongue is like a consuming fire;
[28] His breath is like an overflowing torrent,
Which reaches to the neck,
To shake the nations back and forth in a sieve,
And to put in the jaws of the peoples the bridle which leads to ruin.
[30] And the Lord will cause His voice of authority to be heard,
And the descending of His arm to be seen in fierce anger,
And in the flame of a consuming fire
In cloudburst, downpour and hailstones.

Isaiah 33:10–14

[10] "Now I will arise," says the Lord,
"Now I will be exalted, now I will be lifted up.
[11] "You have conceived chaff, you will give birth to stubble;

My breath will consume you like a fire.
¹² "The peoples will be burned to lime,
Like cut thorns which are burned in the fire.
¹³ "You who are far away, hear what I have done;
And you who are near, acknowledge My might."
¹⁴ Sinners in Zion are terrified;
Trembling has seized the godless.
"Who among us can live with the consuming fire?
Who among us can live with continual burning?"

Isaiah 34:1–4

¹ Draw near, O nations, to hear; and listen, O peoples!
Let the earth and all it contains hear, and the world and all that springs from it.
² For the Lord's indignation is against all the nations,
And His wrath against all their armies;
He has utterly destroyed them,
He has given them over to slaughter.
³ So their slain will be thrown out,
And their corpses will give off their stench,
And the mountains will be drenched with their blood.
⁴ And all the host of heaven will wear away,
And the sky will be rolled up like a scroll;
All their hosts will also wither away
As a leaf withers from the vine,
Or as one withers from the fig tree.

Isaiah 66:15–16

¹⁵ For behold, the Lord will come in fire
And His chariots like the whirlwind,
To render His anger with fury,
And His rebuke with flames of fire.
¹⁶ For the Lord will execute judgment by fire
And by His sword on all flesh,
And those slain by the Lord will be many.

Jeremiah 4:23–28

[23] I looked on the earth, and behold, it was formless and void;
And to the heavens, and they had no light.
[24] I looked on the mountains, and behold, they were quaking,
And all the hills moved to and fro.
[25] I looked, and behold, there was no man,
And all the birds of the heavens had fled.
[26] I looked, and behold, the fruitful land was a wilderness,
And all its cities were pulled down
Before the LORD, before His fierce anger.
[27] For thus says the LORD,
"The whole land shall be a desolation,
Yet I will not execute a complete destruction.
[28] "For this the earth shall mourn
And the heavens above be dark,
Because I have spoken, I have purposed,
And I will not change My mind, nor will I turn from it."

Jeremiah 10:10–13

[10] But the LORD is the true God;
He is the living God and the everlasting King.
At His wrath the earth quakes,
And the nations cannot endure His indignation.
[11] Thus you shall say to them, "The gods that did not make the heavens and the earth will perish from the earth and from under the heavens."
[12] It is He who made the earth by His power,
Who established the world by His wisdom;
And by His understanding He has stretched out the heavens.
[13] When He utters His voice, there is a tumult of waters in the heavens,
And He causes the clouds to ascend from the end of the earth;
He makes lightning for the rain,
And brings out the wind from His storehouses.

Jeremiah 25:30–33

[30] "Therefore you shall prophesy against them all these words, and
you shall say to them,
'The LORD will roar from on high,
And utter His voice from His holy habitation;
He will roar mightily against His fold.
He will shout like those who tread the grapes,
Against all the inhabitants of the earth.
[31] 'A clamor has come to the end of the earth,
Because the LORD has a controversy with the nations.
He is entering into judgment with all flesh;
As for the wicked, He has given them to the sword,' declares the
LORD."
[32] Thus says the LORD of hosts,
"Behold, evil is going forth
From nation to nation,
And a great storm is being stirred up
From the remotest parts of the earth.
[33] "Those slain by the LORD on that day will be from one end of the
earth to the other. They will not be lamented, gathered or buried;
they shall be like dung on the face of the ground."

Jeremiah 46:10

For that day belongs to the Lord GOD of hosts,
A day of vengeance, so as to avenge Himself on His foes;
And the sword will devour and be satiated
And drink its fill of their blood;
For there will be a slaughter for the Lord GOD of hosts,
In the land of the north by the river Euphrates.

Ezekiel 7:7–9

[7] Your doom has come to you, O inhabitant of the land. The time
has come, the day is near—tumult rather than joyful shouting on
the mountains. [8] Now I will shortly pour out My wrath on you and
spend My anger against you; judge you according to your ways
and bring on you all your abominations. [9] My eye will show no

pity nor will I spare. I will repay you according to your ways, while your abominations are in your midst; then you will know that I, the Lord, do the smiting.

Ezekiel 30:1–3, 8

[1] The word of the Lord came again to me saying, [2] "Son of man, prophesy and say, 'Thus says the Lord God,
"Wail, 'Alas for the day!'
[3] "For the day is near,
Even the day of the Lord is near;
It will be a day of clouds,
A time of doom for the nations."
[8] "And they will know that I am the Lord."

Ezekiel 32:7–8

[7] "And when I extinguish you,
I will cover the heavens, and darken their stars;
I will cover the sun with a cloud
And the moon will not give its light.
[8] "All the shining lights in the heavens
I will darken over you
And will set darkness on your land,"
Declares the Lord God.

Ezekiel 38:18–23

[18] "It will come about on that day, when Gog comes against the land of Israel," declares the Lord God, "that My fury will mount up in My anger. [19] In My zeal and in My blazing wrath I declare that on that day there will surely be a great earthquake in the land of Israel. [20] The fish of the sea, the birds of the heavens, the beasts of the field, all the creeping things that creep on the earth, and all the men who are on the face of the earth will shake at My presence; the mountains also will be thrown down, the steep pathways will collapse and every wall will fall to the ground. [21] I will call for a sword against him on all My mountains," declares the Lord God. "Every man's sword will be against his brother. [22] With pestilence

and with blood I will enter into judgment with him; and I will rain on him and on his troops, and on the many peoples who are with him, a torrential rain, with hailstones, fire and brimstone. [23] I will magnify Myself, sanctify Myself, and make Myself known in the sight of many nations; and they will know that I am the Lord."

Ezekiel 39:21

And I will set My glory among the nations; and all the nations will see My judgment which I have executed and My hand which I have laid on them.

Joel 1:15

Alas for the day!
For the day of the Lord is near,
And it will come as destruction from the Almighty.

Joel 2:1–2

[1] Blow a trumpet in Zion,
And sound an alarm on My holy mountain!
Let all the inhabitants of the land tremble,
For the day of the Lord is coming;
Surely it is near,
[2] A day of darkness and gloom,
A day of clouds and thick darkness.
As the dawn is spread over the mountains,
So there is a great and mighty people;
There has never been anything like it,
Nor will there be again after it
To the years of many generations.

Joel 2:10–11, 30–31 (vv. 30–31 quoted in Acts 2:19–20)

[10] Before them the earth quakes,
The heavens tremble,
The sun and the moon grow dark
And the stars lose their brightness.
[11] The Lord utters His voice before His army;

Surely His camp is very great,
For strong is he who carries out His word.
The day of the Lord is indeed great and very awesome,
And who can endure it?
³⁰ "I will display wonders in the sky and on the earth,
Blood, fire and columns of smoke.
³¹ "The sun will be turned into darkness
And the moon into blood
Before the great and awesome day of the Lord comes."

Joel 3:2, 12–16

² I will gather all the nations
And bring them down to the valley of Jehoshaphat.
Then I will enter into judgment with them there
On behalf of My people and My inheritance, Israel,
Whom they have scattered among the nations;
And they have divided up My land.
¹² Let the nations be aroused
And come up to the valley of Jehoshaphat,
For there I will sit to judge
All the surrounding nations.
¹³ Put in the sickle, for the harvest is ripe.
Come, tread, for the wine press is full;
The vats overflow, for their wickedness is great.
¹⁴ Multitudes, multitudes in the valley of decision!
For the day of the Lord is near in the valley of decision.
¹⁵ The sun and moon grow dark
And the stars lose their brightness.
¹⁶ The Lord roars from Zion
And utters His voice from Jerusalem,
And the heavens and the earth tremble.
But the Lord is a refuge for His people
And a stronghold to the sons of Israel.

Amos 5:18–20

¹⁸ Alas, you who are longing for the day of the Lord,

For what purpose will the day of the Lord be to you?
It will be darkness and not light;
¹⁹ As when a man flees from a lion
And a bear meets him,
Or goes home, leans his hand against the wall
And a snake bites him.
²⁰ Will not the day of the Lord be darkness instead of light,
Even gloom with no brightness in it?

Amos 8:8–9

⁸ "Because of this will not the land quake
And everyone who dwells in it mourn?
Indeed, all of it will rise up like the Nile,
And it will be tossed about
And subside like the Nile of Egypt.
⁹ "It will come about in that day," declares the Lord God,
"That I will make the sun go down at noon
And make the earth dark in broad daylight."

Obadiah 15–16

¹⁵ For the day of the Lord draws near on all the nations.
As you have done, it will be done to you.
Your dealings will return on your own head.
¹⁶ Because just as you drank on My holy mountain,
All the nations will drink continually.
They will drink and swallow
And become as if they had never existed.

Micah 5:10–15

¹⁰ "It will be in that day," declares the Lord,
"That I will cut off your horses from among you
And destroy your chariots.
¹¹ "I will also cut off the cities of your land
And tear down all your fortifications.
¹² "I will cut off sorceries from your hand,
And you will have fortune-tellers no more.

13 "I will cut off your carved images
And your sacred pillars from among you,
So that you will no longer bow down
To the work of your hands.
14 "I will root out your Asherim from among you
And destroy your cities.
15 "And I will execute vengeance in anger and wrath
On the nations which have not obeyed."

Habakkuk 2:20

But the LORD is in His holy temple.
Let all the earth be silent before Him.

Habakkuk 3:10–12

10 The mountains saw You and quaked;
The downpour of waters swept by.
The deep uttered forth its voice,
It lifted high its hands.
11 Sun and moon stood in their places;
They went away at the light of Your arrows,
At the radiance of Your gleaming spear.
12 In indignation You marched through the earth;
In anger You trampled the nations.

Zephaniah 1:7–18

7 Be silent before the Lord GOD!
For the day of the LORD is near,
For the LORD has prepared a sacrifice,
He has consecrated His guests.
8 "Then it will come about on the day of the LORD's sacrifice
That I will punish the princes, the king's sons,
And all who clothe themselves with foreign garments.
9 "And I will punish on that day all who leap on the temple threshold,
Who fill the house of their lord with violence and deceit.
10 "On that day," declares the LORD,

"There will be the sound of a cry from the Fish Gate,
A wail from the Second Quarter,
And a loud crash from the hills.
[11] "Wail, O inhabitants of the Mortar,
For all the people of Canaan will be silenced;
All who weigh out silver will be cut off.
[12] "It will come about at that time
That I will search Jerusalem with lamps,
And I will punish the men
Who are stagnant in spirit,
Who say in their hearts,
'The LORD will not do good or evil!'
[13] "Moreover, their wealth will become plunder
And their houses desolate;
Yes, they will build houses but not inhabit them,
And plant vineyards but not drink their wine."
[14] Near is the great day of the LORD,
Near and coming very quickly;
Listen, the day of the LORD!
In it the warrior cries out bitterly.
[15] A day of wrath is that day,
A day of trouble and distress,
A day of destruction and desolation,
A day of darkness and gloom,
A day of clouds and thick darkness,
[16] A day of trumpet and battle cry
Against the fortified cities
And the high corner towers.
[17] I will bring distress on men
So that they will walk like the blind,
Because they have sinned against the LORD;
And their blood will be poured out like dust
And their flesh like dung.
[18] Neither their silver nor their gold
Will be able to deliver them
On the day of the LORD's wrath;

And all the earth will be devoured
In the fire of His jealousy,
For He will make a complete end,
Indeed a terrifying one,
Of all the inhabitants of the earth.

Zephaniah 3:8

"Therefore, wait for Me," declares the LORD,
"For the day when I rise up as a witness.
Indeed, My decision is to gather nations,
To assemble kingdoms,
To pour out on them My indignation,
All My burning anger;
For all the earth will be devoured
By the fire of My zeal."

Haggai 2:6–7, 21–22

⁶ For thus says the LORD of hosts, "Once more in a little while, I am going to shake the heavens and the earth, the sea also and the dry land. ⁷ᵃ I will shake all the nations."

²¹ "I am going to shake the heavens and the earth. ²² I will overthrow the thrones of kingdoms and destroy the power of the kingdoms of the nations; and I will overthrow the chariots and their riders, and the horses and their riders will go down, everyone by the sword of another."

Zechariah 2:13

Be silent, all flesh, before the LORD; for He is aroused from His holy habitation.

Zechariah 12:1–4, 9

¹ The burden of the word of the LORD concerning Israel. Thus declares the LORD who stretches out the heavens, lays the foundation of the earth, and forms the spirit of man within him, ² "Behold, I am going to make Jerusalem a cup that causes reeling to all the peoples around; and when the siege is against Jerusalem, it will

also be against Judah. ³ It will come about in that day that I will make Jerusalem a heavy stone for all the peoples; all who lift it will be severely injured. And all the nations of the earth will be gathered against it. ⁴ In that day," declares the Lord, "I will strike every horse with bewilderment and his rider with madness. But I will watch over the house of Judah, while I strike every horse of the peoples with blindness."

⁹ "And in that day that I will set about to destroy all the nations that come against Jerusalem."

Zechariah 14:2–3, 6–7, 9

² For I will gather all the nations against Jerusalem to battle, and the city will be captured, the houses plundered, the women ravished, and half of the city exiled, but the rest of the people will not be cut off from the city. ³ Then the LORD will go forth and fight against those nations, as when He fights on a day of battle.

⁶ In that day that there will be no light; the luminaries will dwindle. ⁷ For it will be a unique day which is known to the LORD, neither day nor night, but it will come about that at evening time there will be light.

⁹ And the LORD will be king over all the earth; in that day the LORD will be the only one, and His name the only one.

Malachi 4:5

Behold, I am going to send you Elijah the prophet before the coming of the great and terrible day of the LORD.

Matthew 24:29–30

²⁹ But immediately after the tribulation of those days the sun will be darkened, and the moon will not give its light, and the stars will fall from the sky, and the powers of the heavens will be shaken. ³⁰ And then the sign of the Son of Man will appear in the sky, and then all the tribes of the earth will mourn, and they will see the Son of Man coming on the clouds of the sky with power and great glory.

Matthew 25:31–32

[31] But when the Son of Man comes in His glory, and all the angels with Him, then He will sit on His glorious throne. [32] All the nations will be gathered before Him; and He will separate them from one another, as the shepherd separates the sheep from the goats.

Luke 21:25–28

[25] There will be signs in sun and moon and stars, and on the earth dismay among nations, in perplexity at the roaring of the sea and the waves, [26] men fainting from fear and the expectation of the things which are coming upon the world; for the powers of the heavens will be shaken. [27] Then they will see the Son of Man coming in a cloud with power and great glory. [28] But when these things begin to take place, straighten up and lift up your heads, because your redemption is drawing near.

Luke 21:34–36

[34] Be on guard, so that your hearts may not be weighted down with dissipation and drunkenness and the worries of life, and that day will not come on you suddenly like a trap; [35] for it will come upon all those who dwell on the face of all the earth. [36] But keep on the alert at all times, praying that you may have strength to escape all these things that are about to take place, and to stand before the Son of Man.

1 Thessalonians 5:1–3

[1] Now as to the times and the epochs, brethren, you have no need of anything to be written to you. [2] For you yourselves know full well that the day of the Lord will come just like a thief in the night. [3] While they are saying, "Peace and safety!" then destruction will come upon them suddenly like labor pains upon a woman with child; and they will not escape.

2 Thessalonians 2:1–5

[1] Now we request you, brethren, with regard to the coming of our Lord Jesus Christ and our gathering together to Him, [2] that you not

be quickly shaken from your composure or be disturbed either by a spirit or a message or a letter as if from us, to the effect that the day of the Lord has come. [3] Let no one in any way deceive you, for it will not come unless the apostasy comes first, and the man of lawlessness is revealed, the son of destruction, [4] who opposes and exalts himself above every so-called god or object of worship, so that he takes his seat in the temple of God, displaying himself as being God. [5] Do you not remember that while I was still with you, I was telling you these things?

Hebrews 10:31

It is a terrifying thing to fall into the hands of the living God.

Hebrews 12:25–29

[25] See to it that you do not refuse Him who is speaking. For if those did not escape when they refused him who warned them on earth, much less will we escape who turn away from Him who warns from heaven. [26] And His voice shook the earth then, but now He has promised, saying, "Yet once more I will shake not only the earth, but also the heaven." [27] This expression, "Yet once more," denotes the removing of those things which can be shaken, as of created things, so that those things which cannot be shaken may remain. [28] Therefore, since we receive a kingdom which cannot be shaken, let us show gratitude, by which we may offer to God an acceptable service with reverence and awe; [29] for our God is a consuming fire.

2 Peter 3:9–10

[9] The Lord is not slow about His promise, as some count slowness, but is patient toward you, not wishing for any to perish but for all to come to repentance. [10] But the day of the Lord will come like a thief, in which the heavens will pass away with a roar and the elements will be destroyed with intense heat, and the earth and its works will be burned up.

Revelation 6:12–17

[12] I looked when He broke the sixth seal, and there was a great earthquake; and the sun became black as sackcloth made of hair, and the whole moon became like blood; [13] and the stars of the sky fell to the earth, as a fig tree casts its unripe figs when shaken by a great wind. [14] The sky was split apart like a scroll when it is rolled up, and every mountain and island were moved out of their places. [15] Then the kings of the earth and the great men and the commanders and the rich and the strong and every slave and free man hid themselves in the caves and among the rocks of the mountains; [16] and they said to the mountains and to the rocks, "Fall on us and hide us from the presence of Him who sits on the throne, and from the wrath of the Lamb; [17] for the great day of their wrath has come, and who is able to stand?"

Revelation 7:1

After this I saw four angels standing at the four corners of the earth, holding back the four winds of the earth, so that no wind would blow on the earth or on the sea or on any tree.

Revelation 8:1

When the Lamb broke the seventh seal, there was silence in heaven for about half an hour.

Revelation 19:11–15

[11] And I saw heaven opened, and behold, a white horse, and He who sat on it is called Faithful and True, and in righteousness He judges and wages war. [12] His eyes are a flame of fire, and on His head are many diadems; and He has a name written on Him which no one knows except Himself. [13] He is clothed with a robe dipped in blood, and His name is called The Word of God. [14] And the armies which are in heaven, clothed in fine linen, white and clean, were following Him on white horses. [15] From His mouth comes a sharp sword, so that with it He may strike down the nations, and He will rule them with a rod of iron; and He treads the wine press of the fierce wrath of God, the Almighty.

If You Enjoyed This Book, Will You Help Me?

- The best way to recommend reading this book is WORD OF MOUTH, so please tell your friends.

- Are you a writer, blogger, podcaster? Have a website? You may cite up to 150 words.

- POST A REVIEW on Amazon, Goodreads, Facebook, X/Twitter, Telegram, YouTube, and Instagram.

- ADVOCATE by suggesting me for interviews, both in person or via Zoom. I love conversations!

- Ask your bookstore to carry *Be Not Deceived*.

- BUY MORE COPIES to benefit others for gifts and mentoring. Special bulk discounts are available.

- Host a book launch party at your home, church, or small group.

- Look for my OTHER BOOKS, available on Amazon, Barnes & Noble, or my publisher's website: MasterDesign.org/category/jeans/.

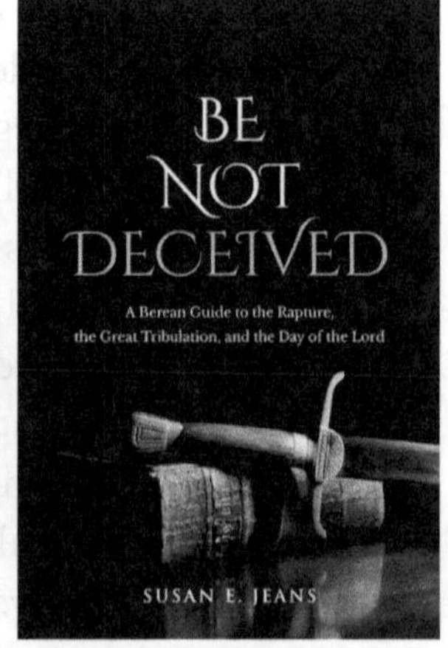

About the Author

Susan E. Jeans graduated (B.A. *summa cum laude*) from the University of North Texas (formerly NTSU) and from the University of Kansas School of Law (J.D.). As an attorney, her work, both for pay and *pro bono*, included:

- handling trusts and estates as a bank trust officer;
- writing contracts and calculating mineral ownership as a landman in an oil and gas exploration company;
- writing employment contracts and policy handbooks for private schools;
- researching, briefing, and motions practice in multi-party environmental litigation.

Susan is also a serious student of Scripture, with more than 35 years of focused Bible study, with a particular interest in the end times. Her training began through Precept Ministries in 1989, marking a turning point in her spiritual development and later leading to twelve years of service as a Precept leader. Her teaching ministry continues through BibleLearningOnline.com.

In addition to this book, Susan is the author of *In the Strength of His Might* and *Does God Matter?*. She and her husband, David, reside in El Paso, Texas, and have two adult daughters and four grandchildren.

www.ingramcontent.com/pod-product-compliance
Lightning Source LLC
Chambersburg PA
CBHW051457030726
47592CB00006B/1983